HEALING
WITHOUT
MEDICINE

Other Books by Albert Amao

Beyond Conventional Wisdom
The Dawning of the Golden Age of Aquarius

HEALING
WITHOUT
MEDICINE

from PIONEERS *to*
MODERN PRACTICE

HOW MILLIONS HAVE
BEEN HEALED *by the*
POWER *of the* MIND ALONE

ALBERT AMAO, PhD
foreword by MITCH HOROWITZ

QUEST
BOOKS

Theosophical Publishing House
Wheaton, Illinois * Chennai, India

Quest Books
Theosophical Publishing House
PO Box 270
Wheaton, IL 60187-0270

www.questbooks.net

Cover design by Great Polo
Cover art: The Rod of Asclepius, a serpent coiled around a staff, is a symbol of
healing and medicine. In ancient Greek mythology Asclepius was the god of
healing and was endowed with the power to cure people.
Image courtesy www.shutterstock.com.
Typesetting by Wordstop, Inc., Chennai, India

Library of Congress Cataloging-in-Publication Data

Amao, Albert.
Healing without medicine: from pioneers to modern practice: how millions
have been healed by the power of the mind alone /
Albert Amao, PhD; foreword by Mitch Horowitz.—First Quest edition.
        pages   cm
Includes bibliographical references and index.
ISBN 978-0-8356-0921-0
1. Alternative medicine. 2. Spiritual healing. 3. Mind and body therapies.
4. New Thought. I. Title.
R733.A54 2014
615.8'52-dc23   2013040018

5 4 3 2   *   15 16 17 18 19 20

Table of Contents

Note

Because of the dynamic nature of the Internet, website addresses or links contained in this book may have changed since publication and may no longer be valid.

The views expressed in this work are solely those of the author and do not necessarily reflect the views of the publisher, and the publisher hereby disclaims any responsibility for them.

Every effort has been made to obtain permission to reproduce material protected by copyright. Where omission may have occurred, we will be pleased to give proper credit in future printings.

This book is devoted to the examination of various forms of mental and spiritual healing. It is provided as a source of information and education only. The content of this book should not be used to diagnose or treat any condition or disease or to serve as medical advice. Nor is it meant to endorse any particular therapy.

The author wishes to give heartfelt thanks to Mitch Horowitz for his support and inspiration, to Richard Smoley for his insightful editing skills, and to Joel Sunbear for revising the initial manuscript.

Foreword

by Mitch Horowitz

In 2010 researchers at Harvard Medical School made a surprising discovery: a significant number of participants in a placebo study reported substantial relief after ingesting a substance that they knew beforehand was nonmedicinal. It was the first major study in which a transparently administered "sugar pill" showed the same therapeutic value as a disguised placebo.

The researchers were wisely reticent about interpreting their data before more studies could be concluded. But the researchers were certain—equally wisely—that their findings deepened and opened new questions about the ability of the mind to affect the experience of illness or discomfort.

The ancestors and antecedents to the Harvard study, and the questions that it raises about healing, can be found in the pages of Albert Amao's book. Most medical researchers are entirely unaware of the spiritual and mystical precursors to contemporary studies of mind-body medicine, the psychology of healing, and the placebo response. Of course, medical professionals might be uncomfortable with the prospect of discovering *any* shared lineage with seekers into the metaphysical. But before a psychological vocabulary emerged in the modern West, the healers described by Amao—mesmerists, hypnotists, positive thinkers, and mystical seekers of the early nineteenth to early twentieth centuries and somewhat beyond—were discovering, in their own ways and using their own language, the same kinds of phenomena that surprised Harvard researchers in the early twenty-first century.

Why should contemporary people, much less medical researchers, care about what a group of self-educated and sometimes eccentric spiritual journeyers were doing in an age before allopathic medicine took its present form? Well, for one thing, these mental healers possessed some extraordinary instincts and insights, which are sometimes validated by current medical science. For example, in the emergent field of neuroplasticity, brain researchers have found that by determinedly redirecting one's thoughts, it is possible to measurably and sustainably divert the electrical impulses of the brain away from certain undesirable patterns, such as those associated with obsessive-compulsive disorder. This same realization appeared in precincts of the New Thought movement in the first decade of the twentieth century, where it was even couched in terminology suggestive of present-day discussions of neuroplasticity. Current medical researchers and historians, not to mention motivated readers, will discover ideas of surprising utility and relevance in the leaves of history that Amao so doggedly turns through.

I have been particularly touched by Amao's depictions of the French therapist Émile Coué (1857–1926), whose reputation is due for a major reassessment. Coué pioneered a method of autosuggestion that involved repeating certain affirmations just before drifting off to sleep at night and just upon awakening in the morning. He was the target of endless mockery for his signature mantra: "Day by day, in every way, I am getting better and better."

What the critics never grasped (and few of them were interested in the experience of Coué's admirers) was that the French therapist possessed a keen insight into a phenomenon sometimes called the "hypnagogic state," when the mind is at its most supple and suggestible. As reflected in Coué's method, this state generally occurs in the moments immediately preceding and following sleep. In the 1970s and '80s, psi researchers— and, in particular, the impeccable scientist Charles Honorton—found that instances of apparent ESP were heightened when the body was induced into a restful state of hypnagogia, or borderline consciousness. Called the *ganzfeld* experiments (German for "whole field"), these clinical studies produced some of the most widely scrutinized and validated laboratory evidence of psi phenomena since J. B. Rhine's card-guessing experiments at Duke University in the 1930s. Avowed skeptic and research psychologist Ray Hyman issued a joint statement with Honorton agreeing on the integrity of the data. (Hyman did not, however, agree that these trials, or any others, produced evidence of ESP.)

Thus, generations before the ganzfeld experiments elucidated the mind's potential in a hypnagogic state, Coué understood that this state of semiconsciousness could harbor therapeutic benefits and might be considered "prime time" for the use of affirmations or other methods of self-reconditioning. Coué is one of the many forgotten pioneers that Amao resurrects in these pages.

It has been widely observed that those who lack knowledge of their past cannot truly understand their present. In twenty-first century America, we routinely reap the benefits of the work of the early mental healers and their experiments into the agencies of the mind. Traces of their efforts can be found in the booming popularity of meditation, stress-reduction therapies, body-mind medicine, neuroplasticity, motivational philosophies, and twelve-step recovery programs. In his deeply humane and historically grounded work, Albert Amao helps us to rediscover the lost threads of our medical and spiritual past—and, in so doing, to recover some overlooked sense of ourselves.

—**Mitch Horowitz**, vice-president and editor in chief of Tarcher/ Penguin books and the author of *Occult America* (Bantam) and *One Simple Idea: How Positive Thinking Reshaped Modern Life* (Crown).

Introduction

The aim of this book is to demonstrate the power of thought to heal the mind and body. I examine the rationale behind so-called mind, spiritual, and faith healing and explain why this kind of treatment works where conventional medicine fails. I also examine the most prominent leaders of the New Thought movement, who used mental and spiritual means to recover their health from supposedly "incurable" diseases, and I describe the mechanism that triggered their healing. Finally, I explain why some people do not respond to any kind of treatment, with medicine or without it.

Mainstream academia should be made aware that mental and spiritual healing is an authentic, American-made phenomenon that originated in and has flourished since the nineteenth century, particularly in New England. This phenomenon continues to develop today through the emerging field of energy psychology, which includes Thought Field Therapy and its derivatives, such as the Emotional Freedom Technique and similar practices.

My main hypothesis is this: *All methods of mind and spiritual healing are self-healing.* Human beings have an inner capacity to heal themselves. Indeed, conventional medicine can be said to heal because it removes obstacles so that the body can regain its recuperative capacity.

In Western civilization, healing by faith and religious belief can be traced back to the beginning of Christianity. In fact, the principles of spiritual healing were behind the teachings and miracles of Jesus Christ.

One thing that merits attention is the fact that prominent religious leaders of what became known as the New Thought movement healed themselves by changing their frame of mind. They subsequently founded religions and philosophical organizations that are still thriving today and have cured millions of followers with mental science.

This book postulates some challenging ideas, such as that Phineas P. Quimby, the father of the New Thought movement, was indirectly healed by his helper, Lucius Burkmar; that Mary Baker Eddy, the founder of Christian Science, was healed by means of autosuggestion using Quimby's metaphysics and by affirmations extracted from the Bible; that Malinda Cramer, cofounder of the Divine Science Church, recovered her health through awareness of the presence of divinity (what depth psychologist C. G. Jung called the *numinous*); that Myrtle Fillmore, cofounder of the movement known as Unity, and William James, father of American psychology, both used affirmations from the Bible to heal themselves, the first from long-standing physical illness, and the latter from depression and hallucinations; and that Jung used self-analysis and self-confrontation to overcome his psychological crises. These statements are fully supported in this book.

My contribution, in addition to psychosociologically analyzing the most conspicuous methods of healing without medicine, is to demystify the mystery that shrouds these occurrences, to find the roots of self-help and self-healing teachings, and to demonstrate the rationale behind mind and spiritual healing.

Furthermore, I try to prove that at the beginning of the twentieth century, America was the leading country in the field of psychology. In the mid- to late nineteenth and early twentieth centuries, America was the land where the New Thought movement came into existence. New Thought arose out of dissatisfaction with the conventional medicine of the time, which in some cases was causing more harm than good. People were also unhappy with dogmatic religious viewpoints and had an enormous desire for new ways of self-exploration and of healing the mind and body. They sought new forms of spirituality and healthy living and ways of unfolding human potential through positive thinking. During this period, many esoteric and metaphysical organizations flourished in America, such as the Theosophical Society, Freemasonry, the Rosicrucian orders, Transcendentalism, and of course New Thought itself. At the same time, alternative methods of cure emerged to serve a public eager for new choices and control over their health and destiny. This led to the origin of self-help and self-healing disciplines and later to the New Age boom. Nowadays self-help and self-improvement constitute a $2.48 billion a year industry including books, seminars, audio and video products, and personal coaching.[1]

As history continues to repeat itself, new labels are given to these discoveries, but the content is essentially the same. The only thing new is the appearance of false healers claiming to heal by the power of the Holy Spirit or other means. James Randi, the American conjurer and debunker known as "The Amazing Randi," has discussed the results of his comprehensive study of evangelical faith healers in his book *The Faith Healers*. This work is highly recommended for learning how some who claim to be spiritual healers deceive naive people.

Others advertise their products or services under a shroud of mystery. For instance, in November 2006, the book and film *The Secret*, by Australian television writer and producer Rhonda Byrne, appeared on the market. The so-called secret is the "Law of Attraction," which has been part of New Thought philosophy for a century. (Incidentally, Esther Hicks, who channels a disembodied entity named Abraham, a major source of Byrne's ideas, states that "the secrets of life have never been a secret. It's like calling the law of gravity a secret.")[2]

Furthermore, since the early 1960s, several channeled entities such as the Guide, Abraham, and Seth have openly taught the concept of the Law of Attraction. It has been a common concept in metaphysical circles and is accessible in the public domain through many books and tapes. I have already argued elsewhere that most of the so-called secrets are in plain sight for those who know how to look for them and have developed their inner resources. In other words, the veil that covers the "secrets" is our own ignorance and lack of spiritual discernment. For further discussion of this subject, the reader may refer to the essay

"Fallacy and Deceptions in Occultism" in my book *Beyond Conventional Wisdom*.[3]

In fact, the biblical assertion that "as man thinketh in his heart, so is he" (Proverbs 23:7, King James Version) encapsulated the basic idea of the Law of Attraction several thousand years ago. James Allen's book *As a Man Thinketh*, published in 1903, describes the Law of Attraction in the following words: "The soul attracts that which it secretly harbors, that which it loves, and also that which it fears."[4]

Contrary to common opinion, the real "secret" is that we humans attract not only what we want but also what we fear. That is, the attraction is manifested according to the core inner beliefs that dwell in our subconscious mind. Unfortunately, most of the time we are unaware of the deep-rooted, self-limiting beliefs that drive our lives. The chapter in this book entitled "New Thought and the Law of Attraction" discusses this phenomenon in detail.

New Thought authors Alan Anderson and Deborah Whitehouse aptly describe the New Thought ideology as "a practical American spirituality." Indeed, New Thought is not only a useful philosophy for right thinking and living, but also a practical religion; it holds that belief and faith play an important role in the restoration of health and success in life. This American philosophy has been the source of many spiritual organizations and churches around the world, including the Unity Church of Christianity, Divine Science, Religious Science, and smaller organizations such as the Quimby Memorial Church. The practical application of New Thought principles to self-help and financial success originated with Charles Fillmore, who with his wife, Myrtle, founded the movement known as Unity in 1889. His work was followed by Napoleon Hill's masterpiece *Think and Grow Rich*, which has been a seminal work for the germination of self-improvement programs and the development of human potential. These ideas were popularized by Dale B. Carnegie's self-improvement courses, Norman Vincent Peale's *The Power of Positive Thinking*, and Joseph Murphy's *The Power of Your Subconscious Mind*.

INTRODUCTION

The most fascinating aspect of writing this book has been to reveal the rational explanation of the healing process that many metaphysical and religious leaders and their followers have experienced applying New Thought principles. Thanks to the contribution of these thinkers and organizations, millions of people around the world have recovered their health free of medicine and improved their personal potential; thus, healing has not been limited to their bodies but has also affected their mental and spiritual well-being. Additionally, the application of these principles as a *motivational device* has proved to have extraordinary value in achieving success in all areas of life. The beauty of this practical philosophy is that it empowers us to become conscious cocreators of our well-being and personal development.

Some New Thought thinkers have held that we all have an inherent inner power that we can employ for the amelioration of our own physical problems as well as those of others. Based on that principle, many wonderful cures took place during the second half of the nineteenth century in New England. The practice of healing without medicine continues to develop in America through the growing field of energy psychology and its variants, including Thought Field Therapy and the Emotional Freedom Technique (EFT).

The role of metaphysics is to attempt to unmask the illusions of reality and penetrate into ultimate reality. Accordingly, I have examined most of the methods of healing without medicine in an effort to discover the factors they have in common. The conclusion is that we all have the power right in our mind to live healthy and fulfilled lives, as well as to shape our future destinies.

Many authorities in the fields of psychology, metaphysics, and other areas of knowledge have pondered the following question: is mind and spiritual healing a matter of spontaneous remission, a placebo effect, or the result of suggestion? This is the question that this book attempts to answer. I invite you to step into the mystery of mind healing—into a mystical and metaphysical world.

INTRODUCTION

While the power of the mind to heal is an important resource, this discussion is not meant as an endorsement for bypassing conventional medicine. If you have, or even think you have, a serious medical condition, please consult your physician. The techniques described herein should be used only as a complement to, and not in place of, the effectiveness of modern medical understanding and technology.

PART ONE

The Antecedents of
Mind Healing

Chapter 1

Franz Anton Mesmer
The Father of Mesmerism

The German philosopher and physician Franz Anton Mesmer (1734–1815) is an important forerunner of the mental healing movement, and his ideas about healing without conventional medicine strongly influenced practitioners on the American continent. Mesmer was a well-educated man who held doctoral degrees in divinity, philosophy, and medicine. He was graduated from the University of Vienna, one of the leading universities in the world at that time. In addition, he showed interest in other areas of science, such as mathematics, physics, and chemistry. He also displayed musical talent, playing glass harmonica, violoncello, and piano. It is even said that Mesmer was a benefactor of the then thirteen-year-old composer Wolfgang Amadeus Mozart. He reportedly helped Mozart when he was having problems raising enough money for the performance of his first one-act opera. Mesmer provided Mozart with the necessary funds, and Mozart's first concert was performed at Mesmer's house.

The modern concept of mental healing in the occidental world started with Mesmer. He was the one who coined the term *animal magnetism*, also known as *mesmerism*. Mesmer's pivotal idea was the existence of a magnetic fluid or ethereal medium in the universe that can be used for therapeutic purposes. The word *animal* in the phrase "animal magnetism" does not have anything to do with the animal kingdom; Mesmer chose the word for its Latin root *anima*, meaning "breath" or "life force." Mesmer wanted to identify a force that emanates from the bodies of living beings, such as humans and animals. In inventing this term, he wanted to distinguish it from magnetism as displayed in the mineral and other inanimate realms.

According to his biographer Stefan Zweig, Mesmer became interested in healing with steel magnets in 1774, when a wealthy foreigner and his wife visited Vienna. The lady was very sick, and her husband asked a Jesuit priest named Maximilian Hell (1720–1792) to treat her with magnets. Hell, who was also a court astrologer, was convinced that there was a magnetic force in the universe connecting all human beings; he also believed that magnetized steel possessed special curative powers. (Today in America there are people who still use magnets as healing tools.) Hell, who was a close friend of Mesmer, informed him about the foreigners' request. Mesmer asked his friend to keep him informed about the results.

Hell later communicated to Mesmer that the sick lady was completely healed with the magnets, and he encouraged Mesmer to use magnetized steel in his medical practice. Mesmer, always eager to try new experiments, asked Hell to give him similar magnets. Subsequently, Mesmer applied the magnets to his patients and, surprisingly, started curing ailments such as sore throat, headaches, and stomach pains. He was astonished at his own success.

Mesmer started developing different techniques of treatment with magnetized steel. He asked his patients to drink magnetized water, and he attached magnets to various parts of their bodies. In addition, Mesmer invented the *baquet* to use in his treatment sessions. The baquet was a huge oak tub filled with magnetized water; iron filings protruded from the wooden top. The patients gathered around the baquet, forming a circle while holding their hands. Mesmer, elaborately dressed, used a wand to point at patients or touch them or stroke them.[1] As a result, people reported experiencing streams of a mysterious fluid running through their bodies, and they were often relieved of their maladies.

Mesmer posited the existence of what he called *magnetic energy* or *magnetism*, a universal invisible energy coming from the stars that permeates living beings. Illness resulted from a disruption of the flow of this universal energy through the body. In this sense, Mesmer was very close to the metaphysical principle of a life force that infuses and animates the whole universe. This concept can be traced back to the Renaissance occultist, mystic, and physician Theophrastus Philippus Aureolus Bombastus von Hohenheim, who is best known as Paracelsus (1493–1541). He disseminated the theory that astrological influences play an important role on human health through a subtle, invisible fluid.

Mesmer was also acquainted with the work of a Catholic priest named Johann Gassner, who performed what he considered to be exorcisms; Mesmer reportedly attended several of these. But Mesmer did not believe Gassner's hypothesis that patients were possessed by demons. Instead, he was convinced that they had emotional disturbances and that the metal crucifix, made of steel and held in Gassner's hand during treatment, magnetized the patients and consequently cured them.

Using these basic ideas, Mesmer experimented with different techniques to generate his cures, such as doing passes and laying his hands on the ailing parts of the patients' bodies. His extraordinary success with this kind of treatment led him to believe he had discovered the long-sought panacea or universal remedy. In any event, his unconventional procedures would heal many conditions where conventional medicine of the time had failed.

Mesmer's fame as a healer grew both in his country and abroad; many people came from distant parts of Europe to be treated by him. Soon many physicians started imitating Mesmer's treatments with magnets and hand passes, also achieving great success in restoring many patients' health. It could be argued that he succeeded at least in part because of collective suggestion, which created a kind of placebo effect. This effect was reinforced by the fact that Mesmer was a physician with professional academic credentials, which was a powerful reason for people to believe in his healing abilities. It was also reinforced by the fact that many people had already been healed by his methods, which inspired trust.

Mesmer's professional life as a healer is well-known, but his association with esoteric schools is unknown to the general public. In 1766, Mesmer received his medical degree with a thesis entitled *The Influence of the Planets on the Human Body*. A decade later, in 1776, he had an encounter with the Count of Saint Germain, who is regarded as the patron of modern esoteric and ceremonial magic. The Count of Saint Germain, also known as Master Rakoczy (or Master R, for short) in occult circles, may have initiated Mesmer in the occult sciences. In any event, Mesmer is said to have had several occult connections:

> Dr. Mesmer was not only a Mason, but was also an initiated member of two powerful occult Fraternities, the *Fratres Lucis* and the Brotherhood of Luxor. The latter was the Egyptian branch of the Brotherhood of Lookshoor in Beluchistan, one of the oldest and most powerful of the Eastern Fraternities. Under the order of the "Great Brotherhood" . . . the Council of Luxor selected Dr. Mesmer to act as their eighteenth century pioneer, later appointing Cagliostro as a helper, with the Count de St. Germain to supervise the development of events.[2]

It is interesting to note that 1776, the year in which Mesmer met Saint Germain, was also the year when he changed his healing paradigm: he abandoned the use of steel magnets and started to work using the idea that the human organism is analogous to a magnet and that the universal energy that flows through this organism can be accumulated according to the laws of magnetic attraction. Furthermore, Mesmer claimed that this energy was the healing force. At this point, he came to the conclusion that his cures were the result of his own magnetic personality. That is, it was not the magnets that were restoring the health of his patients; rather, it was the magnetic energy, accumulated in his own body and passed on to the patient, that was the agent of healing. Here we find the origin of the concept of animal magnetism, which can be understood as "personal magnetism" or "personal influence." This shift in Mesmer's healing paradigm marks a major leap in the evolution of his healing practices and provides a key to understanding the future of mind healing.

In the following year, 1777, Mesmer's career confronted difficulties in Vienna when a blind eighteen-year-old female pianist and composer, Maria Theresia von Paradies, was brought to him to have her eyesight restored. The young lady had been blind since birth, but no physician had been able to find anything wrong with her eyes. She had been under the care of Europe's leading eye specialists for ten years without any improvement. Under Mesmer's care, she gradually recovered her sight, although she lost her ability to play the piano. During the time of treatment she was residing at Mesmer's home. Her mother, influenced by jealous medical doctors, wanted to take her away from Mesmer's care before he completed the treatment. When the young girl refused to leave Mesmer's clinic, the mother struck her across her face, and her blindness returned. Mesmer was accused by the child's father of practicing magic. In this case, it appears that Mesmer succeeded, at least initially, in the treatment because she had an emotional or psychological problem rather than an organic disease.[3] At the time, conditions of this kind were known as hysterical disorders.

This incident put Mesmer under both the scrutiny and the harassment of the scientific circles of Austria, which prompted him to leave Vienna and move to Paris, where he established a medical practice. In Paris, Mesmer also accomplished extraordinary healings and gained some disciples; among them was Dr. Charles d'Eslon. Nevertheless, Parisian opinion was divided between those who thought he was a great physician and those who considered him a charlatan. Although Mesmer failed to get official approval for his healing practices from either the Royal Academy of Sciences or the Royal Society of Medicine, he gained the admiration of important professionals in the French capital.

Mesmer's method of treatment in individual sessions was as follows: He would sit in front of the patient, place his hands on the patient's knees or press the patient's thumbs with his hands while looking fixedly into the patient's eyes. Then, Mesmer would make "passes," moving his hands over the patient's head, forehead, eyes, shoulders, arms, legs, and farther down. He placed his index finger over the forehead, which is considered to be the place of the "third eye." As a result, many patients had peculiar sensations, twitches, or convulsions that were regarded as curative crises.[4] This process is similar to what psychology calls *catharsis*—the release of repressed emotional conflict, generating a curative effect. Mesmer would often conclude his treatments by playing music on a glass harmonica. As a whole, this procedure has many similarities to modern therapies such as Reiki, Therapeutic Touch, energy healing, and music therapy, although their theoretical foundations are different.

The above description suggests that Mesmer's treatment in curing maladies was largely due to his personal influence and suggestion. This is substantiated by the fact that his clinic was carefully furnished in a fashion designed to impress the patients and to put their minds into a state of relaxation—a perfect setting to induce suggestion. Under these circumstances people went into a trance or semihypnotic state that was conducive to healing. Mesmer was indeed a persuasive physician who had the ability to create confidence, which enhances suggestibility. Furthermore, through his mere presence, he was able to create a favorable impression on sick people. His patients saw in him a powerful and accomplished physician with a considerable reputation. This in itself is an indirect form of suggestion.

Mesmer's popularity as a healer continued to grow in France, and he gained an increasing number of followers. This alarmed not only the traditional doctors but also the government. In 1784, King Louis XVI appointed a royal commission to determine the existence of Mesmer's magnetic fluid scientifically. Among the members of this commission were the eminent chemist Antoine-Laurent de Lavoisier and the American ambassador to France, Benjamin Franklin. The commission conducted a series of experiments aimed at determining whether Mesmer had discovered a new physical fluid. The commission concluded that there was no sufficient evidence for the existence of this fluid. They could not verify that the phenomena called "magnetic" were caused by the action of any fluid. The commission also warned physicians who were using Mesmer's method that they could lose their credentials if they continued practicing this therapy.

Nevertheless, as the commission could not ignore Mesmer's healings, it concluded that such healings were the product of the power of the individual's imagination and fantasy. Thus it indicated the power of the imagination and fantasy in restoring health, arriving at a perceptive conclusion regarding the psychological mechanism of healing. Indeed, the commission's conclusion has been validated by modern scientific researches such as the one performed by Dr. Jeanne Achterberg, who has demonstrated the power of imagery in healing. I shall elaborate on this fascinating subject in the chapter entitled "The Role of Imagery in Healing."

Mesmerism and hypnosis are not identical, although currently these words are used more or less interchangeably. The common purpose of these techniques is to induce the patient into a receptive state, which is currently known as an alpha brain state, with the purpose of instilling a *suggestion*. Hypnosis is a process of persuading the patient into a deep relaxation, so he or she becomes amenable to the suggestion given. The operator is thus able to reach the subconscious mind of the patient to remove or eradicate deep-rooted negative habits and to instill a curative idea. Mesmerism, as we have seen, is a technique based on the belief that there is a physical emanation or vital fluid that is transmitted from the operator to the subject. During this treatment, the therapist makes passes and touches affected parts of the body to transmit a fluidic energy. In hypnotism, on the other hand, there is generally no physical manipulation.

Nonetheless, mesmerism is the predecessor of modern hypnosis; the pioneers of hypnosis saw in mesmeric sessions a method of inducing patients into a receptive state of mind. In addition, Mesmer's theory of animal magnetism laid the foundations for modern hypnosis and suggestive therapies. For instance, the Abbé José Custódio de Faria

(1746–1819), one of the pioneers of the scientific study of hypnosis, based his views on Mesmer's work; unlike Mesmer, however, Faria posited that hypnosis is the result of the power of suggestion.

Subsequently, Mesmer's pupil the Marquis Chastenet de Puységur (1751–1825) posited the theory that people, knowingly or unknowingly, exercise personal influence on their neighbors and associates through subtle suggestions. In fact, individuals grow up in a social environment where they are constantly receiving positive or negative suggestions, directly or indirectly, from parents, teachers, mentors, mass media, and so on. These subtle influences are unstated suggestions that engender a kind of waking hypnosis and shape the individual's destiny. One purpose of this book is to emphasize that all human beings are subject to constant influence from their social environment; this can be positive or detrimental to their well-being. By the same token, everyone is also, wittingly or unwittingly, exerting positive or negative influence on family, friends, relatives, and associates.

Chapter 2

The Metaphysical
Phenomenon of New England

New England has played an important role in American political and cultural history. Eight presidents of the United States were born in this region. It produced the first works of American literature, philosophy, and metaphysics and was home to the beginnings of free public education; it is the founding place of some of the oldest and most famous universities in the world, such as Harvard, Yale, and the Massachusetts Institute of Technology. New England parallels European Vienna as an incubator of schools of mind healing. Just as the latter was the epicenter for the development of psychotherapeutic schools that began with Mesmer and were followed by Sigmund Freud's psychoanalysis, Alfred Adler's individual psychology, and Viktor Frankl's logotherapy or existential psychology, likewise, from 1830 to 1880 New England was fertile soil for the emergence of mind healing, American metaphysics, spiritualism, channeling, and religious sects such as the Shakers. This period was also crucial to the destiny of America, as it reached its climax in the American Civil War from 1861 to 1865.

Mind healing, which is part of the New Thought philosophy, is the "practical American spirituality," as Alan Anderson and Deborah Whitehouse have aptly described it. Amazingly, the movement was initiated by an unschooled clockmaker and inventor. The name of this extraordinary New Hampshire–born man was Phineas Parkhurst Quimby (1802–1866). Around the 1850s, Quimby began applying the mental healing modality to cure people based on the metaphysical principle that man creates his own illness in his mind. He boldly hypothesized: "*Disease being in its root a wrong belief, change that belief, and we cure the disease.*" He reduced illness to the condition of belief.

Quimby and Ralph Waldo Emerson represent the roots of the American New Thought movement and American Transcendentalism respectively. Although both men were born in New England within one year of each other (Quimby in 1802 and Emerson in 1803), they did not know each other personally. Their educational backgrounds were quite different. Quimby had practically no formal education, while Emerson was a scholar, a Unitarian minister, and a university professor. Nevertheless, Quimby discovered a mind-based treatment that initiated a new way of healing in America, while Emerson provided the theoretical and metaphysical framework for American Transcendentalism, from which the New Thought movement benefited a great deal. The American philosopher William James encapsulated the essence of New Thought ideology when he described it as "the religion of healthy-mindedness."

To speak of the metaphysical phenomenon of New England is perfectly appropriate because Quimby, Emerson, and Henry David Thoreau were born, lived, and died in New England. Furthermore, Mary Baker Eddy, Emma Curtis Hopkins, and Quimby's disciples Warren Felt Evans, Julius Dresser, and Annetta Dresser were all from New England. The latter three personalities were the initial forces in spreading Quimby's teachings, which eventually developed into the New Thought movement. The prolific New Thought writer Horatio W. Dresser, the son of Julius and Annetta, and Ernest Holmes, the founder of Science of Mind (Religious Science), were also New England natives.

Many New Age holistic therapies, as well as motivational and personal development programs that promote well-being and support the development of human potential, sprang from the New Thought movement. However, the term "New Thought" should not be confused with "New Age." The New Age reached American mass culture in the 1960s, while New Thought came to life in the mid–nineteenth century with the teachings of Quimby. Nevertheless, the New Age arose from the popularization and dissemination of metaphysical and esoteric ideas originally propounded by New Thought, and so it can be seen as a by-product of the New Thought movement. Moreover, the New Age of the 1960s was the result of a protest against the conventional status quo. Its adherents advocated peace and understanding in the world; thus it had a strong socially progressive background, as did Transcendentalism.

From a religious point of view, New Thought expands the narrow boundaries of the traditional interpretation of sacred scriptures and advocates for a broader and more metaphorical understanding of the Bible. From New Thought emerged several religious denominations such as Divine Science, Unity, Christian Science, and Religious Science. In modern times, New Thought has become a practical way of living that draws upon the best of the metaphysical schools and the living religions, including Christianity, Buddhism, idealism, Transcendentalism, and Hindu philosophy.

A common characteristic of many New Thought pioneers is that they suffered from long-standing physical ailments that conventional medicine declared to be incurable. Another common denominator is that they were restored to health by mental and spiritual means and by changing their state of mind. Having had this experience firsthand, they tried to demonstrate these healing experiences for other people. Thus they became teachers of a new way of thinking about healing; some became founders and leaders of New Thought denominations.

The International New Thought Alliance (INTA), an organization formed by several New Thought denominations, depicts modern New Thought as a synthesis of spiritual and scientific principles, and philosophical ideas found in many living religions around the world. In their view, New Thought teaches that people can come into a conscious realization of the divinity within each human being, and to the understanding of the unity of life. The fundamental premise is that God is Mind and that consciousness manifests itself in humans as thoughts and emotions. In turn these thoughts and emotions are expressed in words; words in turn become actions, and actions lead to creation. Thoughts are thus a powerful force and influence our body and environment for good or ill. For the most part, New Thought adherents recognize that illness is real and do not blindly deny reality. But they admonish people to redirect their attention away from their maladies to health and wellness.[1]

The New Thought philosophy has influenced many of the motivational writers and speakers mentioned in the introduction of this book, and figures such as the Frenchman Émile Coué, promoter of autosuggestion. There have been recent new additions to New Thought from teachers who dwell in the "nonphysical" realm. Channeled, disincarnate teachers have been spreading the ideas similar to those of New Thought, heralding a new era known as the Aquarian Age. Among these nonphysical teachers are Seth, channeled through Jane Roberts; the Guide, channeled through Eva Pierrakos; Abraham, channeled through Esther Hicks; and Ramtha, channeled through J. Z. Knight. There is also *A Course in Miracles,* a work reportedly dictated by a nonphysical being claiming to be Jesus Christ. The common characteristic of their messages is that humans create their own reality with their thoughts and emotions (a principle summarized as the Law of Attraction).

The essence of New Thought philosophy can be summarized with the biblical admonition "Seek the kingdom of God, and his righteousness, and all things shall be added unto you" (Matthew 6:33). Right thinking and right doing will pave the way to effectively dealing with life challenges in a positive manner. New Thought philosophy is not limited to healing the physical body, but extends itself to creating financial success and improving relationships and external circumstances; as such its application is unlimited. Many modern New Thought adherents practice what is called *spiritual mind treatment,* also known as *scientific prayer.* This kind of prayer is different from the conventional prayer of supplication, which begs for divine intervention.[2]

PART TWO

American Mind Healers

Chapter 3

Phineas Parkhurst Quimby

The Father of New Thought

Disease is an invention of man.
—Phineas Parkhurst Quimby

The contemporary practical philosophical movement called New Thought and the so-called Metaphysical Movement in America started with Phineas Parkhurst Quimby, who is regarded as the father of the New Thought movement on the American continent. Quimby was born on February 16, 1802, in Lebanon, New Hampshire. He was a clockmaker's apprentice and inventor in New England who attended school for a short period of time; according to authors Willa Cather and Georgine Milmine, Quimby "spent actually only six weeks in school."[1] He was indeed a self-made man with an inquiring and inventive mind.

Quimby contracted pulmonary tuberculosis at a young age, and his liver and kidneys deteriorated as a result of excessive harmful medicine. Disillusioned with medical treatment, Quimby gave up any hope of recovery. He abandoned his business as a clockmaker and retired to his farm, expecting to die. The following is Quimby's own description of his health condition, written around 1863:

Some thirty years ago I was very sick, and was considered fast wasting away with consumption [tuberculosis]. At that time I became so low that it was with difficulty I could walk about. I was all the while under the allopathic practice, and I had taken so much calomel that my system was said to be poisoned with it; and I lost many of my teeth from that effect. My symptoms were those of any consumptive; and I had been told that my liver was affected and my kidneys were diseased, and that my lungs were nearly consumed. I believed all this, from the fact that I had all the symptoms, and could not resist the opinions of the physician while having the proof with me. In this state I was compelled to abandon my business; and, losing all hope, I gave up to die,—not that I thought the medical faculty had no wisdom, but that my case was one that could not be cured.[2]

Several important elements played a key role in Quimby's life that led him to develop his ideas on mental healing. According to Quimby's diary, his doctor prescribed calomel, or mercury chloride, which is toxic. The remedy that Quimby was taking, instead of curing him, was killing him, as he later realized. At the time calomel was used in America as a purgative to cure several maladies, especially yellow fever.[3] Taken in great quantities, the substance has severe side effects, such as loss of teeth and hair, which in fact happened to Quimby. Thus the simple fact that he stopped taking this harmful medication was in itself a positive step toward regaining his health.

Other milestones as well played important roles in Quimby's recovery. At one point he found out that one of his friends had cured himself by doing outdoor physical activities, which included horseback riding. Quimby attempted to emulate his friend, although his severe physical ailments prevented him from riding; instead he tried carriage trips. One day while he was riding in his carriage, the horse stopped and refused to move, so he opted to walk alongside the horse. Suddenly, to his surprise, he found himself walking uphill about two miles by the horse's side.[4] This incident appeared to produce a remarkable impact on his recovery.

The second milestone was when he became acquainted with mesmerism. Dr. Charles Poyen came to America from France to give demonstrations of mesmerism around 1838. Quimby became interested in the theory of animal magnetism and saw in mesmerism an alternative way to regain his health; therefore, he earnestly devoted his time to learning the nuts and bolts of this new "science." Having an inquisitive mind, he quickly learned the mesmeric method. Soon afterwards, he felt capable of practicing mesmerism on his own and began giving public demonstrations in New England, although he was still ill with pulmonary tuberculosis.

In 1840, during a public demonstration of mesmerism, Quimby met a young lad named Lucius Burkmar. This encounter was the turning point in Quimby's life. Lucius was a suggestible boy, who easily fell into a trance under Quimby's direction. They formed a partnership and together gave the most remarkable exhibitions of mesmerism and clairvoyance in New England that can be verified in the newspapers of that time.[5] The procedure was as follows: Quimby would put Lucius into a mesmeric state (or state of trance) with the purpose of clairvoyantly examining the patient's illness. Lucius would diagnose the patient's disease and its location in the body and finally would prescribe the remedies for the cure. In most of the cases, the patient's health was restored.

Clearly Lucius was instrumental in Quimby's psychic demonstrations. But contrary to the common opinion held in the New Thought movement, initially Lucius was the one who was doing the healing. He was the one who was diagnosing the illness and prescribing the remedy to the patient. Quimby's role was limited to inducing Lucius into a trance.

Of course Quimby himself had been diagnosed with a terminal disease; in his own words, he was expecting to die in the near future. At some point the following question likely crossed his mind: if Lucius could clairvoyantly diagnose people's illnesses, could he do the same for Quimby? Lucius was healing other people, so why not test Lucius's method on himself? Consequently, Quimby, with some reservation, asked Lucius about his medical condition.

This point marked the development of Quimby's healing philosophy. He asked Lucius to clairvoyantly scan his kidneys and liver, which were seriously infected. Lucius agreed. Once the examination was made, Lucius announced that Quimby's kidneys were disintegrating, and that he, Lucius, could heal them. Lucius then laid his hands on the infected area, while telling Quimby that he was putting his kidneys back together. A few days later, Quimby again had Lucius examine him clairvoyantly; at this point, Lucius declared that Quimby's kidneys were completely restored to health. Surprisingly, Quimby did not have any more pain. This incident was the decisive moment for Quimby: he started doubting the accuracy of his medical diagnosis. As we see from the above quotation, Quimby himself stated that the physicians had diagnosed him with a terminal disease, and he had given up all hope of regaining his health. However, after Lucius's treatment, his health was restored.

Quimby had his own reservations about his healing. After all, he had been diagnosed by the medical profession as having a terminal disease; how had an inexpert and ignorant lad cured him by laying his hands on him? Analyzing these questions, Quimby concluded that the medical diagnosis was probably wrong. Furthermore, he hypothesized that Lucius in trance was intuitively reading the mind of the patient, rather than clairvoyantly examining him. Quimby started thinking that he might heal himself, but he did not have much evidence to confirm that idea at this point.

After this incident, another event took place that gave Quimby the idea for the development of his future treatment method. During a public healing, Lucius prescribed some expensive medicine to a patient who was unable to afford it. Quimby mesmerized Lucius again and asked him for another prescription. Lucius then prescribed a cheaper medication, which turned out to have the same healing effect. For Quimby, the case was crystal-clear: no matter what kind of medicine Lucius prescribed, it would have had the same effect if the patient believed in it. This theory, later elaborated by Émile Coué, is now known as the *placebo effect*.

In order to determine Lucius's clairvoyant abilities, Quimby induced the lad into a trance using the hypnotic method. Quimby found out that Lucius accepted as true the suggestions given while he was in trance. These experiments convinced Quimby that Lucius, during his clairvoyant examination, was reading the minds of the patients rather than clairvoyantly seeing the illness. Therefore, he discovered that a stronger mind acts upon another's mind by means of what would come to be known as hypnosis. He also realized that the prescriptions given by Lucius were effective *suggestions* to the patients as long as they believed in them. In other words, even if the remedy prescribed did not have any curative value, the healing would take place anyway because the patient believed in the prescription. Here we have another case of the placebo effect in action. Quimby concluded, "Diseases are embraced in our belief."[6]

For Quimby, the problem was the patient's wrong frame of mind. Therefore there was no need for mesmeric sessions to heal; rather what was needed was to change the belief system of the patient. Quimby arrived at this conclusion after recovering his health. The following quotation is extremely important for understanding Quimby's own healing and the events that led to the discovery of mental healing:

> *I had pains in my back, which they [medical doctors] said, were caused by my kidneys, which were partly consumed. I also was told that I had ulcers on my lungs. Under this belief, I was miserable enough to be of no account in the world. This was the state I was when I commenced to mesmerise. On one occasion, when I had my subject [Lucius] asleep, he described the pains I felt in my back (I had never dared to ask him to examine me, for I felt sure that my kidneys were nearly gone), and he placed his hands on the spot where I felt the pain. He then told me that my kidneys were in a very bad state—that one was half-consumed, and a piece three inches long had separated from it, and was only connected by a slender thread. This was what I believed to be true, for it agreed with what the doctors had told me, and with what I had suffered; for I had not been free from pain for years. My common sense told me that no medicine would ever cure this trouble. But I asked if there was any remedy. He replied, "Yes, I can put the piece on so it will grow, and you will get well." At this I was completely astonished, and knew not what to think. He immediately placed his hands upon me, and said he united the pieces so they would*

grow. *The next day he said they had grown together, and from that day I never experienced the least pain from them.*[7] (Italics are mine.)

The italicized sentences illustrate that Lucius had given a powerful suggestion to Quimby when he asked Lucius if there was any remedy for his illness. This question was Quimby's last hope. Lucius's answer was definitively persuasive: *"Yes, I can put the piece on so it will grow, and you will get well."* And the lad proceeded to do his healing, putting his hands over the sick parts of Quimby's body. Quimby held fast to this last hope, as is evidenced by the fact that he checked the status of his recuperation on the following days with Lucius; Quimby was reassured by the young man that he was completely healed. As a result, he felt no more pain. This event was pivotal for the development of mental healing in America. It was the epiphany or "eureka" moment for Quimby. Up to this point, he had been hypnotized by the medical diagnosis that kept him bound to a hopeless belief about his illness. If Lucius had answered Quimby's last hope by saying, "No, there is no treatment or remedy for your illness," Quimby would have continued believing in the medical diagnosis and would possibly have died in a year or so, as he expected:

> I had not the least doubt but that I was as he [Lucius] described; and, if he had said, *as I expected he would, that nothing could be done, I should have died in a year or so.* But, when he said he could cure me in the way he proposed, I began to think; and I discovered that I had been deceived into a belief that made me sick.[8] (Italics are mine.)

Here, in Quimby's own words, is the rationale that led him to the discovery of mental healing. He wrote the following in his manuscript:

> Now what was the secret of the cure? . . . The absurdity of [Lucius's] remedies made me doubt the fact that my kidneys were diseased, for he said in two days they were as well as ever. If he saw the first condition, he also saw the last; for in both cases he said he could see. I concluded in the first instance that he read my thoughts, and when he said he could cure me he drew on his own mind; and his ideas were so absurd that the disease vanished by the absurdity of the cure. This was the

first stumbling block I found in the medical science. I soon ventured to let him examine me further, and in every case he would describe my feelings, but would vary the amount of disease; and *his explanation and remedies always convinced me that I had no such disease*, and that my troubles were of my own make.[9] (Italics are mine.)

This clearly indicates that Lucius persuaded Quimby to believe in the possibility of his healing; by giving a treatment, Lucius indirectly convinced Quimby that there was a remedy for his illness. This was a *powerful suggestion* that cured him. At least for a few moments, Quimby believed in Lucius's treatment and explanation. Lucius was the last resource; Quimby did not have anything to lose but the opportunity to save his life.

Afterward, Quimby realized that the medical diagnosis made him believe that he was severely ill; as a consequence, he had expected to die. He concluded that his beliefs were responsible for the illness, so if his beliefs made him sick, changing his beliefs would make him whole. Quimby never gave any credit to Lucius for his healing. Ironically, Mary Baker Eddy would later likewise deny that she had been cured by Quimby.

These facts indicate that Lucius indirectly cured Quimby. When Quimby was still under the "medical spell" and believed that he was badly sick, Lucius gave him hope and instilled a healing suggestion. This suggestion was reinforced when Lucius laid his hands on Quimby's body and prescribed some kind of medication. Initially, Quimby believed in Lucius, as is verified by the fact that he allowed Lucius to lay his hands over the sick part of his body "to put his kidneys together." *This is exactly how the placebo effect works.* Quimby himself corroborates this reasoning:

At this time I frequently visited the sick with Lucius, by invitation of the attending physician; and the boy examined the patient and told facts that would astonish everybody, and yet every one of them was believed. For instance, he told a person affected as I had been, only worse, that his lungs looked like a honeycomb, and his liver was covered with ulcers. He then prescribed some simple herb tea, and the patient recovered; and the doctor believed the medicine cured him. But I believed that the doctor made the disease; and *his faith in the boy made a change in the mind, and the cure followed.* Instead of gaining confidence in the doctors, I was forced to the conclusion that their science is false.[10] (Italics are mine.)

Quimby's account demonstrates that Lucius, wittingly or unwittingly, was using oral suggestion and placebo very effectively. When the young lad was under a mesmeric state, supposedly mentally reading maladies and prescribing medicine, he was giving very powerful suggestions. It is clear that Lucius cured by virtue of his suggestions when he diagnosed and then prescribed folk medicine that acted as a placebo. These suggestions were all the more compelling for the patient, because Lucius was under a mesmeric state of mind, which made people believe that he was indeed clairvoyantly diagnosing their illness. For people of the time, this was extraordinary—something supernatural, which enhanced their receptiveness to the given suggestions. As Quimby stated above, in many cases he and Lucius visited the house of a sick person and, by request of the attending physician, Lucius performed his "clairvoyant readings." The attending physician usually approved and sanctioned the diagnosis and prescription given by Lucius. This highly enhanced the effectiveness of the suggestion, and inevitably, the healing took place.

Another important consideration is Quimby's *intense desire to get well.* The twentieth-century American esotericist Paul Foster Case has stated that "desires are the most potent form of suggestion." A suggestion is immensely powerful when it is backed up by a strong desire. There is no doubt that Quimby had an enormous desire to regain his health; that is why he became interested in mesmerism and was seeking new methods of healing. This inner desire was ignited when Lucius assured him that he could be healed. Before that he had completely given up any hope of healing and was expecting to die.

After Quimby was restored to health, he concluded that the use of mesmeric treatment and clairvoyant readings was not necessary for a healing. Henceforth he abandoned mesmerism and clairvoyant methods and instead adopted the technique of changing the mind-set of the patient through conscious explanation. Quimby came to understand that disease was in the mind rather than the body. Because ordinary people were oblivious to this principle, Quimby's mission would be to explain that they can heal themselves by changing their negative belief systems. At this point, he reduced disease to the realm of beliefs: since beliefs can be changed, disease can be cured by mental means. Quimby soon arrived at his main hypothesis: "*Disease being in its roots a wrong belief, change that belief and we cure the disease.*" That is the power of the thought over the body. Changing negative thinking will produce a positive effect on the body's neurological, visceral, and cellular systems. Currently this is being confirmed by studies in the fields of neuroscience and epigenetics.

Quimby, convinced of the value of mental healing, developed a technique that might be called *suggestive explanatory treatment.* Quimby's treatment was explanatory; he used to say, "The explanation is the cure." This method consisted of, first, empowering the patient as creator of his condition; second, explaining to the patient how he became sick by fostering wrong beliefs and how changing those beliefs could lead to the restoration of his health; and third, "hammering," or repeating, these ideas until they became ingrained. Quimby's main thesis was "*The false belief is the error.*" Nevertheless, Quimby did not make use of denials as Christian Scientists would later do; this is one of the most important differences between the two systems.

Quimby's suggestive explanatory treatment can be described as follows: He would sit next to the patient and listen attentively to all of his or her concerns. This in itself is a therapeutic component nowadays called the "talking cure." It was later scientifically validated by the psychiatrists Josef Breuer and Sigmund Freud, who incorporated it into his psychoanalytic theory. (This subject will be discussed in detail in the chapter below devoted to Sigmund Freud and psychoanalysis.) But unlike Freud's therapy, in which the patient does most of the talking during the session, Quimby would ask some questions and would intuitively determine the nature of the problem. Then he would explain that the illness was the patient's creation, an error of the mind. He would make clear the mental causes of the malady and then replace the patient's fear with the firm expectation that the illness could be cured. Quimby would repeat his statements until the patient understood or internalized these ideas.

In modern psychology, this procedure can be considered a form of *direct suggestion*. Because of his convincing arguments, Quimby was able to accomplish a significant change in the habitual mental attitude of the patient; as a result, in most cases, recovery was almost immediate. The healing session was concluded with a short period of silent prayer. Because this method of healing was relatively simple, and no medical prescription or physical intervention was used, for some people, it was exceedingly difficult to believe. Consequently, Quimby sometimes would rub or massage the patient's head with wet hands in order to make them believe that *something had been done*. Herein lies the efficacy of the placebo effect. According to Quimby's manuscripts, he never claimed that rubbing patients' heads had any healing effect other than to make them believe that "something was done," that is, to strengthen the patient's confidence in the treatment. Quimby's conviction was that a patient's faith and expectation were essential elements for recovering health.

At this point, he became known as the "New England Doctor." (Although he did not hold any medical degree, Quimby was called "doctor" by his patients and acquaintances as a courtesy; moreover, the title "doctor" was used more loosely than it is today.) "Dr." Quimby summarized his method of treatment in a circular he distributed when he formally established his professional healing practice at the International Hotel in Portland, Maine, in 1859:

My practice is unlike all medical practice. I give no medicine, and make no outward applications. I tell the patient his troubles, and what he thinks is his disease, and my explanation is the cure. If I succeed in correcting his errors, I change the fluids of the system and establish the *truth or health. The truth is the cure.* This mode of practice applies to all cases.[11] (Italics are mine.)

This is the core of mental treatment. Quimby clearly indicated that "what the patient thinks is his disease" and identified that harmful thinking as "his error." Quimby further stated that if he succeeded in correcting the patient's faulty thinking, then he "established the truth" for the patient, and that truth was the cure. What was the error? The wrong beliefs and ideas in the patient's mind.

The following account given by one of Quimby's patients and a pioneer of the New Thought movement, Annetta G. Dresser, illustrates the healing method that Quimby was using when he started his practice in Portland. This treatment can be divided into four stages: (1) empowering, (2) personal persuasion, (3) hammering, and (4) silent spiritual treatment (closing healing). Annetta Dresser describes Quimby's healing method thus:

He seemed to know that I had come to him feeling that he was the last resort, and with but little faith in him or his mode of treatment. But instead of telling me that I was not sick, he sat beside me, and explained to me what sickness was, how I got into the condition, and the way I could have been taken out of it through the right understanding [*empowering the patient*].

He seemed to see through the situation from the beginning, and explained the cause and effect so clearly that I could see a little of what he meant. My case was so serious; however, that he did not at first tell me I could be made well. But there was such an effect produced by his first explanation that I felt a new hope within me, and began to get well from that day [*personal persuasion*].

He continued to explain my case from day to day, giving me some idea of his theory and its relation to what I had been taught to believe [*hammering*], and sometimes sat silently with me for a short time [*silent spiritual treatment*].[12]

The first two steps indicated above are of utmost importance in any kind of treatment, whether mental or conventional. First is the acknowledgment of the patient as a human being, as a spiritual entity, regardless of his or her present condition and background. In humanistic terms, an individual is part of the human community and deserves care and consideration. Second, a charismatic personality radiates positive energy and produces changes in the other person, as we have seen with Mesmer. The third aspect is hammering—impressing the idea on the patient's mind. The fourth is the silent closing of the session, which is a short period of praying and silent treatment. As Horatio Dresser stated, this silent treatment was Quimby's chief discovery.

When Quimby opened his office in Portland, he devoted himself full-time to the enterprise of curing people. Thousands of patients flocked to his office, many of whom were diagnosed as incurable by medical professionals of the time. The period from 1859 to 1865 was the most productive and important chapter of Quimby's life. During this time he performed remarkable healings for many important people in New England. Among the illustrious people who came to his office seeking help were the two daughters of the late judge Ashur Ware;[13] the Methodist minister Warren Felt Evans; Julius Dresser; his wife, Annetta; and Mary Baker Eddy.

Many wonderful cases of healing of incurable diseases were reported in the local newspapers, by independent writers.[14] It was also during this period that Quimby developed a more advanced therapeutic theory: from suggestive explanatory healing, he developed spiritual mind healing. This constituted a quantum leap in the evolution of his healing theory.

Spiritual mind healing is a higher level of therapy; it regards every human as a spiritual being rather than a physical body. Moreover, emphasis is shifted from a mental and suggestive treatment to the spiritual realm. Therefore, the treatment becomes *metaphysical* rather than mental; the change of thought is secondary. Hence this approach does not impose new ideas on the sick person, but rather acknowledges her divine Self, which is never ill. The divine Self is merely seen as entrapped and eclipsed by the physical causes of the illness. Furthermore, Quimby held that all human beings share a guiding principle, which is the "divine wisdom" within. Intuitively and independently, Quimby discovered the principle of a Universal Mind.

Quimby also incorporated biblical principles into his new theory and tried to give an explanation of his healing based on Jesus Christ's teachings. Quimby was able to formulate metaphysical principles through his own intuitive understanding. For instance, he held that all human beings are connected through a "hidden mind" that is accessible to the spiritual healer. For him, all causes were in reality spiritual, and all causation in the physical world comes from an internal rather than an external source. Quimby recognized the supremacy of the spirit over matter and believed that the material world springs from spiritual sources.

For Quimby, every human has two parts: the inner being, what he called Principle-Christ or "scientific" man; and the outward personality, which he called the mortal man. The spiritual being (or Principle-Christ) that dwells in the individual is concealed by the physical or mortal one. Quimby's greatest idea was that a human essentially is a "spiritual being"; he distinguished between the mortal (physical) and immortal (spiritual) being. Horatio Dresser further explains that Quimby addressed the treatment to the "real man, the spirit, who needed to be summoned into power."[15] He intuitively foresaw the existence of what would later be called the subconscious mind, independent of the studies of the Nancy school of hypnosis and long before the works of such figures as Thomson Jay Hudson, William James, and Sigmund Freud.

Quimby resorted to the New Testament to find evidence for his healing method, and he concluded that it was similar to Jesus Christ's. Believing that he had rediscovered the spiritual technique by which Jesus

Christ cured people, he did not want to take credit as the discoverer of this form of treatment. Instead, he tried to follow Jesus's example by healing people in order to mitigate their suffering. That was why Quimby called his therapeutic method "Science of Christ" or "Christ Science." (Note the resemblance to Christian Science.) Hence Quimby abandoned the theory of mental healing—the idea that the power of one person's mind influences another's—and he replaced it with what can be called *spiritual mind healing*. This is his greatest legacy. It is an extraordinary contribution to healing without medicine, a new way to alleviate human suffering. At this point, his fundamental doctrine goes beyond considering a disease the effect of a *wrong belief*. His healing paradigm was now based on a spiritual view of humanity.

Quimby would also request the participation of the patient in the healing process. The patient had to believe in the effectiveness of the treatment. Thus he remained aware that beliefs are of great importance, that most of our beliefs are erroneous, and that God is an invisible Wisdom that fills all space and whose attributes are light, goodness, and love. God is the only reality, everlasting essence, existing in all matter. He wrote, "The true God is benevolent, and could never have created disease. Sickness comes from beliefs and fears and faith is the remedy."[16] This statement is remarkable, because it is close to the metaphysical concept of the existence of a Universal Mind or consciousness.

By the end of 1865, Quimby, overburdened by work, decided to withdraw from his healing practice and moved to Belfast, Maine. An article published in the *Portland Advertiser* gives an interesting account of his retirement. The writer acknowledged that Quimby was well respected by the people who knew him and that "his departure will be viewed as a public loss." The article continues with the following observation:

> That he has manifested wonderful power in healing the sick among us, no well-informed an unprejudiced person can deny. Indeed, for more than twenty years the doctor [Quimby] has devoted himself to this one object; namely, *to cure the sick*, and *to discover through his practice the*

origin and nature of disease. By a method entirely novel and at first sight quite unintelligible, he has been slowly developing what he calls the *"Science of Health."*[17] (Italics are mine.)

The last words of the above quotation are worth noting; we see that the term *Science of Health* was attributed to Quimby's intellectual discovery and was in the public domain before the publication of Mary Baker Eddy's *Science and Health.* This was the first title of her book.

Julius A. Dresser, one of the first pioneers of New Thought, describes Quimby as a humble and "remarkable man . . . to this was united a benevolent and an unselfish nature, and love of truth."[18] This noble and compassionate aspect of Quimby's personality, mentioned many times by the people who knew him, is evidenced in his legacy to future generations. He never thought of copyrighting his discoveries or his teachings; following Jesus Christ, Quimby selflessly gave them to his disciples and to the world. He articulated this intellectual heritage in the following words: "This is my theory, to put man in possession of a science that will destroy the idea of the sick, and teach man one living profession of his identity with life free from error and disease."[19]

Phineas Quimby died on January 16, 1866, at the age of sixty-four, in Belfast, Maine. It is said that his death was the result of excessive work and dedication to his healing profession. His epitaph, taken from John 15:13, accurately describes him as one of great people of this time: "Greater love hath no man than this, that a man lay down his life for his friends" (King James Version). His kindness and devotion to the welfare of his fellow men were well-known. He loved his neighbors and was a genuine seeker of truth. Quimby did not take any credit as the discoverer of mental or spiritual healing; he was content enough believing that he rediscovered the way Jesus had healed people, and saw his mission as teaching and sharing his discoveries with anyone who was interested and ready for them. Currently, several modern scientific disciplines have emerged and are confirming the fundamental theses of the New England healer: neuroscience, new biology (epigenetics), quantum physics, depth psychology, and psychoneuroimmunology (PNI). I will discuss these in later chapters.

Another important figure, contemporary to both Quimby and Mary Baker Eddy, was Andrew Jackson Davis, considered the leading forerunner of American spiritualism. He was born on August 11, 1826, in Blooming Grove, New York, in the Hudson Valley. Davis was influenced by the eighteenth-century mystic Emanuel Swedenborg and by Ann Lee, the founder of the radical religious sect called the Shakers, who settled principally in upstate New York. Indeed the upstate New York of this period, including both the Hudson Valley and the central and western regions, was known as the "burned-over district" because of the many evangelical revivals and spiritual revelations that took place there, including those of Joseph Smith, founder of Mormonism; Jemima Wilkinson, who spoke of a spiritual resurrection; and others.

There are some parallels between Quimby and Davis: both were born into poor families and had very little schooling. While Quimby was a clockmaker in his early years, Davis was a shoemaker. Both became interested in mesmerism after attending public lectures.

Davis's psychic abilities manifested when a local tailor named William Livingston was experimenting with mesmerism. He put Davis into a trance, and as a result Davis found that he was clairvoyant and could understand truths from a higher plane of consciousness. Like both Lucius Burkmar and the "sleeping prophet," Edgar Cayce, fifty years later Davis diagnosed illnesses and prescribed folk medicine while in trance. He was also said to be able to enter into higher levels of consciousness and obtain spiritual knowledge and perceive the laws of the universe. Davis held that after death, all human spirits continue to progress in the spiritual realm throughout eternity. He was apparently also able to see and observe the death process and the way in which the spirit leaves the body and forms a new spiritual being. He even described the hereafter in detail, a state that he was supposedly able to enter at will.[20]

While in trance, Davis dictated many books, the most important being *The Divine Revelations* (1847) and *The Great Harmonia* (1850). In all he wrote around thirty books, which were published while he was alive. His writings included topics such as the seven planes of existence, mental and physical health, astronomy, physics, chemistry, philosophy, education, and many others. As one article puts it, "In his writings about the human body and health, Davis described how the human body was transparent to him in [his] trance state. Each organ of the body stood out clearly with a special luminosity of its own which greatly diminished in cases of disease."[21]

Davis's most remarkable talent was that, unlike other clairvoyants, he was specific in his predictions, and his accuracy was much higher than that of any other seer or psychic of the time. The accuracy of his predictions is reflected in his book *The Great Harmonia*, in which Davis talks about human evolution, a concept that he foresaw nine years before Charles Darwin published his book *On the Origin of Species*. It is also said that Davis also predicted the existence of the planets Neptune and Pluto before their actual discovery.[22] The accuracy of his predictions was far greater than that of other seers and prophets, including Nostradamus and Edgar Cayce. Nostradamus's predictions, for example, are too vague and open-ended, lacking any time frame or concrete geographic specificity.

Although there is no evidence that they ever met or heard of each other, there are some similarities between Quimby's and Davis's teachings. Davis believed that there is only "one Principle, one united attribute of Goodness and Truth." He also asserted that "the Positive Mind is the Divine Intelligence" and "disease is discord." Moreover, "disease is an effect, not a cause." In order for an individual to regain his health Davis recommends "reconciliation with Nature, and not medicines." Indeed, he said, many people have been healed from many maladies by withdrawing from society and going into the sacred temple of nature, to practice contemplation and meditation, or to just be at peace with nature and themselves.

Andrew Jackson Davis died in the year 1910. The same year saw the deaths of both William James, the father of American psychology, and the founder of Christian Science, Mary Baker Eddy.

There is a characteristic common to Lucius Burkmar, Andrew Jackson Davis, and Edgar Cayce. All went into altered states of mind to diagnose and prescribe folkloric medicine; their diagnoses and recommendations, in this author's opinion, served as effective curative *suggestions*. Their interventions were effective because people of the time believed the information they were receiving from them. The belief that this information was coming from a supernatural realm, outside of rational and scientific explanation, enhanced the curative power of their suggestions.

Chapter 4

Warren Felt Evans and Julius and Annetta Dresser

Pioneers of New Thought

While Quimby was undoubtedly the father of the New Thought movement, he never sought to establish any philosophical school or organized church. He was too busy healing people and developing his innovative ideas about life and health. The propagation of his philosophical ideas and method of healing, as well as the development of New Thought, fell initially on the shoulders of three personalities: Warren Felt Evans, Julius A. Dresser, and Dresser's wife, Annetta, née Seabury. All of them, as well as Mary Baker Eddy, came to Quimby as a last resort, seeking relief from their health problems. In 1862, Seabury, Dresser, and Eddy visited Quimby, followed by Evans in the following year. Thus the period 1862–63 was very significant for the evolution of mental healing in America.

Once these individuals were cured by Quimby, they became his students and disciples. Eddy, however, departed radically from her mentor's ideas and developed what can be called a nihilistic type of healing—denying physical reality and consequently illness.

Julius Dresser was born in 1838 in Portland, Maine; he initially intended to become a minister in the Calvinistic Baptist Church. However, when he experienced health problems and conventional medicine of the time did not give him much hope, he learned of Quimby.

Dresser, thinking he had not long to live, went to see Quimby as a last resort. Surprisingly, he was restored to health in a short time. From then on, he became an earnest advocate of this kind of healing and devoted his time to spreading the new gospel.

Dresser held that any spiritual or mental treatment within New Thought requires cleansing negative ideas and thoughts from the conscious mind and replacing them with positive ones, which he called "the truth." These ideas are expressed in the following paragraph:

> There are many ways to give a metaphysical treatment for healing, but there is only one purpose behind any treatment, which is to change the consciousness of the person given the treatment. Generally speaking this is done either by "argument" or by "realization," but the effect is the same. . . . But whatever the method of treatment, what happens is that our own consciousness is changed; where we saw a problem, we now see "Truth established."[1]

Annetta Seabury and Julius Dresser met at Quimby's Portland office for the first time in 1862. Later, in her book *The Philosophy of P. P. Quimby*, Annetta wrote that she heard of Quimby and his wonderful healings in 1860. She also mentioned that although Quimby's unorthodox method of healing was not commonly accepted, Quimby's patients became his friends and his fame as a healer was quickly spreading in the region.[2] This is her account of her healing:

> My own experience with Dr. Quimby was a very interesting one, and attended with most happy results. . . . I went to him in May, 1862, as a patient, after six years of great suffering, and *as a last resort*, after all other methods of cure had utterly failed to bring relief. I had barely faith enough to be willing to go to him, as I had been one of those who were prejudiced against him, and still had more of doubt and fear than expectancy of receiving help. But all fear was taken away as I was met by this good man, with his kindly though searching glance.[3] (Italics are mine.)

Dresser and Seabury married in 1863. They became enthusiastic advocates of Quimby's system and were the first to practice mind healing according to it, practicing it successfully in Boston. They also gave classes on mind healing using Quimby's manuscript as a text. The name used for their classes was "The Quimby System of Mental Treatment of Diseases." The Dressers' basic postulates were that God is omnipresent in the universe and that human beings possess a divine spark within. Individuals have no power of their own, and their role in life is to manifest the Will of God through the qualities of love, mercy, and justice.[4]

In 1887, Julius Dresser published a book entitled *The True History of Mental Science* as a protest against Mary Baker Eddy's claims of being the discoverer of mental healing. This book attempts to reinstate Quimby as the discoverer of spiritual and mind healing in America. In 1895, Annetta Dresser published *The Philosophy of P. P. Quimby*, which describes the background of Quimby's life and works and outlines his healing methods. In that sense, the Dressers made an important contribution to the dissemination of the New Thought philosophy. Both books are early firsthand testimonies of Quimby's mind treatment and give an accurate account of the beginning of mental healing in America.

The other pioneer of mental healing, Warren Felt Evans, was born in Vermont on December 23, 1817. He initially became a Methodist minister and served in different capacities in that denomination. Prior to his encounter with Quimby, he became acquainted with the writings of Emanuel Swedenborg (1688–1772), a Swedish mystic and philosopher who greatly influenced New Thought thinkers including Ralph Waldo Emerson. Evans left the Methodist ministry and joined the Church of the New Jerusalem, a denomination that followed Swedenborg's teachings. During this time, he contracted a serious nervous problem, complicated by a chronic stomach disorder. Conventional medicine was unable to help him. He learned of Quimby, who was becoming increasingly well-known in New England.

Evans visited Quimby at his office in Portland; he was not only healed of his maladies but was deeply impressed by Quimby's teachings, which were close to the metaphysical ideas of Swedenborg. As a result, he became very interested in learning the new method. Familiar with Swedenborg's writings as well as with German idealistic philosophy and the writings of Bishop George Berkeley, Evans was quickly able to comprehend Quimby's spiritual principles. After a few visits he informed Quimby that he wanted to use his healing system. The master, in an attitude of benevolence and unselfishness, agreed and encouraged him to do so.

In 1867, Evans began practicing mental healing in Boston and then in Salisbury, Massachusetts; he also taught the principles of mental healing for several years.[5] It is said that he did not charge for his services and instruction, although he accepted voluntary offerings. In this sense, Evans replicated Quimby's goodwill: he did not deny healing services for lack of money. Like the Dressers, Evans was among the initial promoters of Quimby's method of healing. William J. Leonard, author of *The Pioneer Apostle of Mental Science*, observes about Evans:

> In his estimation, Dr. Quimby was the highest authority in the science of healing, and a man of noble character and purest aims, which Dr. Evans believed were indispensably necessary to bring one into the perfect peace and harmony with the Divine Life required to teach and heal the sick and suffering with success. Not only was Dr. Evans fair enough to honor his master in the science, but, with humility and modesty of the truly great soul, he made no attempt to claim that the truths he presented were absolutely new.[6]

Evans, a prolific writer, disseminated the ideas of mind healing in several works. *Mental Cure: Illustrating the Influence of the Mind on the Body* (1869) was the first on the subject published in America. It was available six years before Mary Baker Eddy's *Science and Health*, published in 1875. *Mental Cure* was an attempt to establish the philosophical and theoretical grounds for mind healing. Evans's writings were also influenced by German idealism and by the philosophies of Bishop Berkeley and Swedenborg. It is probable that Mary Baker Eddy had read this book and assimilated its metaphysical concepts, as it was already well-known in America and abroad when her own book was published. But this assertion will never be confirmed or denied, because she never mentioned or gave credit to anybody as sources for her knowledge and information. Evans authored two other books, including *Mental Medicine*, which was published in 1872, and *Soul and Body*, published in 1875. Both of these were also available before Eddy's *Science and Health*. Therefore Evans was the first to provide a consistent metaphysical explanation for what has become known as New Thought.

As writers Alan Anderson and Deborah Whitehouse indicate, "The writings of Evans were read widely in the United States and abroad. Charles Fillmore, cofounder of Unity Church, considered Evans' works to be 'the most complete of all metaphysical compilations.'"[7] Evans's books were part of the library of the Higher Thought Centre, a British organization based on the teachings of American New Thought.[8]

Horatio Willis Dresser, the son of Julius and Annetta Dresser, was born on January 15, 1866. He later became a prolific writer about New Thought. Like his parents, Horatio was a faithful interpreter and follower of Quimby's philosophy, and he took up their mission to reveal the real origin and history of mental healing in America. Once the Library of Congress made Quimby's manuscripts available to the public, Dresser compiled, edited, and published the work called *The Quimby Manuscripts*.[9]

Chapter 5

Mary Baker Eddy
Founder of Christian Science

I indulge in homeopathic doses of
Natrum muriaticum *(common salt).*
—Mary Baker Eddy

Mary Baker Eddy was the founder of the Christian Science church. She was born Mary Morse Baker in New Hampshire, the same state as Quimby. She was raised in a strict religious home environment with Puritan values and daily Bible readings. Thus she had a strong Christian religious background, and was considered a self-educated woman. She was married three times and went by three married names during the course of her life: Mary Baker Patterson, Mary Baker Glover, and Mary Baker Eddy.

Eddy's childhood and much of her adult life were spent in ill health due to a chronic spinal disease. She spent most of her life seeking healing and tried all the remedial methods available in her time without any success. Traditional medicine did not help her at all. On October 14, 1861, Eddy's second husband, a dentist, Dr. Daniel Patterson, wrote to Quimby, asking him to come to Concord, New Hampshire, to see his wife, who was virtually paralyzed and bedridden. Patterson described her condition as follows: "My wife has been crippled for a number of years by spinal paralysis. She is barely able to sit up, and we shall be so glad, if it is at all possible, to try your wonderful powers in her case."[1]

Quimby was not able to come to Concord. In the spring of 1862, then—Mrs. Patterson wrote to Quimby herself from Rumney, New Hampshire, asking for help.[2] Quimby, busy with his healing practice, perhaps did not pay much attention to her request. As Quimby did not visit her, she went looking for him. Putting together all the money she had been saving and borrowing from relatives and friends, she undertook the journey to meet him.

Author Israel Regardie describes Mary Baker Eddy's physical condition when she came to see Quimby in the following words:

> But here was the pathetic picture of Mary, forty years of age, suffering hopelessly from chronic neurasthenia, poor as a church-mouse, seeking once more the assistance of her family. . . . In order to achieve some alleviation from physical suffering and mental anguish, she had experimented with almost everything. The drugs and medication of the allopath, the mystical attenuations of the homeopaths, countless herbal remedies, mesmeric treatment. All to no avail. She had exhausted almost all the possibilities that her age could offer her in treatment. She had prayed, imploring the high heavens for succor. But the celestial gates were closed fast, and she remained impotent, insecure and ill.[3]

In October 1862, she arrived at the International Hotel in Portland. At the time, she was unable to climb the stairs to the second floor by herself and had to be helped by other people to reach Quimby's office. Among others present in the vestibule of the hotel was Annetta Dresser. She would later recollect:

> It was also at this time, 1862, that Mrs. Eddy, author of "Science and Health," was associated with Dr. Quimby; and I remember the day when she was helped up the steps to his office on the occasion of her first visit. She was cured by him and afterwards became very much interested in his theory. But she put her own construction on much of his teachings, and developed a system of thought which differs radically from it.[4]

Regardie depicts the pathetic circumstances of how Eddy met Quimby and her healing:

> She sat there exhausted and weak. It is said she was shabbily dressed. Every reserve had gone not into presenting a worthy feminine appearance, but simply to get to this office. It seemed as though she were a mere broken vestige of a woman. Phineas P. Quimby gave her a mental treatment and subsequently her health improved quickly, the change on her physical condition was almost instantaneous. Her pain and weakness disappeared, a sense of comfort and well-being immersed into their place. In a week she was able to climb without any help the one hundred eighty-two steps to the dome of the City Hall of Portland, Maine. She was greatly impressed by the magnanimous Quimby.[5]

Exhilarated about her healing, she published several letters in the *Portland Courier*, a local newspaper. In these letters, she described in detail all her previous attempts to obtain relief for her illness, and she gave credit to Quimby for her cure. She even compared Quimby's healing to that of Jesus. In addition to speaking about Quimby's wondrous healing abilities, she published articles and poems in the local newspapers giving testimony of gratitude to him.[6] In a letter published in the *Portland Courier*, she asserted:

> With this mental and physical depression, I first visited P. P. Quimby, and in less than one week from that time I ascended by a stairway of one hundred and eighty-two steps to the dome of the City Hall, and improving *ad infinitum*. . . .
>
> But now I can see dimly at first, and only as trees walking, the great principles which underlie Dr. Quimby's faith and works; *as just in proportion to my right perception of truth is my recovery. The truth which he opposes to the error of giving intelligence to matter and placing pain where it never placed itself*, if received understandingly, changes the current of the system to their normal action; and the mechanism of the body goes on undisturbed.[7] (Italics are mine.)

The italicized sentences indicate how quickly Eddy had absorbed Quimby's instruction. The core of his metaphysical teaching was *not to attribute any power to matter but to the Spirit; mind has power over matter.* After the initial meeting, she was deeply interested in Quimby's theory of mental healing and continued visiting him to learn. She asked questions and sought clarifications. Eager to know how his whole system worked, she wanted to understand how she had been cured without medicine after so many years of unsuccessful conventional treatments. Quimby allowed her access to his manuscripts; she avidly read them and took notes for herself and fully copied his essay entitled "Questions and Answers," in which he described his theory and method of healing. She also submitted her notes to Quimby for correction and approval.

After Quimby's death, Eddy would use his essay to give lessons in mind healing. It is said that Quimby intuitively saw in Eddy an unusual ability to comprehend metaphysical concepts. Reportedly he said about her: "She is a devilish bright woman." Quimby was impressed by her capacity to quickly assimilate his teachings and saw in her an individual who could promote and spread his healing theories.[8] In another letter published in the *Portland Courier*, she wrote:

> P. P. Quimby stands upon the plane of wisdom with his truth. Christ healed the sick, but not by jugglery or with drugs. As the former speaks, as never man before spake and *heals as never man healed since Christ, is he not identified with truth? And is not this the Christ which is in him?* We know that in wisdom is life, "and the light was the light of man." P. P. Quimby rolls away the stone from the sepulchre of error, and health is the resurrection. But we also know that "light shineth in darkness and the darkness comprehendeth it not."[9] (Italics are mine.)

How can this phenomenon be explained in rational terms? Previously, Eddy had unsuccessfully sought every kind of medical treatment, orthodox and unorthodox, but these did not cure her. Quimby was able to cure her, after forty years of chronic poor health, to a condition where she could function. The trip to see Quimby was her last resort and hope; she spent all the money she had borrowed; thus the trip to Portland had to be successful by all means. The rationale for her healing lay partly in her firm determination to get well and in the understanding that the real healer is the Inner Self dwelling in every human being.

Regardie explains Eddy's healing in this way: she suffered from a neurotic paralysis, and with Quimby she experienced a psychological cure as she was released from her emotional distress. "The sickness was a defense, a means of self-protection," according to Regardie.[10] Sigmund Freud might have diagnosed Eddy with a severe case of hysteria, originating in childhood sexual repression due to her strict religious education. (Hysteria has been defined as a mental disorder characterized by emotional excitability or a physical problem, such as paralysis or a sensory deficit, without any organic cause.) According to psychoanalysis, these traumatic experiences and her unfulfilled desires would have caused internal conflict in her subconscious, producing hysterical symptoms.

The healing under Quimby's care can be explained as a combination of suggestion, spiritual explanation of the nature of an illness, and personal influence. Quimby was able to generate in Eddy an emotional discharge that was retained for many years, producing a therapeutic catharsis. Quimby's belief was that illness is only an error of the mind, a wrong belief, and mankind should not attribute any power to matter or illness, but rather to the Spirit.

Regardie acknowledged the profound influence of Quimby on Eddy when he wrote, "For the first time, he had demonstrated to her a method of healing which proved that the mind supremely was able to affect and control physiological function."[11] However, Regardie maintained that Quimby only pointed the way; the philosophical rationale for the modus operandi of mind healing had to be sought somewhere else. This assessment is inaccurate because Regardie was well aware of the fact that Evans had already published three books on mental healing partly based on Quimby's teachings before Eddy's *Science and Health* appeared in 1875. In these books, Evans sought to find a theoretical foundation for mind healing in the ideas of Swedenborg, German idealism, Transcendentalism, and Vedanta, a Hindu philosophy holding that the external reality is *maya*, that is, illusion.

After being cured by Quimby, Eddy returned to Concord.

Quimby died on January 16, 1866. A few weeks later, on February 1, Eddy slipped on an icy street in Lynn, Massachusetts, and injured her spine. She found herself again a "helpless cripple" as she had been before she went to Quimby. The homeopath she consulted, Dr. Alvin Cushing, diagnosed her injuries as a concussion and possible spinal fracture. She was also said to be semihysterical, nervous, and only partially conscious. Since Quimby had just died, she wrote a desperate letter to Julius Dresser, asking him to assume Quimby's role and come to Concord to heal her. Dresser did not feel capable of filling Quimby's role and did not respond to her letter.

Eddy felt lost and powerless without Quimby's sustaining healing power. She was possessed by despair and was horrified by the idea of returning to the sickly condition she had been in before Quimby's healing. Her mentor was gone, and there was no one else able to administer a mental treatment to her. Thus *as a last resort*, she had to depend on her own interpretation of Quimby's method. As we have seen, this use of a *last resort* is a common pattern found in the pioneers of mind healing who cured themselves without medicine.

In human history, it has been observed many times that people rise from the deepest crises in life to find creative solutions or ideas. That seems to have happened here. Since there was no one available to administer mind healing to Eddy, she found that the only solution was to apply Quimby's techniques to herself. Surprisingly, the autotreatment was successful. By February 4, she had regained her health and was able to walk. Later she claimed that she had received a "spiritual revelation" that healed her from her injury.

A similar incident occurred to religious leader Jemima Wilkinson (1752–1819) under different circumstances. Wilkinson, a native of

Rhode Island, is recognized as the first charismatic American-born woman to found a religious group, the Society of Universal Friends, which preached total sexual abstinence. At age twenty-four, Wilkinson suffered from a serious illness, which led to a near-death experience. She mysteriously woke up from a coma completely healed.[12] Wilkinson's experience appears to be an episode of a spontaneous remission similar to the one experienced by Eddy. Wilkinson died when Eddy was nine years old. It is likely that Eddy was aware of Wilkinson's case. Eddy was well acquainted with the religious trends and the alternative therapies of the time, as she was a religious person who sought many forms of relief for her long-standing illness. Indeed psychologist Isaac Woodbridge Riley has written that Eddy was influenced by "'mother' Ann Lee" and accused her of "plagiarism from Shakerism, Mesmerism and Quimbyism."[13] Mother Mary Lee (1736–1784) was the founder and leader of the religious organization known as *Shakers*.

The events narrated by Eddy regarding her "miracle cure" and "revelation" were as follows: reportedly, while she was ill in bed, she asked for her Bible and read an account of one of Jesus's healings. (Previously she had written that Jesus Christ's healings were similar to Quimby's.) She probably recalled Quimby's statement that "illness is an error of the mind" as well as his exhortations "not to place intelligence in matter," "not to believe in the illness," and "not to attribute any power to matter or illness but to the Spirit."

Most likely, the realization and conscious application of these assertions to her own situation were the cause of her epiphany. Thus, through a process of persistent *conscious autosuggestion* using the above statements, reinforced by biblical stories, she was able to recover her health. In other words, she held steadfastly to the metaphysical principle not to attribute power to external conditions or wrong beliefs such as illness. She was able to regain her well-being, and the rest is history. But she did not realize that instead of discovering "Christian Science healing," she discovered the power of autosuggestion, which was unheard of and unknown at that time.

Precisely in the darkest periods, when everything seems gloomy and depressing, when we think there is no way out, a light of hope usually comes from the other end of the tunnel. These incidents serve as learning experiences and provide insightful creative solutions.

Viennese psychiatrist Viktor E. Frankl, a Holocaust survivor, took as a learning experience the time he spent in a Nazi concentration camp. He tried to find the meaning of life in adverse conditions. After his release, he spent most of his life explaining how people, in the most difficult moments of their lives, were able to see the glimmering light at the end of the tunnel that led to their mental and spiritual liberation. The following example given by Frankl describes an event similar to those in which people regained their health after a spiritual epiphany.

> In the mental hospital, I was locked like an animal in a cage, no one came when I called begging to be taken to the bathroom, and I finally had to succumb to the inevitable. Blessedly, I was given daily shock treatment, insulin shock, and sufficient drugs so that I lost most of the several weeks. . . .
>
> But in the darkness I had acquired a sense of my own unique mission in the world. I knew then, as I know now, that I must have been preserved for some reason—however small, it is something that only I can do, and it is vitally important that I do it. And because in the darkest moment of my life, when I lay abandoned as an animal in a cage, when because of the forgetfulness induced by ECT [electroconvulsive therapy] *I could not call out* to Him. He was there. In the solitary darkness of the "pit" where men had abandoned me. *He was there.* When I did not know His Name, He was there; God was there.[14] (Italics Frankl's.)

To summarize, the "spiritual discovery" that Eddy claimed was based on the use of Quimby's technique without recourse to a second person. Since there was no one available to administer mental healing to her, as a *last resort*, she realized that she could apply the metaphysical principles taught by Quimby to herself. That is, she made use of conscious autosuggestion. In this way, she preceded Émile Coué in using autosuggestion for healing.

Incidentally, in the preface of the first edition of *Science and Health*, she wrote: "We made our first discovery that science mentally applied would heal the sick, in *1864*, and since then have *tested it on ourselves* and hundreds of others, and never found it fail to prove the statement made herein made of it" (italics are mine).[15] There is a discrepancy regarding the year of Eddy's alleged "divine revelation" and mental healing. According to the above quotation, it happened in 1864; later she claimed that her discovery occurred on February 4, 1866, three days after falling on the icy street and after her autohealing. If we take the year 1864 (given in the preface of the first edition of *Science and Health*), this would imply that her initial "discovery" took place two years before her famous fall and recovery, when she was still under Quimby's care. She actually wrote a poem in tribute to Quimby after his death, which was attached to the letter she sent to Julius Dresser when she asked him for mental treatment. The poem was published in the Lynn, Massachusetts, newspaper on January 22, 1866, with the following title: "Lines on the Death of Dr. P. P. Quimby, who Healed with the Truth That Christ Taught, in Contradiction to All Isms."[16]

Furthermore, in the preface of the latest official edition of *Science and Health*, she affirms that the "great discovery" of her system was in 1866 and not in 1864, as she had noted in the first edition. This inconsistency is reiterated in her last writing, *Retrospection and Introspection*, in the subchapter "The Great Discovery," where she asserts that in 1866, she became convinced that "all causation was mind, and every effect a mental phenomenon." In the following quotation she finally mentions Quimby, but only as a "magnetic doctor."

> It was in Massachusetts, in February, 1866, and after the death of the magnetic doctor, Mr. P. P. Quimby, whom spiritualists would associate therewith, but who was not in wise connected with this event, that I discovered the Science of Divine metaphysical healing which I afterwards named Christian Science. During twenty years prior to my

discovery I had been trying to trace all physical effects to a mental cause; and in the later part of 1866 I gained the scientific certainty that all causation was Mind, and every effect a mental phenomenon.[17]

In the above statement, she herself acknowledges that "all causation is Mind"; thus we can infer that her healing was not the result of divine revelation but of mental intervention. In addition, her biographers Willa Cather and Georgine Milmine find some discrepancies regarding her "immediate recovery" as well, because her attending physician visited her three times after her "miracle recovery;" thus the recovery was not immediate at all.

It will be noted that although Mrs. Eddy's revelation and miraculous recovery occurred on February third, Dr. Cushing visited her professionally three times after she had been restored to health by divine power. Dr. Cushing says that he visited her on the third day—when, writes Mrs. Eddy, she had her miraculous recovery; and also two days later. In August, seven months after her discovery of Christian Science he was called in to treat her for a cough, and made four professional visits during that month.[18]

This clearly indicates that there are flagrant contradictions about the date of her "famous discovery." If she had found out that all causation was mental, why she was still seeing a doctor after seven months of her "healing"? Establishing the correct date of her presumed "discovery" is extremely important, because the followers of Eddy believe that such a "discovery" was a divine revelation, an inspiration received directly from God. In a letter written in 1877, Eddy suggests that her mission completes that of the New Testament, and she believed that Christian Science had been foretold in the book of Revelation.[19]

In the three years following her fall and healing, Eddy resided in several boarding houses, most of them run by spiritualists (people who seek communication with the spirits of the dead). She described this period as a withdrawal from society. However, both author Stefan Zweig and Eddy's biographers Cather and Milmine reached a different conclusion. They argued that during this period Eddy wandered from home to home taking with her a handwritten copy of Quimby's manuscript "Questions and Answers," in which he described his theory and philosophy of mind healing. During this transient period she came up with the idea of rewriting and expanding "Questions and Answers." She asked people for their hospitality and gained the sympathy of her hostesses by talking about a new system of healing without medicine and reading to them from the manuscript that she was working on.

Stefan Zweig vividly describes these tragic years of Mary Baker Eddy:

> For several years from 1867 onwards, it will be remembered, in her wandering from one house to another, this impoverished woman had continued to carry a precious manuscript among her slender belongings. In her worn valise she had no spare dress. . . . The only thing which, from her point of view, was of priceless value, was this soiled and tattered manuscript, greasy with incessant rereading. At first it has been no more than a faithful transcript of Quimby's *Questions and Answers*, perhaps expanded a little here and there, and provided by Mary Baker Eddy with an Introduction. By degrees, however, the introduction grew longer than the text, while the text itself was, at each recopying, provided with fresh glosses—for this woman possessed by an idea rewrote her strange textbook of mental healing again and again and again. She was never fully satisfied with it. Ten, twenty, thirty years after its first publication, there were still emendations to make, for never could she free herself from her book, or her book from herself.[20]

As she was penniless and without work, she got the idea to give classes based on Quimby's teaching as a way of earning money. She trained a twenty-one-year-old man named Richard Kennedy in the principles of mind cure, and formed a partnership with him so he could start giving classes on mind healing under her supervision in Lynn, Massachusetts.[21] For this enterprise, she already had the material she had copied from Quimby's manuscript, "Questions and Answers." A facsimile of the first page of this manuscript can be found in Cather's and Milmine's book.[22]

Kennedy's classes were successful, and the lecture room was crowded with humble people eager to learn this new technique of mind cure as a way to make extra money. Eddy was supervising behind the curtains.

According to Cather and Milmine, Eddy kept writing and rewriting the manuscript with quotations from and interpretations of the Bible. She constantly rewrote the same manuscript, making amendments and additions until she produced a completely new manuscript. Even after the book's first publication in 1875, she continued making revisions and alterations. In fact, the first edition, which was called *Science and Health*, is substantially different from the later editions; even the title of the book was later changed to *Science and Health with Key to the Scriptures*. The fact that she was continuously inserting new emendations proves that this book was not the result of "divine inspiration," as she claimed, but was the development and maturing of her metaphysical ideas over several years.

Where did Mary Baker Eddy acquire the additional metaphysical information beyond Quimby's ideas? There is strong evidence that she took some of her ideas from Hindu and Neoplatonic philosophies as filtered through Thoreau and Emerson.[23] Israel Regardie believes that during her nomadic years, Eddy came to live at the home of a Hiram Craft, where she apparently had access to a manuscript by the German-American philosopher and metaphysician Francis Lieber entitled *The Metaphysical Religion of Hegel*, dated April 1866. Regardie maintains that "the central thesis, upon which Christian Science is made to stand, is in reality said to be one of the Hegelian concepts as understood and enunciated by Lieber." He further cites Lieber: "For Hegel and his true disciples, there is no truth, substance, life, or intelligence in matter; all is infinite mind. Thus matter has no reality; it is only the manifestation of Spirit. . . . Therefore science is spiritual, for God is Spirit."[24]

Eddy appears to have rephrased this assertion and later incorporated it into *Science and Health with Key to the Scriptures*. The so-called "scientific statement of being" of Christian Science is similar to Lieber's: "There is no life, truth, intelligence, nor substance in matter. All is infinite Mind and its infinite manifestation, for God is All-in-all. Spirit is immortal Truth; matter is mortal error."[25] This declaration is the most important tenet of Christian Science doctrine. It is the formula that must be memorized by its followers and repeated during Christian Science services and Sunday schools.

There is further evidence that Eddy's initial metaphysical ideas were based on Quimby's manuscript. In 1868–70, she resided in Stoughton, Massachusetts and compiled a manuscript known as "Extracts from P. P. Quimby's Writings," on which she based her teachings. "In 1872, while teaching in Lynn, Mass., Mrs. Eddy claimed this manuscript as her own, and in this and other writings she gradually changed the terminology so that it bore less resemblance to Quimby's."[26]

Quimby left manuscripts detailing his discoveries and teachings; in addition, there are many accounts of his healings in local newspapers. Eddy's letters of gratitude published in the *Portland Courier* are hard evidence of her indebtedness to Quimby. He had been practicing mind healing several years before she came to see him, asking for help. It was his treatment that healed her after she had tried conventional medicine and other methods of treatment unsuccessfully for forty years. But after Quimby's death, she declared herself to be the discoverer of mind healing. She expressed profound gratitude to her teacher while he was alive, but once he died, she denied him and went to the extreme of portraying him an imposter.

Quimby's manuscript was examined by editors of *The New York Times* in 1922 and they came to the conclusion: "It was a gigantic task which the editor of *The Quimby Manuscripts* has undertaken when he offers this loosely arranged mass of writings and reflections as not only containing the beginning of spiritual healing, but also the origin of Christian Science."[27]

Regarding the controversial issue of plagiarism, Quimby's son George wrote a letter that shed some light on this issue.

I have a package of Mrs. Eddy's letters to my father, covering a period from 1862 to 1864. . . . In all her letters she gives him full credit for discovering and reducing mental healing to a science. . . . This Mrs. Eddy knew, and this she learned from him, not as a student receiving a regular course as she taught in her college, but by sitting in his room, talking with him, reading his manuscripts, copying some of them, writing some herself and reading them to him for his criticism. In that sense she and many others of his patients were his pupils, in the same way that the disciples were pupils of Jesus.[28]

During the last years of her life, Eddy wrote a reminiscence of the early years of Christian Science. The article is named "Plagiarism," probably to answer the accusations of plagiarism made against her. This piece of writing is crafted in general terms, and it appears that she indirectly rationalized her indebtedness to Quimby without mentioning him at all; otherwise, she would not have had any reason to write it:

If a student at Harvard College has studied a book written by his teacher, is he entitled, when he leaves the University, to write out as his own the substance of his textbook? There is no warrant in common law and no permission in the gospel for plagiarism of an author's ideas and their words. Christian Science is not copyrighted; nor would protection by copyright be requisite.[29]

The irony is that she copyrighted everything, even the term *Christian Science*, which had been coined by Quimby long before her. Eddy's biographers Cather and Milmine, after a meticulous research, agreed with Quimby's adherents who asserted that "Mrs. Eddy obtained from Quimby, not only her ideas, but the very name of her new religion. Mrs. Eddy herself says that in 1866 she named her discovery Christian Science. Quimby, however, called his theory Christian Science at least as early 1863. In a manuscript in that year, entitled 'Aristocracy and Democracy,' he uses these identical words."[30]

The motivations of Quimby and Eddy concerning their metaphysical legacy were substantially the opposite. Quimby never sought to amass money with his teachings, because he thought that it was the divine knowledge taught by Jesus. He was the discoverer of mind healing in America and used this method to alleviate the suffering of people, charging whatever the patient could afford. Sometimes, when the patient was poor, he did not seek monetary compensation.[31]

Eddy employed the same technique to amass a fortune. She was not directly involved in curing people, as Quimby was. Instead, she imparted classes to students, charging certain amounts of money, and she subsequently ordained her students as Christian Science practitioners. (A Christian Science practitioner is a person who has received training in the church's method of mental treatment and is licensed and authorized to administer it.) These practitioners were authorized to give the same classes to others and could also administer mental healing as a way to earn extra income. As a consequence, the number of adherents of this sect multiplied exponentially, not only on the American continent, but also abroad. In a few years after being penniless, Eddy became a millionaire. As Israel Regardie remarks, "Mrs. Eddy may have been selfish, hard driven by lust of power, money-mad."[32]

Another important distinction is that Quimby did not teach his healing system, because of lack of time: he was busy curing people and recording his findings. He never sought to create any church or organized religion, and perhaps he did not realize the magnitude and profundity of his discovery. Eddy, however, was fortunate enough to be associated with bright men and women who under blind faith contributed enormously to the flourishing of "Christian Science" in America and abroad.

Stefan Zweig has brilliantly delineated the differences between Quimby and Eddy. According to Zweig, Quimby's theory was that all diseases are created by the patient's imagination, and the best way of treating them is to change the patient's beliefs regarding his illness. He further stated that Quimby practiced a treatment based "upon the sympathetic and suggestive power of his own personality, whereas Mary B. Eddy being at once bolder and far more absurd, starting from the denial of illness and an insistence upon omnipotence of faith over pain."[33]

Quimby never denied the illness or the fact that people can regain their health under the care of a physician. His method was to cure suggestively by modifying the patient's own feelings and beliefs. By contrast, Eddy went to the extreme of denying the existence of disease. She also denied the existence of evil; for her evil was simply a lie, an error.[34] These are the fundamental differences between Quimby's system and Christian Science. Eddy herself clarifies the essential distinction between her system of thought and Quimby's as follows: "What is the cardinal point of the difference in my metaphysical system? This: that *by knowing the unreality of disease, sin, and death*, you understand the allness of God. This difference wholly separates my system from all others" (italics are mine).[35]

This quotation raises the following question: If "disease, sin, and death" are not real, how would Eddy explain the outbreaks of smallpox, chicken pox, measles, and other diseases in South and North America that killed millions of Native Americans when the Europeans colonized this continent? These infectious diseases could not have been mentally created by the Native Americans because they did not have any idea of their existence. The simple answer is that the European explorers brought those diseases with them to the new continent, and they transmitted them to the Native Americans, who at that time did not have the natural immune defenses against those fatal illnesses common among the Europeans.

Quimby's main postulate was that Jesus Christ was the first mental-spiritual healer. On the basis of that idea, he named his method of healing "The Science of Christ." He entitled a manuscript of his own *Science of Health*, as is evidenced in an article printed in the *Portland Advertiser* in 1865.[36] As Cather and Milmine indicate, Quimby labeled his discovery the "Science of Health and Happiness," and also "Science of Christ" or "Christian Science,"[37] which seemed appropriate because he honestly thought he had rediscovered the way that Jesus Christ used to heal people.

We have already mentioned that Jesus Christ's healing, as it is recorded in the New Testament, was fundamentally faith healing.[38] He asked his disciples and followers to have faith as a requisite for healing. One can even doubt whether Eddy's method of healing should be called "Christian Science," because she claimed that her curing system was not faith healing as such; rather it was based on the denial of the disease. Jesus Christ, as far as we know, never denied reality. He did not try to convince people that their illnesses were not real. Even Christ, in some instances, may have resorted to placebos to heal people; such was the case of the blind man narrated in John's Gospel. In it we read that Jesus Christ formed a piece of mud with his saliva and put it on the eyes of a blind man; then he asked the blind man to wash his eyes in a pool. As a result the blind man was able to see (John 9:6–7). One can only wonder if this miracle was the result of a placebo effect or not; it is up to the reader to decide.

Throughout her career Eddy displayed an attitude of distrust. She went to the extreme of suing and excommunicating from her organization anyone who introduced any improvements to the system or who attempted to mention authors of philosophies or religions other than the Bible and *Science and Health*. Members of this organization were allowed to read only the publications and literature approved by Eddy. Any writing outside the scope of her teachings was considered as heretical and blasphemous to Christian Science doctrine. As we shall see, this was one reason Emma Curtis Hopkins, a prominent New Thought leader, was excluded from Christian Science membership. Along these lines, it is worth quoting Israel Regardie:

> Mr. A. J. Swarts, formerly one of the disciples of Mrs. Eddy, began to publish a magazine called Mental Science Magazine. Mr. Swarts' departure from the sanctum of Mrs. Eddy was the result of his own investigations into the origins of her revelation. He had nothing against her, and equally had no reason for defending Quimby. He was simply

interested in the facts. Swarts paid a visit to Belfast, Maine. After the opportunity of reading excerpts from the popular press concerning Quimby's healing work, and to hear portions of the manuscript read to him by Quimby's sons, he came to his own conclusions. He denounced Mrs. Eddy for plagiarism and for dishonesty—the metaphysics he retained, so becoming one of the early pioneers of the New Thought movement.[39]

As early as 1893, more than fifty years before Regardie's book *The Romance of Metaphysics* was published, psychic researcher and author Thomson Jay Hudson had denounced the false claims of Christian Science. Hudson deemed Christian Science a pseudotherapy because of its absurd conception of reality. With brilliant logic, Hudson uncovered the irrationality of its metaphysical principles. He wrote:

> That system [Christian Science] is based upon the assumption that matter has no real existence; consequently we have no bodies, and hence no disease of the body is possible. It is not known whether the worthy lady founder of the school ever stopped to reduce her foundation principles to the form of a syllogism. It is presumed not, for otherwise their intense, monumental, and aggressive absurdity would have become as apparent to her as it is to others. Let us see how they look in the form of a syllogism: Matter has no existence. Our bodies are composed of matter. Therefore our bodies have no existence. It follows, of course, that disease cannot exist in a non-existent body. . . . Of course, no serious argument can be adduced against such *a self-evident absurdity*.[40] (Italics Hudson's.)

As will be discussed later, Christian Science healings have succeeded mainly because of spontaneous remission as well as individual and collective suggestion. Practitioners prepare the mind of the patient with oral suggestions to receive the necessary mental impressions. The patient is advised to hold a mental attitude of denial of the existence of any disease; she is told to accept the above assertion as a condition for recovery. The patient is not allowed to formulate any objection to the method of treatment; instead, she is asked to blindly believe the practitioner. Rather as in a hypnotic session, the patient is requested to enter a passive and receptive state of mind to listen to the practitioner's instruction. The practitioner usually makes statements about the unreality of the illness; these are repeated over and over until the suggestions sink into the subconscious mind of the patient. At the end of the session, some suggestible patients find some relief, and others feel that they have recuperated. If the healing session is successful, the practitioner is credited with the healing; if he fails, the patient is blamed because she did not hold fast enough to the idea of denying the illness.

There are further inconsistencies in Mary Baker Eddy's ideology that would take another volume to elaborate. For instance, the Christian Science textbook, *Science and Health with Key to the Scriptures*, indicates that in order for healing to take place, a complete passivity is needed from the patient and the operator. Eddy also wrote that the healing would be carried out by itself without human intervention at all, that God would do all the work. Why did she ordain thousands of Christian Science practitioners to perform healing if the recovery could happen by itself? Here is an excerpt from her textbook that corroborates this above assertion: "There is no condition in the body to be rebuilt or straightened or healed. There is nothing to change. There is nothing needed but to see God. Stand still and see the salvation of the Lord."[41] We wonder what explanation she would offer to the parents of children born with congenital organic deformations. Would she still claim there is nothing "to be rebuilt or straightened or healed. There is nothing to change"?

Even in her later writings, Eddy insisted on the unreality of matter.[42] She adhered to the old religious conception of the duality of reality. The pivotal idea of her system is the antagonism between good and evil, spirit and matter, the devil and the Redeemer, etc. She equated matter with evil and spirit with good. She wrote, "If God is Spirit, and God is All, surely there can be no Matter; for the divine All must be spirit."[43] Even following her line of reasoning, it can be inferred that if everything that exists is spirit, then spirit is also manifested in matter as condensed energy. The Bible has recorded God saying at the end of his creation that all "was very good" (Genesis 1:31, King James Version). God did not find anything wrong or evil in his creation.

Undoubtedly, any system of thought earnestly promoted and pursued will always find plenty of followers, no matter how illogical its claims may be. For instance, several religious sects originated in upstate New York in the nineteenth century, including the Shakers and the Mormons. All have or had followers who believe their teachings as given by the founders of these organizations. In the case of Christian Science, by the end of the nineteenth century, the membership was growing steadily and exponentially; churches were spreading into foreign countries. Hudson, a contemporary observer of this phenomenon, reported:

> There is, however, a large and growing class of people, calling themselves Christian scientists, who ignore the fundamental absurdities of the theory of the founder of the sect, and content themselves with the knowledge that the practice produces good results.[44]

Eddy's biographer, Fleta Campbell Springer, has documented in her book *According to the Flesh: A Biography of Mary Baker Eddy* (1930) that Eddy was addicted to morphine. This allegation has been corroborated in Martin Gardner's *The Healing Revelations of Mary Baker Eddy: Rise and Fall of Christian Science* (1993), and Walter Martin's *The Kingdom of the Cults* (2003). Springer and Gardner have written extensively about Eddy's addiction to morphine and her lifelong dependence on morphine pills and shots; this is verified in a diary kept by Calvin Frye, Eddy's personal secretary. Moreover, Miranda Rice, a close friend and former student of Eddy, claimed to have treated her many times with morphine. Rice stated, "I know that Mrs. Eddy was addicted to morphine in the seventies. She begged me to get some for her. She sent her husband, Mr. Eddy, for some, and when he failed to get it she got it herself. She locked herself into her room and for two days excluded everyone. She was a slave to morphine."[45] Furthermore, Eddy's adopted son, Ebenezer Foster, stated in an interview published in the New York *World*, March 12, 1907, that Calvin Frye took a morphine tablet from him and "he followed Frye to Mrs. Eddy's room where she lay screaming and hysterical and saw Frye 'force the tablet into her mouth and hold her firmly down among the pillows.'"[46]

It has been said that Christian Science uses a compelling method of indoctrination on its members and patients to believe in its absurd system as a prerequisite for being healed; this can be considered a kind of waking hypnosis. In addition, the effectiveness of Christian Science in the early years was due, in good part, to generating expectations among naive people and producing a kind of mass suggestion. Over the years, some churches, such as New Jersey's Plainfield Christian Science Church, Independent, have separated from the mother church, the First Church of Christ, Scientist, in Boston, because of the dictatorial and dogmatic rules imposed by the church's leaders. Nowadays, the reduction of the number of churches and membership in this organization is evident. According to medical doctor Stephen Barrett:

> Membership in the Christian Science Church has been declining steadily. The number of practitioners and teachers listed in the *Christian Science Journal* has fallen from about 5,000 in 1971 to about 1,800 in 1996; and the number of churches has fallen from about 1,800 in 1971 to about 1,100 in 2003.[47]

Christian Science developed a method of distance healing called "absent treatment." This kind of treatment is carried out by telepathic means. The procedure is more or less as follows: the operator or healer sits alone and clearly visualizes the patient, who is far away, and then the operator suggests ideas about health to the subconscious of the patient. In most cases, the practitioner uses prayers invoking well-being, as well as reads passages from the Bible and *Science and Health*. Proponents of this treatment argue that telepathic suggestions are made directly to the subjective mind of the patient, bypassing the threshold of the patient's conscious mind. There is no factual evidence for the efficacy of this treatment. However, Thomson Jay Hudson was in favor of it. He stated that he had applied the method of distant treatment with great effectiveness. He argued that the advantage of this procedure is that the patient is in the best condition for the reception of positive suggestions and is not able to contradict them by antagonistic beliefs deriving from the patient's conscious mind. I believe that people who are subconsciously determined to be sick would not respond to this kind of treatment, although it should be kept in mind that any healing will be effective as long as the patient is receptive and willing to accept it.

One serious disadvantage of Christian Science is that the church forbids its patients from employing medical care or using any kind of medicine. This is a dangerous recommendation that can put a sick person at a serious disadvantage. Reportedly, in the past there have been children who died because of practitioners' prohibition of regular immunizations and medical treatment for children. As Hudson observed, "They insist upon the discharge of the family physician, and the destruction of all the medicines in the house."[48] Stephen Barrett recounts:

> Rita and Douglas Swan['s] 16-month-old son Matthew died of meningitis under the care of two Christian Science practitioners in 1977. . . . [Rita] founded CHILD, Inc., to work for legal reforms that can protect children from inappropriate treatment by faith healers. She and a colleague collected and reviewed the cases of 172 children who died between 1975 and 1995 when parents withheld medical care because of reliance on religious rituals. They concluded:
> * 140 of the deaths were from medical conditions for which survival rates with medical care would have exceeded 90 percent. These included 22 cases of pneumonia in infants under two years of age, 15 cases of meningitis, and 12 cases of insulin-dependent diabetes.
> * 18 more had expected survival rates greater than 50 percent.[49]

Although Eddy instructed Christian Science members to avoid doctors and medicine and taught the unreality of pain, suffering, and disease, she herself was frequently attended by medical doctors, particularly in the last years of her life. This was in direct contradiction to the tenets of her religion. In fact, Eddy acknowledged the use of drugs, "I experimented by taking some large doses of morphine, to see if Christian Science could not obviate its effects, and I say with tearful thanks, 'The drug had no effect upon me whatsoever.'"[50] Should we understand this last sentence to mean she might have needed higher doses to feel the effects?

It would be folly to deny the power of drugs and medicine in generating changes in the physical body; they are compositions that have the capacity to alter or release chemical properties in the body that can increase the efficacy of mental healing. Modern New Thought practitioners do not discourage patients from using appropriate medicine. The problem arises when there is an excessive dependency on chemicals that can damage other parts of the body, creating more harm than good. On the other hand, average people are deeply convinced of the power of medicine, and in some cases, their recuperation could be due to a placebo effect. We cannot deny the tremendous scientific advances made in the medical field in diagnosing and treating severe health problems or accidents with severe corporal injuries. In the cases of organic illnesses and physical atrophies, mental healing should be considered as complementary to medical treatment.

Mental healing has been criticized because the patients tend to relapse. Hudson has indicated that in any kind of healing, whether mental or by means of drugs and medicine, the patient is usually at risk of relapsing. In a social atmosphere of incredulity and doubt, a patient cured by mental means has little chance of permanent success. Every doubt existing in the minds of those surrounding him would be conveyed telepathically to the subconscious of the patient, and would operate as a powerful adverse suggestion. Thus reinforcement and support are extremely important for the healing process to be successfully concluded.

In this respect, Christian Science has created an efficient network of support and reinforcement. First, it provides the patient with "healing affirmations" extracted from the Bible or *Science and Health*. These affirmations must be repeated as mantras all day long. Second, they have organized a powerful support system through a network of practitioners who are available at all times. In the event that patients feel any symptoms of relapse, they are instructed to call the practitioner immediately to receive a "healing affirmation" suitable to their health condition. Third, the patient is requested to attend Sunday services and Wednesday testimonial meetings at a local Christian Science church. The Wednesday meetings are devoted explicitly to sharing "healing testimonies" from members of the church who were cured with this method. These gatherings are powerful suggestions that heighten the confidence of the patient; they constitute potent verbal suggestions that enhance the healing process; they can be defined as an effective form of waking hypnosis. If a person does not participate in or resonate with the mental environment of this "festivity of gratitude," he or she will likely feel inadequate. In some cases, the mental pressure of the group environment will eventually lead newcomers to stand up and articulate fake testimonies in order to be part of the community.

Some believe that the affirmations extracted from the Christian Science textbook or the Bible would work as mental narcotics to help the patient endure illness and life's difficulties. If patients find themselves in difficult situations, they are supposed to contact the practitioner immediately by telephone. The practitioner "straightens out" the thinking of the individual with affirmations extracted from the textbook or the Bible, which act as a new "mental medicine." The patient pays fees to the practitioner for these consultations.

During its initial years, Christian Science grew rapidly, thanks to a momentum of immense collective suggestion, of which the movement's leaders took advantage. They organized the newcomers into classes, delivered lectures, assigned practitioners to patients, and gave instructions on how to treat themselves with affirmations and prayers. Knowingly or unknowingly, the practitioners were training their patients in the methods of autosuggestion without having a clear concept of the principles of mental healing. Nevertheless, the practitioners were using them effectively.

Although the method of healing propounded by Christian Science is illogical, thousands of people have benefited from it. Some of these cures have been verified by the medical profession. However, the healing was effected mainly by a collective suggestion and autosuggestion (the placebo effect). In many cases, the healing was the result of a spontaneous remission; we should never underestimate the tremendous recuperative power of the body to regain health. In most cases, the healing was the result of what I call *derivative benefit*, which is a form of indirect healing, resulting from an autosuggestion produced by witnessing others being cured. Since the death of Eddy in 1910 and the consequent decline of fervor, the egregore (collective psychic energy) of this institution has been weakened; thus current reports of mind healing by Christian Science practitioners are few. (I will discuss the egregore in the chapter below entitled "The Concept of the Egregore.")

In the end, we have to acknowledge Mary Baker Eddy as one of the first female American religious leaders with national and international stature. In 1910, she founded the *Christian Science Monitor*, a newspaper that is respected around the world for its editorial integrity and insightful news. (Although it was originally a daily, financial difficulties have reduced its frequency to weekly as a print publication.) Finally, Eddy should be recognized for her organizational skills in creating a church that expanded internationally. She died of pneumonia on December 3, 1910.

Eddy displayed similar characteristics to those of Freud, in addition to the fact that their theories are both flawed. Both were extremely stubborn and fixed-minded regarding their supposed "discoveries." Eddy regarded illness as an illusion, Freud considered religion an illusion—a "universal obsessional neurosis." Although both were subject to severe criticism and rebuttal by their contemporaries, they held steadfast to their theories. Freud never retracted his viewpoint of the sexual genesis of neurosis or his thesis that religion originated from the killing of a primeval father and the ensuing sense of guilt. Eddy held unwaveringly onto her belief that illness was unreal and that evil was simply a lie. Finally, Eddy was addicted to morphine, as Freud was to cocaine, albeit these drugs at the time were legally used for medical purposes.

Chapter 6

Emma Curtis Hopkins
Teacher of Teachers

If Quimby is the father of New Thought, Emma Curtis Hopkins is usually considered to be the movement's teacher of teachers. She was born in Killingly, Connecticut, in 1849 and passed away in 1925. Having health problems in her early life, she became interested in Christian Science, which at the time was booming. In December 1883, after a healing session with Mary Baker Eddy, she enrolled in Christian Science classes. In order to pay for her classes she worked on the *Christian Science Journal*, the official magazine of the Christian Science church. In September 1884, she became the publication's editor. However, already having much knowledge of metaphysics, she never went on to the advanced classes.

In 1886, Hopkins was ordained as a Christian Science practitioner, and she started teaching and providing mind treatment in Chicago. However, in 1888, Eddy excommunicated Hopkins because she was mentioning other sources besides the Christian Science textbook in her teachings. Eddy used to excommunicate rivals, as she put it, "for being mind-quacks who were spreading abroad patchwork books, false compendiums of my system crediting some ignoramus or infidel with teaching they have stolen from me. The unweaned suckling whines while spitting out the breast-milk which sustained him."[1] Ironically, this assessment could also be applied to her.

CHAPTER 6

Highly self-educated in metaphysics, Hopkins was familiar with the philosophy of German idealism, Transcendentalism, and the Hindu Vedanta. In addition to giving credit to the pioneers of New Thought, she was trying to find theoretical and metaphysical grounds for validating methods of mind healing other than those in the Christian Science textbook. During this time, New Thought as a movement was still in its infancy, and Quimby's ideas were rough material that needed an ideological and philosophical basis to be presented as a coherent system to the educated public.

After her excommunication in 1888, Hopkins founded her own school, called the Emma Curtis Hopkins College of Metaphysical Science. One has to keep in mind that at that time, all the teachings that later became part of the New Thought movement were initially called "Christian Science" because Quimby used the terms "Christian" and "Science" in his mental treatments and manuscripts. After Mary Baker Eddy copyrighted the name "Christian Science," other New Thought leaders had to find new names for their own organizations.

Hopkins was a charismatic teacher and an excellent speaker and spiritual leader. She inspired and motivated future founders of New Thought churches and organizations. Among them were Charles and Myrtle Fillmore, founders of Unity, currently the largest denomination in the New Thought movement. Hopkins was also the inspiration for Malinda Cramer, cofounder of the Divine Science Church, and for Dr. H. Emilie Cady, author of the influential book *Lessons in Truth*. She was also the spiritual mentor of Ernest Holmes, the founder of the Religious Science movement. Her influence on the future of New Thought is undeniable.

Charles Fillmore, who knew Hopkins personally, portrayed her as having a powerful personality that inspired wellness with just her presence, like Mesmer and Quimby before her:

She is undoubtedly the most successful teacher in the world. In many instances those who enter her classes confirmed invalids come out at the end of the course perfectly well. Her very presence heals and those who listen are filled with new life. Never before on this planet have such words of burning Truth been so eloquently spoken through a woman.[2]

In essence, Hopkins's teaching is similar to the esoteric doctrine that affirms the oneness of humanity. Her basic postulate was that one underlying truth runs throughout all major religions. As she puts it:

> *There is one indestructible substance pervading all things from the remotest star to the nearest dust particle....* It can only be recognized by the mind ... and only the understanding power of the mind can make it useful. He who by any manner ... handles this substance and realizes its nature as his nature soon finds himself experiencing vital renewal throughout body and mind.[3] (Italics Hopkins's.)

Hopkins's masterpiece is *High Mysticism*, a twelve-lesson series on the wisdom of the ages. In her book *Scientific Christian Mental Practice*, she foresaw the advent of women in spiritual and public affairs. This assessment seems appropriate considering the emerging presence of women in philosophy and religious leadership in the mid-nineteenth century in America. Among these personalities were Jemima Wilkinson, the first American-born woman to found a religious movement; Margaret Fuller, the first authentic feminist in America and a member of the Transcendentalist movement; and, of course Mary Baker Eddy. They would be followed by Malinda Cramer and the Brooks sisters, founders of the Divine Science Church, whom we shall examine in the next chapter.

Chapter 7

Malinda Cramer and
the Brooks Sisters

Founders of the Divine Science Church

Malinda E. Cramer (1844–1906) was the cofounder of the Church of Divine Science; she is also considered an important figure of the New Thought movement. Cramer, who was born in Greensboro, Indiana, and moved to San Francisco in 1870, resembled Mary Baker Eddy in three respects: (1) both were long-time invalids, Cramer for about twenty-five years,[1] Eddy for about forty years; (2) both had spontaneous remissions after a severe health crisis; and (3) each resorted to spiritual means as the last option for the recuperation of her health. In both cases, the healing was produced as a result of earnest prayer and autosuggestion in the middle of a desperate situation. As we have already seen, one common characteristic of New Thought leaders is that they sought mental and spiritual healing *as* the last alternative, after they exhausted all conventional methods of treatment.

That is the case with Cramer as well. After many years of unsuccessful care from the conventional medicine of the time, one day she made the bold decision not to seek further medical attention. At that time, 1885, her process of recuperation was independent of New Thought and Christian Science influence. Her decision marked the beginning of a spiritual adventure that led her to regain her health from an "incurable" condition. Cramer herself explains the turning point in her life in an

1894 article entitled "Spiritual Experience." Her account shows how a strong resolution to regain health can trigger spontaneous remission. It also provides the rationale behind her healing.

> It was early one morning in the year 1885, during an hour of earnest meditation and prayerful seeking, that I asked the following questions in faith, believing that they would be answered, with a willingness to abide the decision, whatever it might be. "Is there any way out of these conditions? Is there any power in the vast universe that can heal me?" The immediate and all-convincing response was not an audible voice, but was an intuitive response by the life-giving spirit, which penetrated the body through and through, and which illumined and vivified its every atom with newness of life. From the depths of Divine perception and understanding I was caused to know and realize that if I got well it would be by the power of the Infinite Spirit. I arose from my chair, and walking the floor said, "If, if, if I ever get well, then there is *one* way out of these conditions; then I must *seek* that way. . . .
>
> The answer to my earnest inquiry, as to whether there was any power that could heal me, was an all absorbing realization of a presence not heretofore realized. *This presence was more than personal; it was omnipresence, and was so real, and so vivifying and illumining, that I became It. I realized It to be my Life, my Being, my health, knowledge and power. It was as a "consuming fire,"* in that all things became It, and were this Presence manifested. Simultaneous with finding myself in God, I experienced the indrawing of all things; that is, that all are embraced within one eternal God and Father, or One Infinite Source and Cause, and as I looked out over the Infinite's Creation, I beheld what to me was "a new heaven and a new earth."[2] (Italics are mine.)

Thus meditation and prayer, supported by a firm desire to get well, led her to realize the presence of the Divine Spirit and to understand that if she ever got well, it would be by the power of that Spirit. This is a mystical experience that Carl Jung called an encounter with the *numinous*—the realization of the presence of the divinity. Like many spiritual sages, Cramer became aware of the omnipresence of the Divine Spirit. This presence "was real, and permanent. It was so vivifying and illumining I knew I was one with it. . . . It was a 'consuming fire' in that all things became it, and were this One Presence manifested."[3]

In metaphysical circles, the principle of causation states that nothing happens by chance; everything has its cause and effect. The notion that events occur at the right time is similar to the saying, "When the student is ready, the teacher will appear." This principle applies to Malinda Cramer: she was intellectually prepared to understand metaphysical principles as well as the rationale of her healing through the "numinous" experience.

In passing it should be mentioned that meditation and prayer could also be considered means for effective autosuggestion. In fact, Divine Science minister Joseph Murphy considers scientific prayer to be an act that conveys a specific image to the subconscious mind.[4]

After her healing, Cramer attended Emma Curtis Hopkins's classes in metaphysics in San Francisco. Hopkins's teachings provided Cramer with the rationale and solid metaphysical background for her own spiritual experience and healing. As a result, Cramer began teaching on her own. In 1888, she and her husband, Charles, founded the Home College of Divine Science in San Francisco to provide instruction in Divine Science and its therapeutic application, which they described as "Jesus Christ's method of healing."[5]

A similar revelation took place in Pueblo, Colorado, with Nona Brooks (1861–1945). Brooks had been in Chicago for a medical consultation for a severe throat illness, and was told by her physician that she needed an operation. Instead of going to surgery, Brooks was persuaded by a friend to attend Hopkins's classes on "High Mysticism." After several sessions with Hopkins, Nona suddenly found herself healed and returned home to Pueblo.

Subsequently to that, a mental healer named Kate Bingham began to give informal classes on New Thought teachings. The individuals who attended the classes included the Brooks sisters: Nona, Fannie Brooks James (1854–1914), and Althea Brooks Small (1848–1906). On the third day of attending Bingham's lectures, Nona Brooks, who had had a relapse of her throat ailment, was healed again.[6] These experiences gave her faith in mental and spiritual treatment. Her faith became solid when she observed other people were healed by these means; as a result, she began her healing ministry, based on New Thought principles.

Nona Brooks and her two sisters, who resided in Denver, Colorado, came across Cramer's teachings in San Francisco. Consequently, they started corresponding and eventually founded the earliest New Thought denomination, the Church of Divine Science. The metaphysics of this school emphasizes that God exists in every person as a divine spark; through understanding and focusing on that divine presence, one can be healed and transformed.[7]

In addition to being influenced by Hopkins, Malinda Cramer was well acquainted with the books of Warren Felt Evans. Her memoirs indicate that she had also read the Bhagavad-Gita, works on the Qabalah, a system of Jewish mysticism, and the writings of the seventeenth-century German visionary Jacob Boehme. Authors C. Alan Anderson and Deborah G. Whitehouse aptly synthesize the essence of Divine Science teachings as follows:

> The chief Divine Science emphasis is on the omnipresence of God, or simply Omnipresence. Everything follows from this. Divine Science proclaims to those who follow a commonsensical belief: "We have the same idea of substance; you call it matter; we call it Spirit."[8]

Two other significant figures emerged from the Divine Science organization: Emmet Fox (1886–1951) and Joseph Murphy (1898–1981). Both of them were influential speakers and prolific New Thought writers. Fox, born in Ireland, practiced most of his spiritual ministry in the United States. He was well-known for his Divine Science church services held in New York City. Murphy was minister-director of the Church of Divine Science in Los Angeles for twenty-eight years. In addition, he was an international motivational and prosperity speaker for many years.

Chapter 8

Charles and Myrtle Fillmore

Founders of Unity

Like many of the figures we have examined so far, Charles Fillmore and his wife, Mary Caroline Page Fillmore, known as "Myrtle," were both healed of long-standing illnesses by New Thought teaching before they became active advocates of the philosophy. Charles was born in St. Cloud, Minnesota. At the age of ten, he had an ice-skating accident that dislocated his hip and left him with a shrunken leg. Myrtle contracted tuberculosis at an early age, and to recover from it, she spent the years 1877–78 in Denison, Texas, where she met Charles. They married in 1881, and moved to Kansas City, Missouri. In 1886, Charles found himself in a financial crisis after having had a successful real estate business. At the same time, Myrtle was suffering from tuberculosis.

Under these circumstances, a friend recommended that they attend a lecture given by a New Thought proponent named Eugene B. Weeks. The impact of Weeks's teachings on the Fillmores would become profound. They became committed to the new way of thinking, and as a result Myrtle progressively regained her health and Charles's financial situation improved significantly. Anderson and Whitehouse describe how the Fillmores initially became interested in New Thought:

> A young woman dying of hereditary tuberculosis attends a lecture in 1886, leaning heavily on her husband's arm. He himself with a severe limp, having damaged his hip in a childhood skating accident that left him with a withered leg. The woman emerges from the lecture with

a new and powerful belief: *I am a child of God and I do not inherit sickness.*

Two years later, with no further medical intervention, the woman is completely well. Her husband's leg, no longer withered, has grown three inches longer, and the constant pain has disappeared. The husband and wife begin a ministry that becomes worldwide, healing and prospering many thousands of people.[1] (Italics are mine.)

While New Thought teachings were helping Myrtle to recover from her tuberculosis, Charles used the prosperity teaching of New Thought to improve his financial troubles. Surprisingly, he became successful in his speculations; the small amount of money he invested in stock in the bankrupt Missouri Pacific Railroad was multiplied exponentially. They attributed these events to Myrtle's prayers and involvement with New Thought. These events were the turning point in the Fillmores' lives.

The healing of Charles and Myrtle Fillmore appears to be the result of a conscious realization of the spiritual essence of human beings, which is never ill. This realization involves switching the focus of the mind from conditions like illness and poverty and directing it to ideas of physical wholeness and prosperity. In the case of Myrtle, before her awareness of the New Thought ideology, her subconscious mind had been tied to the idea that she had inherited tuberculosis. By an act of unintentional autosuggestion, she herself promoted the manifestation of that illness. However, using the powerful counteracting statement "*I am a child of God and I do not inherit sickness,*" she gradually recovered her health. That affirmation served as a potent suggestion to her subconscious mind. Likewise, Charles used the same principle on his own behalf, by switching the focus of his mind onto prosperity rather than being hypnotized by a belief in the lack of money and poor health. In both cases, their involvement in group prayers and in New Thought philosophy were a potent reinforcement for their physical healing and financial recovery.

In 1889, Charles abandoned his business enterprise to devote himself full-time to organizing prayer groups; this movement would later be called "Silent Unity." In addition, in the same year, he began publishing the magazine entitled *Modern Thought*. Fillmore's teachings were essentially Christian although he had read extensively in Eastern philosophy, esoteric thought, and occultism.[2] This could be why he accepted the writings of the esotericist and New Thought pioneer William Walker Atkinson (1862–1932) for publication in *Modern Thought*.

A short digression is appropriate here to mention the influence of Atkinson on the New Thought movement, as well as on American esoteric organizations. He started his own periodical, called *New Thought*, and was a prolific writer, authoring more than one hundred books on religious, spiritual, and occult topics. Special attention deserves to be given to his books on Eastern philosophy, written under the pen name Yogi Ramacharaka. The book *Fourteen Lessons in Yogi Philosophy and Oriental Occultism*, initially published in Chicago in 1904, is highly recommended. This book was the first in which he attempted to reconcile his religious beliefs with science and contemporary philosophy and ignite his metaphysical search for a spiritual understanding of the role of humanity in the universe.

In 1889, Charles and Myrtle Fillmore founded the movement known as Unity (informally, Unity Church) in Kansas City, Missouri. During his life, Charles wrote extensively on metaphysical matters and became known as an American mystic for his contributions to the interpretation of biblical Scripture. In 1891, the magazine *Unity* was created as an organ of the church. This was the magazine in which Harriet Emilie Cady (1848–1941) published her famous serial articles entitled *Lessons in Truth*. Posthumously, these articles were compiled and printed as a book with the same name, and they are regarded as influential in the Unity movement. After the deaths of Myrtle and Charles Fillmore, Unity continued to grow into a worldwide organization.[3]

Charles Fillmore relied heavily on the power of prayer for the attainment of health and prosperity. His books *Christian Healing, The Science of Being, Mysteries of Genesis*, and *Mysteries of John* give an accurate idea of the quality and lucidity of his thought. In the beginning of the second chapter of *Christian Healing*, he sets out the basic principle of his philosophy:

1. The foundation of our religion is Spirit, and there must be a science of Truth. The science of Truth is God thinking out creation. God is the original Mind in which all real ideas exist. The one original Mind creates by thought. This is stated in the first chapter of John:

2. In the beginning was the Word [Logos—thought-word], and the Word was with God, and the Word was God. The same was in the beginning with God. All things were made through him; and without him was not anything made that hath been made.

3. Eadie's biblical Cyclopedia says: "The term Logos means thought expressed, either as an idea in mind or as vocal speech."

4. An understanding of the Logos reveals to us the law under which all things are brought forth—the law of mind action. Creation takes place through the operation of the Logos. God is thinking the universe into manifestation right now. Even He cannot create without law. The law of the divine creation is the order and harmony of perfect thought.

Chapter 9

Ernest Holmes

Founder of Religious Science

Ernest Holmes, founder of the Church of Religious Science, is one of the last important theorists of the New Thought movement. Born in Maine, the youngest of nine sons, at the age of eighteen he left school and set out on his lifelong spiritual quest. He went to Boston, worked in a grocery store, and pursued his studies by himself. Later he discovered the writings of Emerson, who profoundly influenced him.

Ernest Holmes's work represents the culmination of the seminal ideas of the previous New Thought writers. In his masterpiece *Science of Mind*, he summarized the best of worldwide metaphysical and religious concepts and harmonized them with New Thought. As he expressed it:

> The Science of Mind is not a special revelation of any individual, it is, rather, the culmination of all revelations. We take the good wherever we find it, making it our own in so far as we understand it. The realization that Good is Universal, and that as much good as any individual is able to incorporate in his life is his to use, is what constitutes the Science of Mind and Spirit.
>
> We have discussed the nature of The Thing as being Universal Energy, Mind, Intelligence, Spirit—finding conscious and individualized center of expression through us—and that man's intelligence is this Universal Mind, functioning at the level of man's concept of it. This is the essence of the whole teaching.[1]

CHAPTER 9

The entire book *Science of Mind* is the development of the key ideas expressed here. Again and again, Holmes emphasized the basic principle that we are surrounded by the Universal Mind, that is pure Intelligence, which reacts and responds to our thoughts. Here, in this one sentence, is the essence of the metaphysical conception of the world and the New Thought philosophy: wittingly or unwittingly, our thoughts create our external circumstances. This metaphysical principle holds that the whole universe and everything within it is the manifestation of One Mind. This Universal Mind is known by different names such as life force energy, Universal Consciousness, Spirit, and prana. Jesus Christ called it "Our Father." These are only different names for what has sometimes been called the "One Thing."

For Holmes, "The premise upon which all mental work is based is perfect God, perfect man, perfect being."[2] A mental practitioner has to acknowledge first that she is a perfect being and then regard her patient as a perfect entity living in a perfect universe governed by a perfect law. Thereafter, the practitioner must proceed to change the negative thoughts and beliefs that are binding the sick man to his suffering.

Holmes, who coined the expression *spiritual mind healing*, was also deeply influenced by the English metaphysician Thomas Troward (whom we shall examine in chapter 13), and often acknowledged his indebtedness to Troward. Dr. Donald Curtis, a close friend and associate of Holmes, recalled Holmes as saying: "Sixty percent of the *Science of Mind* is Troward."[3]

Another influence, as we have mentioned, was Emerson, who propounded the concept of self-reliance, which was important for emerging American intellectuals who needed to break their cultural and ideological dependence on European influence. Emerson's teachings directly influenced the development of the New Thought movement in the early twentieth century. In fact, the young Holmes adopted Emerson's concept of self-reliance as the guiding principle in his life. It is said that Holmes even entertained the idea that he could have been the reincarnation of Emerson.[4]

Holmes's inquisitive mind and his quest for truth led him to different areas of knowledge, including literature, science, philosophy, and religion. A painful long-term throat ailment was healed when he applied the healing principles of New Thought to himself. At this time, he began attending the Christian Science "Mother Church" in Boston and started performing his first mental healings. But Holmes focused on the concept of the mind as the operative healing agency, which was a clear departure from Christian Science's denial of physical reality.

Holmes did not depend exclusively on external information given by books but also sought confirmation through information received during his meditation sessions. In fact, it could be said that wisdom gathered from the Inner Teacher is more reliable than that gained from more familiar sources. This is the method practiced by mystics, sages, and masters of wisdom on a regular basis. Here again Emerson's concept of "self-reliance" comes into play, urging one to trust in knowledge acquired by inner means. Regarding this aspect, Curtis writes:

> He [Holmes] learned simultaneously on both outer and inner levels, for he was not only attentive to the world around him, but he was also developing a rich inner life due to his practice of meditation. In meditation, he listened carefully to inner instruction and considered it the authority for his spiritual unfoldment. When he read the works of ancient and modern teachers, philosophers, and scientists, he was delighted to discover confirmation of the teachings he had received directly during his quiet contemplation.[5]

Holmes's ideology was also influenced by such New Thought figures as Christian D. Larson, Ralph Waldo Trine, Horatio Dresser, and Phineas Quimby. Among these, Holmes was particularly impressed with the writings of Christian D. Larson (1874–1962), who was a prolific author on metaphysical matters. Holmes also had the privilege of taking classes for a short period of time from Emma Curtis Hopkins.

It can be said that Holmes's masterpiece, *Science of Mind*, is a summary of the teachings of Emerson, Troward, and Larson, with overtones of

Vedantic philosophy. It has been said that Holmes was not an original thinker, but he was a great synthesizer who drew much inspiration from the best of many philosophies and religions around the world. This is confirmed by Curtis, who asserted that Holmes never claimed to be an innovator.

> He [Holmes] learned, borrowed, and absorbed from everyone and everything. He was an avid student but not strictly a scholar. He could intuitively grasp great concepts and he had the exceptional ability to synthesize the knowledge received in meditation.[6]

Science of Mind is the textbook of Religious Science, and it is also used by other New Thought organizations. Although Religious Science philosophy is based on Jesus Christ's teachings and the Christian Bible, some leaders of this organization do not consider themselves to be traditional Christians, because its teachings are also heavily influenced by Hindu philosophy and other worldwide religions.

Hopkins, influenced by the Vedanta, postulated the existence of a universal life force that permeates the whole universe. The conscious awareness of this universal energy in our lives can be manifested in a renewal of vitality in mind and body. By contrast, Malinda Cramer regained her health by using meditation and prayer to experience the omnipresence of the Divine Spirit. Charles Fillmore strongly relied on prayer, faith, and spiritual discernment for healing and prosperity. Holmes, tying these strands together, taught the existence of a universal life force energy pervading our universe and responsive to our thoughts. He also considered it a *sine qua non* for any healing to consider the sick person as a human being, a perfect child of God, no matter what his or her present condition might be. The metaphysical postulate behind that is "perfect God, perfect man, and perfect being." In other words, the key for any spiritual mind healing is to regard a person, first of all, as a spiritual entity, perfect right here, right now.

At this point, it is useful to elaborate on the connection between healing and religious experiences. Historically, healing and religion have been interrelated; ever since the onset of human civilization, shamans have invoked spirits and communicated with the spiritual world for medicinal purposes. It is customary for an ailing individual to resort to a higher power or to the divinity to ask for help to alleviate his trouble, because he feels powerless. Likewise, since the onset of the New Thought movement, mind healing in America has been closely connected to religion. Quimby thought that he had discovered how Jesus Christ healed people—through faith—and Quimby and his successors have relied on Christ's teachings and the Bible as a spiritual support for their methods of healing. Furthermore, most prominent New Thought leaders founded their particular organizations on spiritual principles. Hence the modern New Thought movement is an authentic form of practical American spirituality that incorporates the teachings of the Christian scriptures and the best of the world's religions.

PART THREE

Pioneers of Mind Healing

Chapter 10

Ambroise-Auguste Liébeault and Hippolyte Bernheim

The Nancy School of Hypnosis

Prior to the study of hypnosis and healing by suggestion, it is useful to examine the study of somnambulism or sleepwalking, which was the prelude to the discovery of the Law of Suggestion and the subconscious mind.

The first experiments in this area were conducted by Marquis de Puységur. A former disciple of Mesmer, Puységur was the first person to study the sleeplike trance called somnambulism.

A typical example of somnambulism can be described as follows: A sleeping individual arises from bed and, with his eyes closed, walks around the rooms of his house and sometimes performs some simple tasks. Once he has carried out these actions, he quietly returns to his bed and continues sleeping as if nothing had happened. The following day, he has no recollection whatsoever of what he did while he was in the state of somnambulism.

At that time, the 1780s, sleepwalking and somnambulism were considered inexplicable. But in 1784, Puységur accidentally encountered the phenomenon of somnambulism when he was practicing mesmerism with a young shepherd named Victor. When Puységur stroked his fingers, the young boy suddenly fell into a deep sleeping state. Alarmed, Puységur attempted to wake the boy by calling his name and shaking his arms, but he did not respond and continued to be in a profound state of sleep. But Puységur noticed that the youth's sleep was not of the ordinary kind: when he ordered him to do something such as stand up or walk around, he obeyed without hesitation as if he were awake.

How can we explain a somnambulistic incident, a person who under a sleeping trance performs deeds that he would not do awake? What or who leads the sleepwalker to perform such actions? These are legitimate questions, and the logical explanation is that when the conscious mind is absent the subconscious directs our actions. Under these conditions, a person cannot be held accountable for his or her actions.

Puységur found that a person executes the suggestions given in the state of hypnosis. Hence it was obvious from the above was that the human mind is composed of two selves: the conscious and the subconscious. Contrary to the conventional wisdom of the time, it was proved beyond a reasonable doubt that the subconscious mind plays an active role in human life. These experiments also showed that most "unnatural" mental phenomena and inexplicable behavior could be traced to the subconscious mind. Up to this point, the subconscious had been regarded as a kind of mental attic where memories of past experiences dwelled, having no influence on people. However, as we now know, the subconscious mind is the source of dreams, of automatic thoughts, of habitual thinking, and is the repository of memories that can be brought to consciousness under special circumstances. In the subconscious mind, there is an interaction of mental forces and instinctual drives that are expressed when the censorship of the conscious mind is removed. By the same token, the subconscious is the fountain of inspiration, inventiveness, and knowledge.

This discovery of the dual structure of the mind served to unmask the false prophets, charlatans, pseudo-occultists, necromancers, and spiritualists who supposedly practiced communicating with the spirits of the dead. What they were doing was employing the power of the subconscious in order to mislead people, making them believe something supernatural was occurring. Incidentally, Carl Jung argued that disembodied spirits "from the psychological angle, are unconscious autonomous complexes which appear as projections because they have no direct association with the ego."[1]

In passing, we should also mention the English physician James Braid (1795–1860), who developed and scientifically demonstrated the phenomenon of hypnosis to academic circles throughout Europe. Braid, who based his theory on Mesmer's ideas, coined the word *hypnosis*, which comes from the Greek word *hypnos*, meaning "sleep."

In mid-nineteenth-century France, the school of suggestive therapies appeared, represented by the Nancy school of hypnosis, founded in 1866 (coincidentally the year of Quimby's death) by Dr. Ambroise-Auguste Liébeault (1823–1904). It is so called to distinguish it from the Charcot school, also known as the Paris school, led by the renowned French neurologist Jean-Martin Charcot at the Salpêtrière Hospital in Paris. Charcot used hypnotism to investigate the causes of hysteria, and the Paris school regarded hypnosis as a particular form of induced hysteria.

Liébeault is considered by many to be the father of modern hypnotherapy. Liébeault elaborated and expanded on the ideas of Puységur and Faria, who were among the first to argue that suggestion, rather than magnetic fluid, was the operative cause of success in mesmerism. Like Puységur and Faria, he held that hypnosis was a normal phenomenon induced by suggestion, in contrast to mesmerism, which portrayed hypnotic trances as manifestations of magnetism. Liébeault became a medical doctor in 1850, but instead of practicing medicine, he devoted himself to the study of hypnotism. He settled in Nancy, where he opened a free clinic for the treatment of poor patients by suggestion. The results of his investigations were published in his seminal 1866 work *Sleep and Certain Analogous States*.[2]

Hippolyte Bernheim (1840–1919) was also a French physician and neurologist. Born in Alsace, he eventually moved to Nancy, where he met and later collaborated with Liébeault at the university there. Bernheim was a well-known authority in the field of hypnosis and published several books on the subject. The first to introduce suggestive therapy to the scientific world in Europe, he described his method of treatment as follows:

> We try to make him [the patient] believe that these symptoms no longer exist, or that they will disappear, the pain will vanish; that the feeling will come back to his limbs; that the muscular strength will increase; and that his appetite will come back. We profit by the special psychical receptivity created by the hypnosis, by the cerebral docility, by the exalted ideo-motor, ideo-sensitive, ideo-sensorial reflex activity, in order to provoke useful reflexes, to persuade the brain to do what it can to transform the accepted idea into reality.[3]

Hence the Nancy school characterized hypnosis as a heightened state of suggestibility, akin to sleep, which allows impressing suggestions upon the mind of the patient. Incidentally, Freud, in the early stages of his professional life, visited the Nancy school to learn suggestive hypnosis therapy. He was so interested in this method of healing that he took one of his female patients with him to be treated with hypnosis. In a letter addressed to his friend and confidant Wilhelm Fliess, Freud stated his intention to "translate Bernheim's book on suggestion."[4]

Chapter 11

William James

The Father of American Psychology

Without any doubt, William James and Thomson Jay Hudson are the leading pioneers of American psychology. Although James was born in New York City, he lived most of his life and made his intellectual contributions in New England. Interestingly, Ralph Waldo Emerson was his godfather. James studied medicine at Harvard University, but he never practiced, devoting most of his time to teaching, writing, and giving conferences on psychology, philosophy, and religion. He attempted to bridge the differences between science and religion. "Science and religion are both of them genuine keys for unlocking the world's treasure house," he wrote.[1] James was the first American philosopher and psychologist who fully understood the intimate connection among body, mind, and spirit.

Strangely, although, as he admitted, James never took a single class in psychology, he became a renowned teacher of the subject and wrote the groundbreaking textbook *The Principles of Psychology*, which had profound influence throughout America and Europe and which became the most influential textbook in the history of American psychology. The two volumes of *The Principles of Psychology* laid out many of the foundations for the future development of this discipline, which was then in its early stages. James was a scholar with vast erudition, who covered many disciplines, among them psychology, philosophy, religious experience, and mysticism. He was also the founder of the American philosophy of pragmatism.

Unfortunately, James tends, to a certain extent, to be neglected. He needs to be reinstated to his rightful position in history for his contributions to this field, including the theory of functionalism. In psychology, functionalism is the opposite of structuralism: the former is interested in explaining how the mental process operates while it is in action, while the latter aims to describe the structure of a mental process in a state of passivity. Paradoxically, the theory of functionalism, which has its foundation in a rational, theoretical basis, is less well-known and popular than the materialistic Freudian theory of psychoanalysis, which has many theoretical flaws, as we will see.

James's most important contribution to religion and spirituality is *The Varieties of Religious Experiences*, a comprehensive study of religious and mystical experiences published in 1902. Here James's concern was not with religious institutions, but with the emotions and feelings which mystical experiences generate. James was careful about revealing his own religious convictions in his writings, perhaps because the academic circles of the time were becoming increasingly materialistic. Ludwig Feuerbach, for instance, had published his highly critical *Essence of Christianity* in 1841; Charles Darwin's *Origin of Species* came into print in 1859, and Karl Marx's masterpiece *Das Kapital* was published in 1867. These works were the favorite intellectual food for the academic circles of James's time.

From James's diary one can infer that he had deep knowledge of Christian scriptures and used biblical passages to overcome and heal mental crisis and depression:

> Whilst in this state of philosophic pessimism and general depression of spirits about my prospects, I went one evening into a dressing-room in the twilight to procure some article that was there; when suddenly there fell upon me without any warning, just as if it came out of the darkness, a horrible fear of my existence. . . . I have always thought that this experience of melancholia of mine *had a religious bearing.* I mean

that the fear was so invasive and powerful that *if I had not clung to Scripture-texts like "The eternal God is my refuge," etc., "Come unto me, all ye that labor and are heavy-laden," etc., "I am the resurrection and the life," etc., I think I should have grown really insane.*[2] (Italics are mine.)

The above passage clearly reveals James's strong religious inclination and his use of biblical passages as healing affirmations, similar to that of Myrtle Fillmore and other New Thought leaders. It also suggests that James used prayer in his private life. According to scholar John C. Durham, in *The Varieties of Religious Experience* James suggests that "spiritual energy" is transferred from the supernatural to the natural world during what he calls "genuine prayer."[3]

James was one the few philosophers who sympathized with and intellectually supported the New Thought movement, which he characterized as the "religion of healthy-mindedness." He acknowledged the importance of New Thought when he stated, "The greatest discovery of my generation is that a human being can alter his life by altering his attitude of mind," which is one of the movement's main tenets. He also emphasized that New Thought was a genuinely religious movement. He provided a few cases of dramatic "mind cures," and suggested that the medical profession and psychology should pay more attention to such phenomena.

In *The Varieties of Religious Experience*, James distinguishes between a person characterized by optimism or "healthy-mindedness" and the pessimist or "sick soul." According to him, a person's moods exert a powerful effect on his or her physical well-being. Thus the "healthy-minded" religious person has a deep sense of the goodness of life and is predisposed to see others as fundamentally good; the gloomy individual, on the other hand, tends to see the negative side of reality and to find unhappiness in any situation in life, no matter how secure he or she may be.

The most fascinating part of *The Varieties of Religious Experience* is the chapter entitled "Mysticism." In fact, the introduction to the 2004 Barnes and Noble edition indicates that "the chapter on mysticism is more widely read than any other because it is often included in anthologies on religious experience and mysticism."[4] According to James, there are four characteristics of mystical experience: (1) ineffability, meaning that it defies expression—its quality is directly experienced, and it cannot be imparted or transferred to others; (2) it has a "noetic quality," that is, it incorporates a mystical sensation that presents itself as a state of knowledge; (3) it is transient; and (4) the person who has the experience cannot control its coming and going.[5]

Like Jung, for whom the "human psyche is 'by nature religious,'"[6] James finds religious experience to be useful to humanity and considers religion to be "*the feelings, acts, and experiences of individual men in their solitude, so far as they apprehend themselves to stand in relation to whatever they may consider the divine*" (italics James's).[7] Furthermore, he observes that religious experiences *connect human beings with an ineffable and greater dimension*, a reality that is not accessible to our normal cognitive faculties. This clearly indicates that he acknowledged the existence of a spiritual dimension that is beyond physical sensation. It also reinforces the belief that he had transcendental experience in his life, as is proved by the following passage describing an experience that he underwent in New York State's Adirondack wilderness:

> The temperature was perfect either inside or outside the cabin, the moon rose and hung above the scene before midnight; leaving only a few of the large stars visible, and I got into a state of spiritual alertness of the most vital [kind] . . . I spent a good deal of [the night] . . . in the woods, where the streaming of moonlight lit up things in a magical checkered play, and it seemed as if the Gods of all the nature-mythologies were holding an indescribable meeting in my breast with the moral Gods of the inner life. . . . It was one of the happiest . . . nights of my existence.[8]

James suffered from many illnesses throughout his life, which might be one reason he became interested in New Thought. There are indications that James used the principles of this "religion of healthy-mindedness" on himself. He made positive references to New Thought writers such as Horatio Dresser, Ralph Waldo Trine, and Henry Wood. He defended the New Thought movement and criticized orthodox religion for being narrow-minded. Regarding Christian Science, he wrote, "Christian Science, so-called, the sect of Mrs. Eddy, is the most radical branch of mind-cure in its dealing with evil. For it 'evil is simply a lie, and anyone who mentions it is a liar.'"[9]

James was also the leading American proponent of pragmatism in philosophy and functionalism in psychology. Here are two aspects of pragmatism that are of interest: He defines true beliefs as "those that prove useful to the believer"—that is, the value of any truth depends upon its use to the person who holds it. The other assertion is, "I choose to believe in free will." With this simple declaration James also attempted to deal with the time-honored philosophical argument of free will. Reducing the issue of free will to the level of belief, he wrote: "My first act of free will shall be to believe in free will."[10] In other words, an individual first has to be aware of her free will and believe in it.

James spent almost his entire academic career at Harvard; he was a professor of several subjects, such as physiology, anatomy, psychology, and philosophy. During his last years, he was increasingly afflicted with cardiac pain, which worsened in 1909. He died of a heart attack on August 26, 1910, at his home in New Hampshire.

In passing, we should mention another prominent American psychologist: John B. Watson (1878–1958), founder of the school of behaviorism. This school is opposed both to the metaphysics of New Thought and to functionalism in psychology. By the turn of the twentieth century, Watson posited that psychology did not have a subject matter; he wanted something measurable, concrete, and observable. He proposed the concept of "behavior" as a subject matter for the discipline. This thesis was expanded on and perfected by B. F. Skinner (1904–90). Skinner contended that the phenomena of behavior are external to the person and have nothing to do with the individual's interior world. It would appear that these two figures viewed the subject matter of psychology upside down. They did not take into account an individual's motivations or beliefs. According to the behaviorist school, a person is like an automaton, responding only to external circumstances.

Sociologically, behaviorism, which has been highly influential, is a typical expression of a consumerist-capitalist society. Behavioral psychology holds the concepts of "conditioning behavior," "rewarding," and "reinforcement" as integral elements of its system. These concepts can be used manipulatively by corporations to maximize their productivity. In addition, this theory focuses on the consequences and the effects of the behavior and not on the original motivations of the behavior, which are thoughts or beliefs. The subject matter of psychology *should* be thoughts and beliefs. It is thoughts and beliefs that dictate human behavior, and not the other way around. But this discussion goes beyond the scope of this book.

Chapter 12

Thomson Jay Hudson
The Scientific Working Hypothesis

The truth liberates and cures.
—Erich Fromm

At the end of the nineteenth century, psychology was in its infancy. It was not yet considered a science because it lacked a scientific theory that could satisfactorily explain the variety of psychological disturbances and psychological phenomena. At this point an obscure American, an unknown lawyer and journalist working at the U.S. Patent Office appeared named Thomson Jay Hudson. He published his landmark book, *The Law of Psychic Phenomena*, in 1893, with the noble intention "to raise Psychology to the domain of exact sciences." He is indeed a precursor of depth psychology in America.

Any discipline that claims to have a scientific status needs a working theoretical structure that can pass the test of verification, much like the heliocentric or gravitational theories that explain the natural laws of the universe. Although James had laid down the basis for a scientific method of studying psychology in academic circles, an overarching theory was still missing that could explain all the range of psychological phenomena that were considered paranormal or supernatural, including healing by faith, mental means, magic, witches, shamans, divine intervention, miracles, and so forth. Before Hudson, nobody had proposed a satisfactory working hypothesis to explain these psychological phenomena.

Before the discovery of the Law of Suggestion by Liébault and his disciple Bernheim, it was difficult to differentiate between the conscious and the subconscious mind. However, hypnotic experiments established that the subconscious mind is incapable of discrimination: it does not have the ability to formulate its own premises, and its role is to follow what is conveyed to it by the conscious mind. Thus, in general terms, the subconscious mind is subordinate to the conscious mind because it always carries out the suggestions given by the conscious mind. Nowadays, this theory is accepted as true in metaphysical circles, esoteric psychology, and New Age thought.

Before the studies of Liébeault and Berheim, the understanding of the mind's structure and the differentiation of the conscious and subconscious were beyond the scope of science. The subconscious mind was called "unconscious" because it was regarded as completely inert and dormant, a passive reservoir of forgotten memories in the human mind. However, the opposite is true: the subconscious, far from being an attic for past experiences, is the primal factor out of which human behavior and life are fashioned. It is from the subconscious mind that automatic thoughts, irrational fears, conditioned behaviors, prejudices, and emotions spring. This theory was later confirmed by independent studies conducted by Hudson, Freud, Jung, and Thomas Troward, who all agree concerning the active role the subconscious mind plays in human life.

Around the same time as Hudson's book was published, the earliest attempts to scientifically explain occult phenomena were being made by Jung in Europe and James in America. At the beginning of the twentieth century, Jung obtained his doctoral degree with a thesis entitled *The Psychology and Pathology of So-Called Occult Phenomena*, published in 1902, in which he described cases of double consciousness, twilight states and somnambulism, pathological dreaminess, pathological lying, and other phenomena.[1] This was the same year in which *The Varieties of Religious Experience* was published, in which James also examines a wide range of mystical experiences, such as trance, mediumship, ghostly phenomena, and mind healing. However, a scientific working hypothesis explaining these phenomena was missing.

Hudson's book *The Law of Psychic Phenomena* was a best-seller in America and Europe. According to the publisher, this book had appeared in forty-seven editions by 1925. This fact indicates that Hudson's psychological theory had a profound influence from the time of its inception. It was especially influential for metaphysical and esoteric writers such as Thomas Troward, Paul Foster Case, William Walker Atkinson, Christian D. Larson, H. Spencer Lewis (founder of the Ancient and Mystical Order Rosae Crucis, or AMORC), Norman Vincent Peale, Ernest Holmes, and other prominent leaders of New Thought.

The fact that James's *Principles of Psychology* (1890) and Hudson's *Law of Psychic Phenomena* (1893) both appeared before Freud's publications is clear evidence of American leadership in the field of psychology at that time.[2] Ironically, academic and scientific circles in America "venerated and idolized" Freud for his role in the discovery of the dual structure of the human mind and the function of the subconscious in human behavior. But they did not acknowledge the contributions of Hudson, who posited the existence of the subconscious mind long before Freud. It seems that the worldwide academic community was mesmerized by the theories of sexual repression and the Oedipus complex, which were highly sensational subjects at that time. Perhaps another reason was that America was a young nation, and European scholars did not want to pay much attention to the thinkers of the new continent.

It should be noted that in 1896, Hudson's book *The Laws of Psychic Phenomena* made its way to Vienna, birthplace of Mesmerism and psychoanalysis. In the Introduction to Samuel Weiser's 1968 edition, Erwin Seale states that the American writer Arthur Abell was in Vienna gathering information for his book *Talks with Great Composers*. Abell had been introduced by a friend to the great German composer

Johannes Brahms. During the interview, Brahms confided to Abell that he received inspiration through the subjective mind and showed him Hudson's book, which was lying on top of his piano.[3] Remember that was 1896, meaning that this book was already known in the same city where psychoanalysis was in full gestation. One can only wonder, if a great musician had possessed and cherished Hudson's book, why were Freud, his colleagues, and disciples not aware of it? Or had they known about it but simply ignored it?

Since the publication of *The Law of Psychic Phenomena*, the psychic spectrum, which includes spiritualism, magic, mesmerism, somnambulism, miracles, faith and mental healing, madness, mediumship, automatic writing, multiple personality disorder, and extrasensory perception, was no longer relegated to the domain of the paranormal or supernatural, because now these phenomena could be explained as unusual or extraordinary expressions of the subconscious mind. Hudson demystified and provided a rational explanation for them.

For these reasons, Hudson should be considered as a genuine forerunner of modern psychology, metaphysics, and esoteric psychology. Most authorities give credit only to Freud, neglecting Hudson as well as the Nancy school. For example, the renowned sociologist and psychotherapist Erich Fromm writes: "Freud was the first to have made this discovery the center of his psychological system and he investigated unconscious phenomena in the greatest detail, with astonishing results."[4] Stefan Zweig also holds that it was Freud who discovered the subconscious, claiming that the "fundamental transformation and vast expansion of the area in which our mental energies are known to operate, has been Freud's supreme act of genius."[5]

But in fact Freud was not the discoverer of the unconscious mind and its importance for understanding conscious thought and behavior. James had already mentioned the terms "unconscious" and "subconscious" in *The Principles of Psychology*. Moreover, Boris Sidis, a student of James, published *The Psychology of Suggestion: A Research into the Subconscious Nature of Man and Society* in 1898, one year before the publication of *The Interpretation of Dreams*. (James's introduction to the book is dated November 1, 1897.) In chapter 12 of his book, entitled "The Double Self," Sidis had already posited the dual structure of the mind and the fact that the subconscious is an active, intelligent element in the mind.

The approaches of Hudson and Freud to the theory of the dual structure of the mind come from different perspectives. Freud's was based on the interpretation of dreams, while Hudson's was based on the theory of hypnosis and suggestion. There are still other ways to access the subconscious mind. One is through ceremonial rituals and special symbols used in occult and esoteric groups such as the Hermetic Order of the Golden Dawn, which flourished in Britain in the last decade of the nineteenth century.[6] Furthermore, the American Qabalist Paul Foster Case propounded a systematic meditation on the symbolism of the Tarot cards for the cleansing of negative traits in the subconscious and the understanding of mental processes. (See his works cited in the bibliography.)

Freud's conception of man was decidedly materialistic; he identified himself as an atheist, while Hudson's perspective was metaphysical and spiritual. Like the adherents of New Thought, Hudson believed that the main issue was the nature of the beliefs and ideas stored in the subconscious mind, and he praised the benefits of hypnosis in achieving mental well-being. Freud was aware of the benefits of hypnosis in the healing of mental disorders, but he was disappointed with this method, as he was unable to hypnotize patients properly.

Hudson believed that the Nancy school had conducted a vast array of investigations and systematized the information in a coherent system, setting out on the royal road to understanding the entire field of psychological phenomena. This made it possible to formulate a coherent hypothesis. Thus he came to the conclusion that *suggestion and the subconscious were the key elements to explaining most psychological phenomena*. This principle was later confirmed by Troward and subsequent writers in esoteric psychology, metaphysics, and New Thought. Hudson put forward his breakthrough hypothesis in the following terms:

1. A human being has two minds: the *objective mind* (conscious) and the *subjective mind* (subconscious). Each one is endowed with separate and distinct powers; each one is capable, under certain conditions, of independent action.

2. The subjective mind is constantly amenable to control by suggestion.

3. The subjective mind is incapable of inductive reasoning.

In this way, Hudson established a scientific basis for understanding many types of psychic phenomena that, at that time, did not have any explanation. He also propounded the basic theory underlying the metaphysical and psychological basis of mental healing. These principles, which furnished psychology with a useful and workable theory for the understanding of many mental and physical diseases, raised the discipline of psychology to the level of science.

A corollary hypothesis is that the conscious mind has the ability to have dominion over the functions and sensations of the physical body, "and that power can be invoked at will and applied to the alleviation of human suffering."[7] This assertion is extremely important for comprehending the metaphysical theory that mankind has the power to positively influence the functions of the body, and that this can be done at will. It is also a key premise for understanding the dynamics of the interaction of the conscious and subconscious mind. Thus Hudson did not exaggerate when he said, "These propositions together furnish the key to the whole science of psychology."[8]

Modern mental and behavioral scientists concur with esoteric psychology's viewpoint that the subconscious is in charge of every function of our bodies. It controls the heartbeat, the breathing process, the circulation of blood through the body, the production of sugar by the liver, the assimilation of the food and its conversion into energy, the reproduction of cells, the instinctual mechanism of self-preservation, and so on. None of these functions depends on our conscious awareness. Along these lines, esoteric psychology postulates that the subconscious is the agent that carries out the healing process, and medicine merely sets up a chemical reaction to which the real healing power of the body reacts in response.

There is an old occult aphorism that proclaims, "Nature unaided fails." Nature in this case is the physical body, which needs the mind's intervention to maintain optimum health and improve itself. In addition, the key for any healing is a *firm desire* to regain one's health. This attitude implies a positive *expectation* and willingness on the part of the patient to *change* his habitual way of thinking. These are the favorable conditions for the operator to implant a powerful *healing suggestion* in the patient's subconscious mind.

Although, as we have noted, the subconscious mind is incapable of inductive reasoning, it is capable of *deductive reasoning*. This is another key point to consider in mental and spiritual healing. The subconscious arranges and works on the information (beliefs, presumptions, biases, unstated conceptions, etc.) accepted wittingly or unwittingly by the conscious mind. The subconscious draws conclusions from the information already existing therein. It will make its deductions from irrational or erroneous beliefs as well as from those that are true. If the mind fosters wrong presumptions and false beliefs about humanity and life, the subconscious works based on those premises.

The reasoning process of the subconscious resembles the classical Aristotelian syllogism, a form of deductive reasoning in which a conclusion is derived from two stated premises. A classic example, given by Aristotle himself, is as follows:

First premise: All men are mortal.

Second premise: Socrates is a man.

Conclusion: Therefore Socrates is mortal.

However, if the premises are wrong, the conclusion is going to be incorrect, because the subconscious cannot discriminate between what is wrong and right or between what is false and true; it accepts any information supplied by the conscious mind as absolutely true. It infers its conclusions on the basis of the information already accepted by the conscious mind, regardless of the accuracy of that information. Consequently, if somebody holds the false belief that Latinos are lazy, the subconscious will reason as follows:

First premise: All Latinos are lazy.

Second premise: Juan is Latino.

Conclusion: Therefore, Juan is lazy.

The subconscious mind is not equipped with the faculty of discerning which ideas are good or bad for the person's well-being. For example, if someone believes that cancer is hereditary, then the subconscious thinking would reason thus:

First premise: All cancers are hereditary.

Second premise: John's father died of cancer.

Conclusion: John will most likely die of cancer.

On these premises, John will unwittingly have a subconscious tendency to create a self-fulfilling prophecy. It will be reinforced by the mass media and the social environment, which often support this kind of view, as well as by conventional medicine, which says that if the parents had a certain disease, the children will have a propensity to develop the same one. Under such powerful suggestions, which are "false evidence," John's subconscious will do its best to create such a malady. In his daily conversation, John might talk to his friends and relatives about how his parents died from cancer, how the illness runs in his family, and so forth. Unfortunately, many people who believe that illnesses are hereditary will sooner or later manifest them as self-fulfilling prophecies.

Unstated or hidden beliefs can originate in the social environment as well. If people commonly believe that the human life span is only sixty years, an individual will program his mind to live until around that age. The accumulated collective experience of the human race is also a factor: Ernest Holmes called this "race-suggestion," defined as "the tendency to reproduce what the [human] race has thought and experienced."[9]

If a person has put his faith in a particular belief, no matter how absurd or illogical it may be, his subconscious mind will do its best to manifest it accordingly. If this belief is reinforced by collective thinking, for instance, at a gathering of people such as a Christian revival meeting or an evangelistic tent healing, the atmosphere of the meeting could activate the creative imagination of an individual and the restoration of health is most likely to follow. Likewise, if a person strongly believes that a special herb or medicine will do the healing, this fact will enhance his capacity to regain his health. The above give some hints to understanding mental healing, as well as all the systems known as faith healing, mesmerism, Christian Science, and other suggestive therapies. The common denominator is *belief* and *suggestion*; they are the agents that activate the curative powers of the body. Interestingly, Paracelsus encapsulated this principle in the following words:

> Whether the object of your faith be real or false, you will nevertheless obtain the same effects. Thus if I believe in Saint Peter's statue as I should have believed in Saint Peter himself, I shall obtain the same effects that I should have obtained from Saint Peter. But that is superstition. Faith, however, produces miracles; whether it is a true or a false faith, it will always produce the same wonders.[10]

This clearly explains the absurd beliefs held by dogmatic religious sects, political organizations, and fanatical social groups. And as Voltaire said, "He who believes in absurdities will commit atrocities." If an individual overtly or covertly accepts the suggestion of a wrong premise, the logical conclusion will be incorrect. Once that suggestion or belief is settled in the subconscious mind, the individual will automatically screen out any evidence that contradicts it. She will instinctively search for confirmation of her preconceived notions. She will mechanically seek out events and experiences confirming her biases and preconceptions and will be oblivious to all facts or ideas conflicting with them. Thus her personal view of reality will be arranged according to what she wants to see and hear.

Here, we have arrived again at an extremely important factor—the *belief system*. Beliefs and attitudes fostered by an individual, knowingly or unknowingly, will eventually be expressed in his body or in his external circumstances. This principle applies to all areas of life, such as relationships, success, and human potential. Beliefs pave the way for the future manifestation of things expected. Thoughts and words are energy, and consequently are powerful instruments of manifestation, because they represent the expression of inner beliefs. First come the thoughts, then the words, then the actions; words and actions are an extension of thoughts.

Since the subconscious controls the automatic functions of the body, the logical inference is that the subconscious can also restore it to health and keep it well. Its power can be awakened by mental means, that is, by *suggestions*. Moreover, we live in a social environment where we receive suggestions from multiple sources. The kind of health and the external circumstances we find ourselves in at this moment are the results of suggestions we have been submitting to the subconscious mind all our lives. Furthermore, subconscious healing power is not limited to psychosomatic and nervous illnesses, but extends to every organ of our bodies, even to the reconstruction of bones and damaged tissues, as we have seen from the case of Charles and Myrtle Fillmore. Neuroscience has even demonstrated that the body has the capacity to reshape severe brain injuries in response to what it thinks and imagines. This issue will be further discussed in pages ahead.

Hudson was one of the first who, following the investigations of the Nancy school of hypnosis, demonstrated scientifically that the structure of the mind is dual; that is, an individual functions as two distinct selves— the conscious and the subconscious—each one apparently working independently of the other. This would explain somnambulism or sleepwalking. In this case, the sleepwalker's awareness is absent and he or she performs some actions under the direction of the subconscious mind.

From this, it can be further inferred that an individual possesses a threefold structure: the conscious, the subconscious, and the physical body. The conscious mind apprehends reality through the five physical senses, and its main function is discrimination. In contrast, the subconscious operates on the basis of information given it by the conscious mind, without discerning the accuracy of the information submitted. The subconscious does not question any of the information handed to it by the conscious mind; it accepts without hesitation every statement, no matter how absurd.

The work of the subconscious mind is perceived when the physical senses are relaxed; for instance, during natural sleep, the subconscious continues to perform its functions in maintaining and restoring the physical body from the wear and tear of the day. For Hudson, the conscious mind is merely a function of the brain, while the subconscious mind goes beyond the domain of physical reality where time and space have no bearing; it stores the wisdom and experiences of the race memory.

Another contribution made by Hudson to the field of mental healing is his classification of the types of nonmedical healing. He found six categories: (1) prayer and religious faith, (2) the "Mind Cure," (3) Christian Science, (4) spiritism, (5) mesmerism, and (6) suggestive hypnotism.[11] Most of these items have been already discussed in previous pages, so there is no need for further clarification, except for spiritism. This is based on the belief that the spirit of a dead person communicates through a medium.[12] To the above codification should be added another entry, spiritual mind healing, which is a modern form of healing practiced by New Thought practitioners.

These different methods of healing are based upon different perspectives, and each one fits a different kind of people according to their idiosyncrasies. In other words, one method will work for some and not for others. However, the common denominator in all these treatments is that they do not use any kind of medicine, and all of them have as their sole purpose impressing the subconscious of the patient with the healing idea.

Regarding the lasting effect of mental healing, Hudson acknowledges that some patients have a tendency to relapse. However, he argues that a patient treated with traditional medicine also has a risk of relapse, and in some cases the secondary effects of the drugs and medicine can do more harm than good. Consequently, conventional medicine may sometimes heal one part of the body and damage another. The truth of the matter is that with any kind of treatment, the patient may relapse. The success of mental methods depends on the patient's ability to hold steadfast to the idea of recuperation and not allow the negativity of the social surroundings to neutralize the effects of healing. Hence the patient should not discuss his or her healing with others who may induce doubt.

Some students of occultism approach metaphysical studies with the idea of surrendering their will and conscious mind to the direction of the subconscious. This is dangerous, because the subconscious cannot direct itself. The person who allows his subconscious to control him runs the risk that dormant, anarchic, and destructive forces in the psyche will express themselves at the least expected times in devastating ways. When the conscious mind surrenders its dominion over the subconscious, the person becomes at the mercy of untamed primeval instincts, which could result in mental illness. As Hudson wrote, the "subconscious cannot direct itself, nor can direct us. Its marvelous powers must always be definitely limited if they are to do us any real good. The unrestrained expression of the subconscious is insanity."[13]

Hudson also advises those who seek to communicate with the dead or with disembodied spirits that they risk putting themselves at the mercy of negative influences or under the control of harmful forces that could endanger their mental wellness.[14]

Chapter 13

Thomas Troward

Founder of Mental Science

Thomas Troward exercised a tremendous influence on American New Thought writers, especially, as we have seen, on Ernest Holmes. Troward was born of British parents in Punjab, India, which at the time was under British rule. He was raised and educated in England. At age of twenty-two, in 1869, he returned to India and successfully passed the Indian civil service examination. He became assistant commissioner and then was quickly promoted to divisional judge in the Punjab, where he served for the next twenty-five years. After his retirement in 1896, he devoted his time to studying the Bible, writing metaphysical essays, and painting. He also deepened his studies in metaphysics, philosophy, and religion. He already had profound knowledge of the Bible, the Koran, and the Hindu scriptures. He learned Hebrew in order to read the Bible in its original tongue.

When Troward returned to Europe, it seems that his destiny was already laid out for the mission that he had to accomplish. According to the New Thought author Harry Gaze, Troward was discovered in London in 1902 by Mrs. Alice Callow, who was an honorary secretary of the Higher Thought Centre (an organization that was inspired by the ideas of the American New Thought writers). Troward happened to be at a tearoom in London. Gaze, a close friend of Troward, witnessed his initial meeting with Callow, and he vividly narrates the casual encounter in the following terms:

In a corner sat a little gentleman, rather bald, and perhaps you would say somewhat homely. . . . A lady, approaching that period designated by race habit "middle-age," entered the tearoom. . . . Addressing the absorbed writer, she said, apologetically, "You don't mind, sir, I trust?" and accepted his studious silence as consent to her taking her place at his table. She gave her order to the waitress. Too busy to notice her appearance on the scene, the gentleman worked away at his manuscript, writing in very large script, perhaps to help his vision in the somewhat dim light.

He was aroused from his preoccupation by an exclamation of surprise from the newcomer at the table, "Why, sir, you really must pardon me for my apparent rudeness, but you wrote so large and so close to me I could not help seeing your words. What you are writing is Higher Thought or Divine Science, isn't it?"

The writer seemed in no way disturbed but, on the other hand, quite amused and interested. "Why, madam," he declared, "I trust it really is *higher* thought, and certainly not lower thought. But what do you mean by Higher Thought?"

"Well," she said, "I must explain my thoughtless interruption of your work. I am the secretary of a new organization at Kensington, called the Higher Thought Centre, where we study and listen to lectures on metaphysical Truth applied to health, spiritual unfoldment, and successful living." The philosopher was duly impressed.[1]

As a result of this informal meeting, Troward accepted an invitation to visit the Higher Thought Centre and to attend some of its meetings. Gaze, who knew the Centre, depicts it as a place that consisted of connecting rooms furnished with folding chairs and a platform for lectures and classes. In addition, there was a library of metaphysical books and a reading room. On the library table were abundant New Thought materials from the United States, including copies of publications such as *Mind, The Arena, Boston Ideas, Positive Thought, Unity, Universal Truth, Nautilus,* and the *Exodus.* On the shelves were books by pioneers of New Thought and Divine Science such as Henry Wood, Charles Brodie Patterson, Elizabeth Towne, Julius Dresser, Emma

Curtis Hopkins, Malinda Cramer, Warren Felt Evans, Ralph Waldo Trine, and Emilie Cady. At the time there was practically an invasion of the New Thought ideology into England.[2]

According to the foreword of the book *Thomas Troward: An Intimate Memoir of the Teacher and Man*, it was Gaze who provided the missing link to Troward's metaphysics regarding the relationship between the conscious and the subconscious mind by giving Troward a copy of Hudson's *Law of Psychic Phenomena*.[3]

The Higher Thought Centre was one of London's chief metaphysical groups. Its members held meetings on a regular basis to study and listen to lectures on metaphysical matters as applied to health and spiritual unfoldment, based on the teachings of the New Thought movement. Troward found himself among like-minded people, in a mental and spiritual environment where he could safely express his metaphysical ideas. The members of the Centre, in turn, found him a wise and congenial man. He visited this place every time he went to London.

Troward's encounter with Callow was certainly not coincidental. The members of the Centre recognized in him a learned individual, and they invited him to speak. As a result, in 1904 Troward delivered a series of lectures at Queen Street Hall in Edinburgh, Scotland. These talks are known today as the *Edinburgh Lectures on Mental Science*, which were followed by the *Dore Lectures* in 1909. Through these talks, Troward laid down the metaphysical foundation for the modern New Thought movement.

Troward adopted Hudson's working hypothesis about the dual nature of the human mind. In fact, this idea was the foundation for Troward's Edinburgh lectures. In these lectures Troward also corroborated Quimby's discovery about mental healing. Troward found, as Quimby had a half-century before him, that the basis of all healing lay in changing the frame of mind of the patient. Troward also held that *the subconscious in every human being is the creative faculty*. He understood that the subconscious has the natural tendency to build, maintain, and rebuild the human body, as well as to keep it in good shape.

Troward held that *the human subconscious creates whatever consciousness impresses upon it*. Therefore Troward's position is similar to Quimby's: healing is a matter of changing wrong beliefs, but most of the time an individual cannot do this without a solid conviction of the falsity of the old beliefs. Synthesizing Quimby's ideas, Troward said that wrong beliefs externalize as sickness. Whereas people erroneously think that the illness is the primary cause to be healed, in fact the primary cause is the belief that has settled in the subconscious mind. The disease is simply the consequence of wrong ideas.

The power of beliefs in creating illnesses and curing them is masterfully explained by Troward:

> Whatever personality[4] the objective mind impresses upon it [the subconscious], that personality it assumes and acts up to; and since it [the subconscious] is the builder of the body, it will build up a body in correspondence with the personality thus impressed upon it. These two laws of the subjective mind form the foundation of the axiom that *our body represents the aggregate of our beliefs*. If our fixed belief is that the body is subject to all sorts of influences beyond our control, and that this, that, or the other symptom shows that such an uncontrollable influence is at work upon us, then this belief is impressed upon the subjective mind, which by the law of its nature accepts it without question and proceeds to fashion bodily conditions in accordance with this belief. Again, *if our fixed belief is that certain material remedies are the only means of cure, then we find in this belief the foundation of all medicine*. There is nothing unsound in the theory of medicine; it is the strictly logical correspondence with the measure of knowledge, with which those who rely on it are as yet able to assimilate, and it acts accurately in accordance with their belief that in a large number of cases medicine will do good, but also in many instances it fails. Therefore, for those who have not yet reached a more interior perception of the law of Nature, the healing agency of medicine is a most valuable aid to the alleviation of physical maladies. The error to be combated is not the belief that, in its own way, medicine is capable of doing good, but the belief that there is no higher or better way.[5] (Italics are mine.)

For Troward, there is a crucial difference between holding an idea in the conscious mind and holding one in the subconscious mind. The conscious mind perceives things as being related to time and space, whereas the subconscious has no reference to time and space. Troward goes on to say that man's spirit is unconditioned; therefore "he is not subject to illness; and when this idea is firmly impressed on the subconscious mind, it will externalize it."[6]

To the question, why is it that many people do not heal quickly with mental treatment? Troward replies that they have been holding the idea that illness is a natural condition since childhood; one treatment cannot eradicate a conviction held for many years. The new belief needs time to penetrate down to the innermost depths of the subconscious mind. Hence it is important for the healer to strengthen the new conviction until the cure is produced.

To the above answer it can be added that in many cases the illness has been built into the body for many years without the person's awareness; therefore the body also needs time to heal itself, provided that it gets the needed rest and the proper nutrients. The problem is that some people are impatient and want a quick fix. When the healing does not occur quickly, they interfere with the body's natural curative process by ingesting harmful chemicals or by forcing the body into activities for which it is not yet prepared. As a consequence, they aggravate the situation. This impatience can also manifest as a feeling of anxiety and insecurity about the outcome. This attitude is a powerful counterproductive suggestion to the subconscious mind. The key in most cases is to give the body the time to cleanse itself from the harmful elements that created the sickness.

In cases where the patient is unable to practice self-healing, Troward recommends the use of a competent practitioner of mental or spiritual treatment. One obstacle that Troward found to a successful treatment of mind healing is the misconception of the separateness of human beings. Some practitioners consider themselves to be entities completely apart from the patient. They may also hold a certain sense of superiority.

These are all mistakes. At the collective, subconscious level there are no personal demarcations or borders between humans. Such mistaken beliefs hinder the positive rapport between the two subconscious minds that is necessary for healing, because during this process, the two people are communicating at the subconscious level.

The process of removing the mental barrier between operator or healer and patient involves establishing rapport. This is possible because the universal subconscious is present at every point of space and time. For this reason, once the operator realizes that the barriers of external personality between himself and the patient have been removed, he is able to impress healing ideas into the patient's subconscious mind.

Here is an extremely important thing to keep in mind in a healing session: if the operator directs his mind toward the unhealthy condition of the patient, he will not have much success because he is focusing on the illness and not on the outcome of a healthy situation. Furthermore, to achieve permanent healing, the practitioner must regard and acknowledge the spiritual being of the patient rather than identify her with the outer personality. Troward admonishes:

> We must therefore withdraw our thought from the contemplation of symptoms, and indeed from his corporeal personality altogether, and must think of him as a purely spiritual individuality, and as such entirely free from subjection to any conditions, and consequently as voluntarily externalizing the conditions most expressive of the vitality and intelligence which pure spirit is.[7]

Troward advises that in order to get conscious cooperation from the patient, the operator needs to instruct the patient in the general principles of Mental Science. In some cases, that may not be advisable because the principles might be contradicted by the patient's existing prejudices. In such instances, absent or long-distance treatment appears to be the most effective. Here it does not matter if the patient is in the presence of the operator or in a distant place. According to Troward, treatment during sleep has been found to be effective because the patient's whole system is naturally in a state of relaxation, which prevents her from offering any conscious opposition to the treatment.

These ideas had already been established by Hudson in *The Law of Psychic Phenomena*. Troward agrees with Hudson that the best time to impress the subconscious with healing thoughts is just before the patient falls asleep and right after waking up in the mornings. He warns that the student should be on guard against a common mistaken belief held by some writers and teachers of metaphysics, who regard themselves as using their personal willpower to perform healing or other wonders. The authentic practitioner of mind healing should keep in mind the following admonition:

> No doubt intense willpower can evolve certain external results, but like all other methods of compulsion it lacks the permanency of natural growth. The appearances, forms, and conditions produced by mere intensity of willpower will only hang together so long as the compelling force continues; but let it be exhausted or withdrawn, and the elements thus forced into unnatural combination will at once fly back to their proper affinities; the form created by compulsion never had the germ of vitality in itself and is therefore dissipated as soon as the external energy which supported it is withdrawn.[8]

Healing by personal charisma or influence by mental means does not have lasting effects. According to Troward, the operator who cures through mental powers alone is appealing to the corporeal body but not to the spiritual being. This statement could well be applied to Mesmer, whose type of treatment was transmitting a fluidic energy from the practitioner to the corporeal body of the patient while neglecting the spiritual side. For Troward, a genuine and integral healing should consist of the following steps:

1. To consider every patient as a spiritual being. In the spiritual realm, every soul is whole and perfect at every moment and place.
2. To empower the sick person to awaken his or her inner capabilities for the process of healing.

3. To instill a healing suggestion into the subconscious mind of the patient.

Metaphysical writers and critics have written abundantly about Troward, but few have realized that he was a genuine Rosicrucian. The Rosicrucian order was supposedly founded in Germany by one Christian Rosenkreutz (in English, Christian Rose Cross), who is probably an allegorical figure. This organization came into public awareness at the beginning of the seventeenth century. Troward gives hints in his writings of his profound admiration for Rosicrucianism; for instance, there is a striking remark at the end of his Edinburgh lectures, where he gives a brief account of the founder of the fraternity. He indicates that Christian Rosenkreutz had summarized "*all his knowledge in the words: JESUS MIHI OMNIA.*"[9] These words, which literally mean "Jesus is all things to me," were written on the sarcophagus in the center of the crypt of Christian Rosenkreutz, according to the seventeenth-century Rosicrucian tract *Fama fraternitatis* ("The Fame of the Brotherhood"). This clearly shows the Christian roots of the fraternity.

Jesus Christ set the standard for measuring a genuine Christian when he said, "By their fruits ye shall know them" (Matthew 7:20). Troward demonstrated that he possessed insightful knowledge in metaphysical and mystical matters and shared his knowledge openly in the Edinburgh and Dore lectures. Troward wrote in the Edinburgh lectures, "And now his followers await the coming of 'the Artist Elias,' who shall bring the Magnum Opus to its completion. 'Let him that readeth understand.'"[10]

"The artist Elias," according to Paul Foster Case, is a reference to the self-liberation to be accomplished by the individual. The "artist Elias," of whom it is said that he shall return and "restore all things" (Matthew 17:11), accomplishes what is known as the Magnum Opus, or the "Great Work." Therefore Troward is alluding to the Great Work, which is the "creation of a new man by himself." This is the ultimate goal of a true spiritual seeker. The Great Work, also known as the Great Art of the Rosicrucians, is, according to Case, the work of those who know "the secret of regeneration. Thus they can use the law that has evolved man out of the lower kingdom to take man farther, out of the limitations of his natural state."[11]

In the same series of lectures Troward also asserted:

> Among such records explanatory of the supreme mysteries three stand out pre-eminent, all bearing witness to the same ONE Truth, and each throwing light upon the other; and these three are the Bible, the Great Pyramid, and the Pack of Cards.[12]

Those who are familiar with esoteric literature will immediately recognize that when Troward mentions the "Pack of Cards," he is not referring to the ordinary playing cards, but to the Tarot cards, which are also known as the Tarot keys. These keys are powerful mental tools for meditation and personal transformation. The intriguing thing is that Troward is putting the Tarot on the same level as the Bible and the mysteries of the Great Pyramid.

At this point it is a good idea to caution neophytes and all students who approach esoteric and occult studies seeking personal advantage that the authentic Western mystery schools, such as the Hermetic Qabalah, alchemy, and most branches of the metaphysical disciplines, are rooted in the teachings of the Holy Bible and Jesus Christ. As we have seen, the original Rosicrucian order was fundamentally a Christian organization. Likewise, the Knights Templar were established in medieval times to protect Catholic pilgrims so they would have access to the sacred city of Jerusalem. Freemasonry is also rooted in Christian teachings, as was the Hermetic Order of the Golden Dawn, which flourished at the end of the nineteenth century. This group, which indelibly influenced all areas of modern Western metaphysics, occult philosophy, and ceremonial magic, claimed to be a direct successor of the Brotherhood of the Rosy Cross.[13] The beginner would do well to heed this consideration in order to avoid future disenchantments.

Chapter 14

Émile Coué

Autosuggestion and the Placebo Effect

Autosuggestion is an instrument that we possess at birth, and in this instrument, or rather in this force, resides a marvelous and incalculable power.

—Émile Coué

The French pharmacist and psychologist Émile Coué (1857–1926) is considered the father of applied conditioning or applied psychology. He popularized the concept of autosuggestion and methodically explained the placebo effect to the scientific circles of his time. Nowadays the placebo effect is commonly used in clinical trials and medical settings; it has even become a cliché in psychological treatments and marketing strategies.

Although Coué was a pharmacist, he was interested in hypnosis. He visited the Nancy school of hypnosis and studied extensively with Liébeault and Bernheim. As we have seen, this school promoted the method of healing known as *suggestive therapies*. Coué, furnished with the knowledge he acquired at the Nancy school, developed his own therapeutic technique based on the work of Faria, who postulated the importance of suggestion and autosuggestion in the healing process. Coué thought that hypnosis was not needed as long as the patient consistently repeats constructive affirmations similar to mantras. He reportedly cured thousands of people with this method.

The origin of the placebo theory goes back to Bernheim's experimentations with suggestive therapies. He narrates the story of a man with paralysis of the tongue, which was deemed incurable because of its resistance to several methods of treatment. Finally, when the man visited a doctor, the doctor told him that he would try a new instrument of his own invention to cure him. He further stated that this instrument had rendered excellent results in healing other people. Then the doctor asked the patient to close his eyes and open his mouth. While the man had his eyes closed, the doctor introduced a pocket thermometer into the patient's mouth. The patient believed what the doctor told him, because once he was told to open his eyes, he exclaimed joyfully that he was able to move his tongue freely.[1] By saying that *this instrument had rendered excellent results in healing other people*, the doctor conveyed a powerful suggestion to the patient. The patient believed it, and the healing took place.

Coué had a similar experience when he was working as a pharmacist. One day, while he was in his drugstore, a customer showed up and wanted to buy a certain medicine that required a medical prescription, but the customer didn't have one. Nevertheless, the customer insisted on buying the medicine. Coué, who was unable to sell the medicine without a prescription, improvised a solution inspired by what he had learned at the Nancy school. He recommended a different product to the buyer, saying that he had a new remedy as effective as the one the customer was requesting, and no medical prescription was required. The customer purchased the alternative medicine and left the pharmacy. The product sold was sugar pills with no medicinal value at all.

A few days later, the customer returned and happily exclaimed that the medicine sold by Coué had healed him completely; he also said there was no limit to how fantastic this new wonder drug was. After the customer left, Coué was perplexed by the effectiveness of the suggestive therapy. He had just confirmed what we now know as the placebo effect. However, as a professional, he wondered: What really healed the customer? Was it the belief in the fake "remedy," or was it his determination to regain his health? Why had a product without any curative properties healed the man?[2] The answer is that the hidden suggestion given by Coué made the patient believe in the fake medicine; this suggestion was enhanced by the patient's desire to regain his well-being.

This incident was the turning point in Coué's professional life. He realized the importance of this experience and developed his method of curing people by what is called *conscious autosuggestion*, that is, using positive affirmations, which must be constantly repeated. In academic circles, this is known as the theory of applied conditioning. Coué's theory would have a positive impact on the lives of millions of people throughout the world. His teachings came into vogue in America and Europe and were reportedly responsible for thousands of remarkable healings at the beginning of the twentieth century.

Coué soon concluded that there was no necessity for any intermediary between the patient and the illness: the patient could apply her own suggestions and heal herself. The theory behind the idea of autosuggestion is that positive affirmations, as long as they sink into the subconscious, have the capacity to change the individual's frame of mind and imagination and gradually alleviate her physical condition.

Coué believed that every person can heal himself by using the method of autosuggestion. Thus, in effect, *every healing is self-healing*. He postulated, "The patient always does his own suggestion anyway. The need for some outside operator is only an aid toward the acceptance of a suggestion." As we have seen, the method of Christian Science—denying the existence of matter and thus denying the existence of illness—is another form of suggestion, however irrational. The crucial point is to make the patient *believe* in the possibility of recovery of health and to instill that belief into the subconscious mind. In Coué's method, positive affirmations were the essential tool to reach and influence the subconscious mind. For this purpose, he elaborated a series of affirmations that became famous all over the world, including his best-known: *Day by day, in every way, I am getting better and better.*

Science is now verifying the profound influence of thoughts and emotions in restoring the body's well-being. Currently, the principle of autosuggestion is becoming recognized in the medical community, although many fail to acknowledge its effectiveness as a therapeutic agent. Properly understood and applied, autosuggestion through positive affirmations enables all people to treat themselves, or at least to maintain a proper mental attitude towards obtaining good effects. For instance, affirmations made in the state of mind known as the alpha level (the meditative level) tend to be more powerful than those made at the beta level, which is the state of the waking mind. Many minor aches and pains can be alleviated by proper autosuggestion. After hypnotic sessions, professional hypnotists usually teach their patients appropriate affirmations and self-hypnotic techniques so that they can continue the treatment at home and prevent any relapse. Of course, the affirmations have to be tailored to the patient's idiosyncrasies and specific needs.

Coué's masterwork, *Self Mastery through Conscious Autosuggestion*, became very popular in America and Europe. Coué, like the mental healers who preceded him, regarded the subconscious mind as the most powerful factor in the human personality. To demonstrate the power of the imagination and the subconscious mind, he offered this example:

> Suppose that we place on the ground a plank 30 feet long by 1 foot wide. It is evident that everybody will be capable of going from one end to the other of the plank without stepping out of the edge. But now change the conditions of the experiment, and imagine this plank placed at the top of the towers of high buildings. [A person] would not be capable of walking even a few feet along this narrow path if the person is not an acrobat or skillful in walking in situations like that; before taking two steps, he would begin to tremble and it is most likely he would fall to the ground. Why is it then that a person would not fall if the plank is on the ground, and why should he fall if it is raised to a height above the ground? Simply because in the first case one imagines that it is easy to walk on the plank, while in the second case the fear takes possession of the imagination. The dizziness is entirely caused by the picture one makes in his mind about the fear of falling. Let us now

consider the case of a person suffering from insomnia. If he does not make any effort to sleep he will quietly fall asleep; on the contrary if he tries to force himself to sleep by his will, the more efforts he makes, the more restless he becomes.[3]

This illustration demonstrates the influence of the subconscious and the imagination over human behavior. Here is another example that shows the power of the imagination: Close your eyes and imagine having a juicy yellow lemon in your hands. Now imagine putting the fruit on the kitchen table, getting a knife, and cutting the lemon in two halves; see with your mind's eye the juice coming out of the lemon. At this point, your mouth is likely to water.

These two examples show that the subconscious mind does not distinguish whether the object of the imagination is real or not. In either case, the physical reaction will correspond to the mental images the person is providing to the subconscious mind. Likewise, if a person holds negative ideas and bitter emotions for many years, these will sooner or later be manifested in his or her physical condition. (I will discuss this further in the chapter entitled "The Role of Imagery in Healing.")

It is said that Coué was a Freemason and a member of an esoteric school that practiced hypnosis and mesmerism. Although there is no conclusive proof of this, we can infer its veracity from his teachings. For instance, Coué wrote that human beings possess within themselves a force of incalculable power. This force is managed through thinking and feeling; when it is not properly directed and controlled it can be prejudicial to one's well-being. By contrast, if individuals have mastery of themselves, they can direct this universal force in a conscious manner to free themselves from the bondage of physical limitations and illnesses. This kind of knowledge is definitely what we would call *metaphysical*.

Coué's most relevant contribution to applied psychology is his thesis that an individual can control his or her body and external circumstances with positive affirmations through autosuggestion. This confirms the second principle of Hudson's working hypothesis. Furthermore, Coué proposed applying autosuggestion to developing human potential, changing negative behavioral traits, and healing oneself from minor illnesses. He also recommended being aware of one's way of thinking. According to Coué, once conscious autosuggestion has been mastered through practice, it can be an effective means of eliminating negative habits and behaviors as well as improving the quality of our lives. Coué recommends the following steps for a practical application of autosuggestion for self-healing. For instance, in the event of pain, the suggestion must first be made that *the pain is about to cease*; then, that *it is already ceasing*, and finally, that *it has ceased*. These suggestions should be made in the form of spoken words and reinforced by clear visualization and feeling the end result. The intention of self-healing should persist until the desired effect is produced. A constant affirmation that the pain is gone, without a clear visualization of the desired outcome, will make the effort ineffective.

In our society, we are constantly bombarded by suggestions of all kinds. We receive these suggestions from our friends, mentors, and the mass media, all of which are beyond our control. Big pharmaceutical companies spend billions of dollars on advertising, creating fictitious illnesses and promoting their remedies for these maladies. This negative social environment needs to be countered with persistent positive affirmations. One very potent suggestion is the interpretation an individual gives to daily life experiences, because the subconscious mind will elaborate its deductions from such interpretation.

The self-healing process should be performed in full confidence that the symptoms will not return. At the first symptoms of an illness, an individual should begin with an energetic course of autosuggestion. The body has a tremendous capacity to heal itself, and natural self-healing occurs when the conscious mind is at rest and does not interfere with the healing process. While the most potent time for suggestion is just before falling asleep and just after waking up, the suggestion will be effective as long as there is a harmonious relationship between the conscious and the subconscious mind. No cure ever was or ever can be achieved by mental means unless the subconscious mind of the patient is impressed with a belief in the efficacy of recovery.

At this point, it can be confidently affirmed that most cases of healing by mental means are the result of *suggestion and autosuggestion.* This statement has been confirmed by scientific studies, which have demonstrated that the mind is the charioteer of the physical body and not the other way around.

Chapter 15

Sigmund Freud

Father of Psychoanalysis

The best-known representatives of depth psychology and mental healing are William James, Sigmund Freud, and Carl Gustav Jung. They exerted a profound influence on the field of mental therapeutics in America that deserves our special attention. In addition, there are some common characteristics between their philosophies and those of New Thought. All of them regarded the subconscious mind as the most important factor in human well-being. Freud's approach was to make conscious the repressed sexual and aggressive drives from the subconscious mind through a talking therapy and free association of ideas. Jung's theory aims to uncover the negative elements of the subconscious mind, which he calls the *Shadow*, through the interpretation of dreams, folklore, and collective symbols that he called *archetypes*, and consciously integrate them into the personality. Freud and Jung share another common characteristic with many leaders of American New Thought. The first is that they healed themselves by mental means. For Freud and Jung, the healing was not of physical ailments but of psychological and inner conflicts. The second is that they created systems of healing without medicine.

Many years ago, a magazine published an interesting article discussing the results of an investigation conducted in some universities in America. Researchers found that many students of psychology entered their studies to resolve their own inner problems. More recent studies revealed dramatic information about the rate of psychiatrists' suicides, a sign that many mental health professionals also have strong unresolved psychological problems. According to one study, among 18,730 physician deaths during a five-year period, 1967–72, there were 953 psychiatrist suicides. The same article further states that "psychiatrist's suicides [grow] regularly, year-by-year, at rates about twice those expected; and these differences are statistically significant."[1]

Sigmund Freud was born in Freiberg, Moravia, in what is now the Czech Republic, on May 6, 1856, to Jewish parents. His family moved to Vienna only a few years after he was born, and he spent most of his professional life there. In 1881, he was graduated from medical school and worked in the Vienna General Hospital for a few years. Here he was supervised by the famous physiologist Ernst Wilhelm von Brücke, whose influence on Freud led to the future development of psychodynamics, which describes the processes of the mind whereby repressed emotions lodged in the subconsciousness surface into the patient's consciousness. These repressed inner conflicts create psychological problems. This concept was the cornerstone for the development of psychoanalysis.

Before Freud founded the psychoanalytic school, hypnosis was more or less synonymous with psychotherapy. Mental treatment was done by hypnosis. In fact, after graduating from the university Freud visited both the school of Paris and the Nancy school of hypnosis. Freud learned hypnosis from of them, especially under the direction of Jean-Martin Charcot (1825–93), a prominent French neurologist who did pioneering research on hysteria. Freud stayed with Charcot for four months in 1885–86.[2] He was strongly interested in hypnosis at the time, and he even thought about improving his mentor's technique. The following paragraph, from a biographical introduction to Freud's book *The Ego and Id*, corroborates this assertion:

> From October 1885 to February 1886, Freud worked in Paris with the celebrated French neurologist Jean-Martin Charcot, who impressed Freud with his bold advocacy of hypnosis as an instrument for healing medical disorders, and no less bold championship of the thesis

(then quite unfashionable) that hysteria is an ailment to which men are susceptible no less than women. Charcot, an unrivaled observer, stimulated Freud's growing interest in the theoretical and therapeutic aspect of mental healing.[3]

Afterwards, Freud was influenced by Josef Breuer (1842–1925), an Austrian physician who accidentally discovered the therapeutic treatment known as the "talking cure." Freud refined this technique with the interpretation of dreams and developed it into what is now known as psychoanalytic treatment. Freud regarded the interpretation of dreams as "the royal road to the understanding of unconscious mental processes."

Breuer discovered the talking cure in the following way: he found that one of his patients, Bertha Pappenheim (later known in a famous case study as "Anna O."), regained her health from hysterical symptoms by talking to him about her daily life problems, past traumatic experiences, and emotions during her therapeutic sessions. These talking sessions served as her "chimney sweeping," as she herself described it later to her friends.

Prior to coming to Breuer, Anna O. was under treatment by other neurologists without much success. She had been accused of faking her symptoms, and her doctors refused to provide any further therapy. But under the compassionate and attentive listening of Breuer, she obtained relief from partial paralysis, hallucinations, and unfounded fears. In conversations with her friends about her recuperation, she asserted that Dr. Breuer had discovered the "talking cure," implying that the entire therapeutic session, the "chimney sweeping," consisted only of talking about her problems. Thus she was actually the one who coined the name for this kind of mental treatment.

Breuer discussed this experience with the young Freud, who in turn theorized that mental disturbances could be overcome by exploring the inner world of the patient. This was the beginning of psychoanalytic theory. Freud abandoned the hypnotic method and devoted himself to the talking cure as a therapeutic method of treatment. He included in his system the free association technique and the analysis of dreams to uncover past traumatic events buried in the subconscious mind. Freud theorized that the origins of neurosis (phobias, fears, panic attacks, and other mental disturbances) were traumatic experiences that happened in childhood. These traumatic events were usually forgotten and dwelled in the depths of the subconscious mind, hidden from conscious awareness, usually as conflicting forces. The key to healing was to make the unconscious content become conscious.

Thus the purpose of psychoanalytical treatment is to help the patient uncover past traumatic experiences through a long session of talking therapy, interpretation of dreams, and free association. In this way personal concerns and anxieties are exposed to conscious awareness, as are the original causes of the disturbances. Once the forgotten conflict emerges from the subconscious mind, the therapist assists the patient in confronting it, and in doing so, produces a phenomenon known as *catharsis* (Greek for "purification"). In psychology, catharsis is a process of discharging the entrapped emotional energy and consequently facilitating the release of internal emotional conflicts. This process helps eliminate underlying inner conflicts, enabling the patient to progressively restore his or her mental well-being.

The emotional energy trapped in the subconscious mind is usually not present to the consciousness of the individual and acts behind the curtains. Freud called this *repression*. When this energy is channeled toward a creative direction as a subterfuge, it is called *sublimation*. Through the talking cure and the interpretation of dreams, the therapist is expected to find the origin of the emotional problem. Then the therapist reinterprets the significance of the traumatic event and generates the release of emotional energy, freeing the emotional disturbances. Nevertheless, *the patient heals herself*; the role of the therapist is to facilitate that healing.

Incidentally, the process of releasing repressed negative emotional energy was rediscovered in America in the 1970s through the systems known as *energy psychology* or *energy medicine*. Here a key concept is that most physical maladies are related to emotional suppression or repression. This system borrows from the Chinese concepts of acupuncture and meridians. Oriental medicine associates specific maladaptive emotions with disturbances in the flow of energy that runs through the physical body.[4] Energy psychology is gaining a wide range of acceptance in medical and psychological circles for the treatment of psychological, emotional, and physical ailments. I will discuss it further in chapter 27 below.

Freud's early notion that hysteria was caused by repressed memories of sexual abuse makes more sense than his later notion that hysteria was caused by repressed memories of incestuous desires.[5] Charcot was reportedly the first to note that the source of a neurotic patient's behavior lies in the peculiarities of his or her sex life. This observation deeply impressed Freud and was the pivotal idea in the development of psychoanalysis.[6] This hypothesis was reinforced when Freud found that most of his female patients were victims of sexual abuse at early ages. The idea of sexual drives and their repression became the fundamental engine of human behavior in Freud's philosophy.

Freud's therapeutic technique of interpretation and reconstruction of the symbolic language of the subconscious can become biased and arbitrary, because the patient is subject to the therapist's own prejudices. The therapist interprets and manipulates the patient's association of ideas and symptoms according to his own level of expertise. The patient regards the clinician as a medical doctor, a professional trained to heal the sick person; one word, one sentence uttered by the clinician, as well as any statements of approval or rejection, will inevitably have a powerful impact on the patient's well-being. Hence there is a risk of inadvertently implanting false memories in the mind of the patient. In this sense, there is not much difference between the interventions of the psychoanalyst and those of the hypnotic therapist. Indeed Freud's psychoanalytic treatment can be seen as technically similar to partial hypnosis. The session, as practiced by Freud, consists of making the patient feel calm and relaxed. The patient is reclined on a special couch, comfortable and in a receptive state; she might even have her eyes closed. The patient does not see the therapist, who is seated behind her; the patient only hears a voice coming from "somewhere else."

This method of freeing negative emotional contents from the subconscious mind is a kind of self-exploration and self-discovery that can take many years, and its effectiveness depends on the patients' own capacities for insight and their honest desire to confront their own "devils and witches." Psychoanalytic treatment has been criticized because it does not go beyond the mental or psychological exploration of the traumatic events in a person's life; it is limited to examining and unearthing past psychological traumas, reframing them, and expecting relief. Consequently, in most cases this kind of therapy is not conducive to integral healing because it does not take into account the spiritual dimension of the human being. Another drawback of psychoanalytic treatment is that it can take many years with uncertain results. As some authors have indicated, this treatment can consume huge amounts of money and time.

In the past decades, the fundamental tenets of psychoanalysis as a scientific method of treatment have been seriously questioned.[7] Currently, Freud's theory of repression is seriously questioned by authorities in the field of psychology.[8] After several years of investigating the theory, Israeli professor Yacov Rofe concluded that that there is no empirical confirmation to support it. In a paper published in the American Psychological Association's *Review of General Psychology*, Rofe boldly concluded that Freud's theory of repression "should be dropped."[9]

The writer Stefan Zweig, an enthusiastic admirer of Sigmund Freud, had already acknowledged the limitations of psychoanalysis as a comprehensive method of healing because of its heavy materialistic viewpoint. Zweig wrote:

> Psychoanalysis can throw light on mental facts, but it cannot warm the human soul. The only thing it can give is health, but health alone does

not suffice. To be happy, to be creative, man must always be strengthened by faith in the meaning of his own existence. Psychoanalysis, however, has no opiate to offer as has Christian Science; it can promise no ecstasies of intoxication. . . . It make makes no promises at all; offers no consolation. . . .

Unquestionably psychoanalysis tends to rob man of his god, perpetually reminding him that he is a perishable creature bound for ever to this somewhat inhospitable planet, and that can hardly be regarded as a cheering prospect. Candour can enrich the intelligence, but it can never fully satisfy the feelings, can never make us long to excel ourselves—the maddest and yet the most necessary of our desires. Even as a bodily organism, man cannot live without dreams.

Zweig further states that a materialistic theory, in this case psychoanalysis, cannot provide a sense of meaning that enables humans to endure life's adversities as religion does.

This hunger of the soul for faith can find no nutriment in the harsh, the cold, the severe, the matter-of-fact sobriety of psychoanalysis. Analysis can give knowledge and nothing more. For the very reason that it has no place for faith, it can only supply us with facts; with realities, but never with a philosophy. This is the limitation. No other psychological method can so successfully lead man into the recesses of his own ego; but, being an intellectual discipline and not an affective one, it can never lead him back to altitudes that transcend his own ego. It dissolves and subdivides and separates; it shows to each life its own meaning; but it is incompetent to weave these separate strands into a common meaning.[10]

Consequently, Zweig proposes the term *psychosynthesis* instead of "psychoanalysis" as a more comprehensive concept.

The term *psychospirituality* could be even more appropriate than Zweig's psychosynthesis, since it goes beyond the materialistic Freudian worldview. Incidentally, psychiatrist Viktor Emil Frankl (1905–1997), a Holocaust survivor, proposed the term *existential analysis* or *logotherapy*.

This treatment aims to be an integral psychotherapeutic system that includes the spiritual dimension of a human being.

Another of Freud's admirers, the sociologist and psychoanalyst Erich Fromm, put forward the term *humanism* as a solution to man's alienation in modern societies. Fromm's book *Greatness and Limitations of Freud's Thought* examines Freud's life and work at length. Fromm questions Freud's dualistic thinking as he describes human consciousness as struggles between two extremes; he also finds a discrepancy between early and later Freudian theory. In his early work, Freud described human drives as a tension between desire and repression, but in his later work, he distinguished human drives as a struggle between the will to live and the will to die—the *eros* and *thanatos* instincts.

A further limitation of the psychoanalytic theory is that it is directed only to the healing of emotional and mental disturbances, while New Thought practitioners are able not only to cure physical and emotional maladies but also to give the patient a sense of spiritual meaning. Freud's theory was heavily influenced by Charles Darwin's theory of evolution and by Freud's university professors, who had a reputation for being tough-minded positivists who despised any metaphysical or spiritual speculation. Modern psychologists strongly question Freud's method, and they even argue that the theory of psychoanalysis does not qualify as scientific.[11] Author Frederick Crews goes further, considering Freud the "major villain responsible for the ills of contemporary psychotherapy."[12] Along the same lines, Thomas Szasz, in his book *The Myth of Psychotherapy*, argues that "psychotherapy as medical treatment is an illogical and immoral practice that has had disastrous economical and existential consequences."

To use Freudian psychoanalytic parlance, we can suggest that Freud's theoretical system is, in great part, a form of *transference*, a projection of his own inner shadows and conflicts onto his psychological theory. As with any human being, Freud's traumatic incidents in his childhood were the primary constituents of his personal viewpoint of life. He found some features in his patients' pasts that were similar to his own, and from these he generalized a widespread pattern for humanity—for instance, regarding repressed sexual drives as the engine for all human activity.

Freud's biographical information shed some light on his psychological "discoveries," such as the sexual etiology of neurosis, sexual repressions, and his famous Oedipus complex, on which the whole paradigm of his psychoanalytical theory rests. (Freud took this name from Sophocles' ancient tragedy *Oedipus Rex*, in which Oedipus unknowingly kills his biological father.) According to the theory of the Oedipus complex, children feel sexual attraction toward their parents of the opposite sex and hostile feelings toward their parents of the same sex. This complex, if unresolved, would lead to the genesis of different psychological and mental disturbances.

Freud claimed that his clients usually reported repressed memories of sexual abuse in early childhood. He originally posited childhood sexual abuse as a general explanation for the origin of neuroses and hysteria, but later on he abandoned this so-called "seduction theory" to emphasize the Oedipus complex as the primary cause of hysteria and other neurotic symptoms. Paradoxically, the Oedipus complex seems related to Freud's own psychological conflicts. It appears that Freud may have had a serious "father complex" of his own, which strongly influenced his psychological theories. His Oedipus theory is based on the idea that a child is jealous of his father. Moreover, in his book *Religion: The Future of an Illusion*, he theorized that man invented religion as a need for a protective father. In *Totem and Taboo* he argued that early humans (the "primal horde") killed their tribal father, usurping his hierarchical position. In *Moses and Monotheism*, Freud claimed that Moses, whom he regarded as the Hebrew primal father, was murdered by the Israelites in the wilderness, and so on. His work gives many indications of a deep underlying conflict with the father figure.

There is further support for the above thesis: after Freud's father passed away, Freud went through a period of deep personal crisis; as a result, he became engaged in exploring his own dreams, childhood memories, and the dynamics of his personality development. During this self-analysis, he remembered the hostility he felt toward his father and the sexual attraction he had toward his mother. Freud generalized this issue and applied it to the whole of humanity. Thus an event that happened to him was generalized as a universal event. This assertion is corroborated by a letter he wrote to his close friend and confidant, Wilhelm Fliess, on October 15, 1897:

> A single idea of general value dawned on me. I have found, in my own case too, [the phenomenon of] being in love with my mother and jealous of my father, and *I now consider it a universal event in early childhood*, even if not so early as in children who have been made hysterical.[13] (Italics are mine.)

Freud went to the extreme of trying to impose his sexual theory on his pupil Carl Jung as sacrosanct dogma. For a time, Freud considered Jung as a kind of crown prince to his psychoanalytic heritage and wanted Jung to follow Freud's materialistic psychological principles. Jung recalls a conversation regarding this matter:

> I can still recall vividly how Freud said to me, "My dear Jung, promise me never to abandon the sexual theory. That is the most essential thing of all. You see, we make a dogma of it, an unshakable bulwark." . . . In some astonishment I asked him, "A bulwark—against what?" To which he replied, "Against the black tide of mud"—and here he hesitated for a moment, then added—"of occultism." He said that to me with a great emotion, in a tone of a father. . . . It was the words "bulwark" and "dogma" that alarmed me . . . that no longer has anything to do with scientific judgment; only with a personal power drive.[14]

Freud's tendency toward fixed ideas was also noticed by William James. He met Freud in 1909 at Clark University, in Worcester, Massachusetts, where both Freud and Jung had been invited for a conference. Freud delivered some lectures about his theory of dreams and psychoanalysis to his American colleagues. In a letter to a friend, James reported that he and Freud took a short walk at one point, which was interrupted when James got sick and had to leave right away. James said that Freud's theory of dreams did not convince him at all and that he had the notion that Freud was "a man obsessed with fixed ideas."[15] James's initial enthusiasm for Freud fell into disenchantment.

Freud was a product of his time and social environment, a Viennese society with strong Catholic and Victorian values (reportedly, in his time Viennese society was eighty percent Catholic). He lived in a social environment characterized by extreme religious and moral principles and by a patriarchal society in which women and children were viewed as possessions of the head of the household. At this time the church considered it a sin even to hold an innocent conversation with a female counterpart relating to a sexual topic. Women were not supposed to talk about sex at all, and it was unusual even to acknowledge that women could have sexual desire. To think about sex in this environment was a sin to be punished with eternal condemnation in hell. Undoubtedly this environment, with its extreme moral repression, generated emotional problems for many people. Herein lies the greatness of Freud: under the cover of a scientific discovery he exposed the bigotry and cynicism of false Victorian moral values. Indirectly, he also denounced child sexual abuse, which was unaddressed at that time in European society. Freud initially stood alone in his task, although he later obtained the support of colleagues such as Jung, Otto Rank, Alfred Adler, and others.

Freud's most important contribution to psychology was his notion of human sexuality as a natural biological need. He discovered a pattern in his patients: people who developed neuroses and serious emotional problems in their adult lives were commonly women with a history of sexual abuse when they were children.[16] He was bold enough to propound his theory of sexual repression, the Oedipus complex, and child sexual abuse in a society characterized by bigotry and puritanism.

One can imagine the huge difference between Victorian times and modern society. At that time it was taboo to talk about sexual abuse, and there were no children's rights. Even in our contemporary society, with its strict laws and education, incidents of child sexual abuse are still common. At the turn of the twentieth century, it was common for adult men, including parents, relatives, adult siblings, and even religious representatives, to sexually abuse children, and such incidents were kept as family secrets. People lived in two different worlds, one of extreme religious values and the other of secretiveness about their sexual needs. In child psychology, it is well known that child victims blame themselves for these happenings. This kind of abuse undoubtedly created severe emotional disturbances in the adult lives of victims.

Although Freud's theories were flawed, they have had a tremendous impact on all areas of modern activity, including art, law, music, and sculpture, as well as on psychology and psychiatry.

It is also well documented that ever since he was a student Freud had a tendency to experiment with cocaine (at that time the use of the drug for medical purposes was not illegal). In fact he became addicted to it. Freud wrote papers on coca, explaining its virtues and promoting its use as both an analgesic and a stimulant.[17] In addition to writing articles on the antidepressant qualities of the drug, Freud was influenced by his friend Wilhelm Fliess, who recommended cocaine for the treatment of the "nasal reflex neurosis."[18] Freud sincerely believed that cocaine would work as a panacea for many disorders and recommended it to his close family and friends. Some critics have even suggested that most of Freud's psychoanalytical theory was a byproduct of his cocaine addiction.[19] E. M. Thornton wrote a book entitled *The Freudian Fallacy: An Alternative View of Freudian Theory*, whose purpose was to present evidence of Freud's addiction to cocaine, which she did. She also audaciously states that Freud's "theories were the direct outcome of this [cocaine] usage."[20]

Author Frank Cioffi, who investigated Freud's legacy for many years, published the results of his investigation in his book *Freud and the Question of Pseudoscience*. He examines the legacy and the legitimacy of psychoanalysis as a psychological discipline, demonstrating that Freud's accounts of the development of his psychoanalytical theories have no scientific foundation. The American psychiatrist Thomas Szasz, known as an anti-Freudian critic of psychiatry and psychotherapy and author of *The Myth of Mental Illness* and *The Myth of Psychotherapy*, goes so far as to argue that there is no such thing as mental illness; it is only a metaphor.[21] Psychotherapy amounts to little more than the talking cure, personal influence, and suggestion. The reader interested in the subject would do well to consult the above-mentioned books.

Chapter 16

Carl Gustav Jung
Doctor of the Soul

Carl Gustav Jung was a Swiss psychiatrist and the founder of analytical psychology, also known as Jungian psychology. Although the roots of what has come to be called depth psychology can be traced to the Nancy school of hypnosis and to Thompson Jay Hudson, the theoretical contributions of Freud and Jung have been influential as well. Jung and James went further, as they took psychology into the realm of metaphysics and religion. One of Jung's major contributions is that he demonstrated the mythic foundations of our daily life.

There are similarities between Carl Jung and William James. In addition to their interest in the paranormal, mind healing, mysticism, and religious experiences, both were spiritually independent and did not attend organized religious ceremonies. They respected all religions and considered them important mechanisms for the functioning and well-being of societies. James was convinced of the existence of authentic religious experiences, while Jung proclaimed that the human psyche is "by nature religious." Both Jung and James studied the major religions of humankind. They are sometimes now characterized as *transpersonal psychologists*, as they incorporated spirituality and religious experiences into their psychological perspectives. Interestingly, both Jung's and James's fathers were deeply interested in the theology of Emanuel Swedenborg.

Jung was raised in an environment conducive to the study of occult matters. He had psychic abilities since early childhood—he played with imaginary friends and had visions and psychic experiences that were unusual for children of his age. Jung's father was a minister; his mother had an interest in the paranormal and encouraged him to pursue his studies in the occult. Jung's cousin, Helene Preiswerk, was a medium in séances attended by his family.[1] His interest in the occult is evidenced in his doctoral dissertation, *On the Psychology and Pathology of So-Called Occult Phenomena*, which discusses Preiswerk's séances.

Jung was a rather solitary child; starting with his first year at the gymnasium in Basel, Switzerland, he was the object of harassment by his classmates. To avoid going to school, he used sickness as an excuse; as a result he remained at home for six months, until he overheard his father speaking worriedly to a visitor about his future and his ability to support himself.[2] At this point he understood that he would need to have a good education to earn his way in life. Jung initially thought of studying archeology, but changed his mind and opted to study medicine at the University of Basel.

Jung defined himself as an empiricist. His mission in life was to understand how the human psyche works, and to do that he explored the symbology of dreams, folklore, alchemy, mythology, religion, and philosophy. Jung can be seen as the psychologist who inspired much of the New Age: he coined many now-familiar terms, including *archetypes*, the *collective unconscious, introvert* and *extravert*, and *synchronicity*. These terms are frequently used in almost every current book on Tarot, astrology, alchemy, and esoteric psychology.

It is said that Jung did not have plans to pursue psychiatry as a profession because it did not have a good reputation at the time. However, he became very interested in this subject when he was studying a psychology textbook at the University of Basel. He identified with some of the psychological issues described in the book and wanted to find an explanation for them, as well as for the paranormal issues he had experienced as a child and teenager. In time, he became convinced that this would be the field that he would undertake as his career.[3]

In 1906, psychology was still in its early stages of development. This was the year when Jung read Freud's *Interpretation of Dreams*, and he was impressed by its similarity to some of his own ideas. In the same year, Jung sent to Freud a collection of his early publications entitled *Studies in Word Association*.[4] This event was the beginning of an intense correspondence, exchange of ideas, and collaboration between the two that lasted for more than six years. They met for the first time in March 1907, when at Freud's invitation Jung visited him at his home in Vienna. They had much in common to share and talk about. Freud cancelled his medical appointments for the day to devote time to his guest. Jung's diary describes this meeting:

> We met at one o'clock in the afternoon and talked virtually without a pause for thirteen hours. Freud was the first man of real importance I had encountered; in my experience up to that time, no one else could compare with him.
>
> What he said about his sexual theory impressed me. Nevertheless his words could not remove my hesitations and doubts. I tried to advance these reservations of mine on several occasions, but each time he would attribute them to my lack of experience. Freud was right; in those days I had not enough experience to support my objections.[5]

Freud, seeing in Jung a future disciple and considering him a kind of son (there was a difference of nearly twenty years between the ages of the two men), expected to leave the development of psychoanalytical theories on Jung's shoulders. However, from the beginning of their friendship, Jung disagreed about the sexual genesis of hysteria, which he expressed in his first letter to Freud in 1906. "It seems to me," wrote Jung, "that though the genesis of hysteria is predominantly, it is not exclusively, sexual. I take the same view of your sexual theory."[6]

Freud expected eventually to convince Jung of the sexual origin of hysteria and the importance of sexual repression to understanding hysteria and neurosis. Freud replied as follows:

> Your writings have long led me to suspect that your appreciation of my psychology does not extend to all my views on hysteria and the problems of sexuality, but I venture to hope that in the course of the years you will come much closer to me than you now think possible.[7]

Freud had a strong preconceived notion against anything related to the paranormal and to parapsychology, to which Jung was strongly inclined. In several instances, Jung tried to call Freud's attention to these issues, but he obtained only an adverse reaction. During his third visit to Freud's home, he had the following experience:

> It interested me to hear Freud's views on precognition and on parapsychology in general. When I visited him in Vienna in 1909 I asked him what he thought of these matters. Because of his materialistic prejudice, he rejected this entire complex of questions as nonsensical, and did so in terms of so shallow a positivism that I had difficulty in checking the sharp retort on the tip of my tongue. It was some years before he recognized the seriousness of parapsychology and acknowledged the factuality of "occult" phenomena.
>
> While Freud was going on this way, I had a curious sensation. It was as if my diaphragm were made of iron and were becoming red-hot—a glowing vault. And at that moment there was such a loud report in the bookcase, which stood right next to us, that we both started up in alarm, fearing the thing was going to fall over on us. I said to Freud: "There, that is an example of a so-called catalytic exteriorization phenomenon."
>
> "Oh, come," he exclaimed. "That is sheer bosh."
>
> "It is not," I replied. "You are mistaken, Herr Professor. And to prove my point I now predict that in a moment there will be another loud report!" Sure enough, no sooner had I said the words than the same detonation went off in the bookcase.[8]

In the early years of their friendship, Jung was an active collaborator with Freud in the development of the psychoanalytic organization, and he became the first president of the International Psychoanalytic Association. Eventually, Jung's and Freud's theories diverged tremendously because of their opposing philosophical perspectives. Freud's notion of life was eminently materialistic and positivistic. (Positivism is a doctrine that postulates that corporeal perceptions are the only admissible basis of human knowledge.) Jung's, by contrast, was metaphysical. He held that human beings could be wholly understood only through their spiritual dimension, while Freud regarded spirituality and religion as products of neurosis.

The publication of Jung's book *Psychology of the Unconscious* in 1912 intensified the ideological differences between them. In addition to their differences about the origin of neurosis and about parapsychology, Freud conceived of the unconscious solely as a repository of repressed sexual drives and aggressive feelings, while for Jung, the subconscious was the storehouse not only of repressed emotions and feelings, but also of all the creative forces of human beings, where the archetypes reside. The archetypes are defined as primeval patterns or image-forms dwelling in the subconscious mind.

Furthermore, Jung posited that the human psyche was composed of three levels: the *conscious mind* (or ego), the *personal subconscious* (or unconscious), and the *collective unconscious* (or universal subconscious). The subconscious holds both memories that are easily brought to mind and those that have been buried deep in the layers of the mind. The collective unconscious is the storehouse of all the experiences of humankind; it is the race-memory that spans the history of humankind from its early stages of development. The concept of the collective unconscious is similar to the Hindu concept of the Akashic Record, which is considered to be the reservoir of all human experiences. Jung held that people can have access to this collective unconscious through the personal subconscious. Extraordinary people who have excelled in different areas of life, such as artists, poets, inventors, and geniuses of all kinds, directly or indirectly have accessed this universal record, which is a fountain of inspiration and creativity. One example is the phenomenon of surrealism in art, in which the artist uses the subconscious as a source of inspiration.

Contrary to Freud's conception that religion is the expression of human neurosis,[9] Jung considered religions to be similar to collective mythologies, seeking to explain the existence of a higher spiritual dimension. Jung regarded religion as positive and necessary for human welfare, whereas Freud deemed it a detriment to mental health. As Thomas Szasz writes: "In Jung's view religions are indispensable spiritual supports, whereas in Freud's they are illusory crutches."[10]

As a result of these irreconcilable differences the personal and professional relationships between these two men ended in 1913. After their falling-out, Jung withdrew from his professional activities to reexamine his psychological theories. During this period he underwent a process of deep self-exploration. Although many authors consider this retreat from society a time of psychological breakdown, the truth is that this period was the most productive of Jung's life. He stated that this was the phase of experimentation, a voluntary confrontation with the shadows of his subconscious mind, which was an integral process of personal transformation. During this time he began working on his "occult journal," in which he recorded everything he thought, felt, and practiced. Jung himself considered this large, red, leather-bound tome, now known as *The Red Book*, to be the most important work he produced. His heirs kept the manuscript in a vault and refused to publish it until 2009.

Jung describes this period of his life as follows:

The years . . . when I pursued the inner images, were the most important time of my life. Everything else is to be derived from this. It began at that time, and the later details hardly matter anymore. My entire life consisted in elaborating what had burst forth from the unconscious and flooded me like an enigmatic stream and threatened to break me. That was the stuff and material for more than one life. Everything later was merely the outer classification, scientific elaboration, and the integration into life. But the numinous beginning, which contained everything, was then.[11]

At this time Jung also developed his system of analytical psychology as well as his most important contribution: the theory of *individuation*. Individuation, in Jung's view, is an integral process of development within a human being. It is similar to what some esoteric schools have called self-realization or the Great Work. This method involves a psychological process of purging the negative contents of the subconscious, transforming them, and integrating them into the whole personality in order to create a balanced and harmonious individuality. The process of self-realization implies a profound course of self-analysis, which includes the confronting the "witches and devils" that dwell in the subconscious mind, resolving their antagonisms, and integrating them into a whole identity rather than having dual or multiple personalities. It is at this point that an individual comes into equilibrium and realizes his or her own essence.

During his own individuation process Jung drew many mandalas, which form part of *The Red Book*. (*Mandala* is a Sanskrit word that literally means "circle." Mandalas are geometrical figures used as means for focusing attention in order to attain deeper levels of meditation.) He understood the meaning of these mandalas and the universality of their symbology after reading an ancient Taoist tractate called *The Secret of the Golden Flower*, which was translated from Chinese into German by Jung's close friend Richard Wilhelm.[12] Jung wrote a lengthy introduction discussing the meaning and message of this book, which some authors regard as the "Holy Grail of Chinese yoga."

In this sense, Jung became a doctor of the soul. He went far beyond the healing of mental disorders into the metaphysical realm. For Jung, the healing of a person is not restricted to alleviating suffering from emotional or physical problems, but involves the thorough restoration of the human being. By encountering the archetypes, an individual can become connected to the collective subconscious and eventually experience the numinous—the presence of the divine. In a letter to a friend, Jung wrote: "The main interest of my work is not concerned with the treatment of neurosis but rather with the approach to the numinous . . . [which] is the real therapy."[13]

Furthermore, Jung believed that the human essence is universal and all humanity shares the same ultimate origin. Myths and religion play an important role in explaining, in a metaphorical sense, the process of reintegration with the spiritual source. He postulated that the meaning of life can be found in myths, folklore, culture, and religion. This was the one reason for him to study these disciplines. With his concept of the collective unconscious, Jung opened a completely new world to psychology. It would no longer be restricted solely to the study of the psyche, perceptions, and behavior, but it would now be open to a whole new dimension, to an uncharted psychic and spiritual world. According to Jung, the primary mission of a human being in life is to unfold his or her deep innate potential, which is in essence spiritual. Each of us has to experience the process of unfoldment, like the caterpillar that transforms into a butterfly.

In his book *Psychology and Alchemy* (1944), Jung analyzed the symbols of medieval alchemy and found a direct relationship to the process of individuation. The alchemical process is the transformation of the impure personality (lead) into a perfected soul (gold). Thus it is similar to the main goal of Freemasonry, to work on the rough stone of one's personality to become the perfect cubic-shaped stone.[14] In alchemy, the individuation process is known as VITRIOL, the acronym of the Latin *Visita interiora terrae; rectificando invenies occultum lapidem*: "Visit the interior of the earth (the subconscious) and by rectifying (purifying) you will find the hidden stone." Freemasonry represents this concept in symbolic form with the "Chamber of Reflection," where the candidate for the first degree is seated at a table with a skull. Here he is to reflect on the nature of physical death and the ephemeral nature of life.

The Latin term *solve et coagula*, meaning "dissolve and coagulate," is the first phase of the Magnum Opus, or Great Work, to which Troward alluded. This practice demands that the aspirant dissolve all petrified misconceptions, negative race memories, and sense of separateness. He has to be born again as a regenerated person. The concept is similar to Jesus Christ's saying "Except a man be born again, he cannot see the kingdom of God" (John 3:3). Christ also stated that the kingdom of God is within, but in order to dwell in that kingdom one must enter as a newborn child.

Jung found great similarities between the Magnum Opus of occultism and the individuation process. The work was to be directed to the subconscious mind, which undergoes a process of purification and integration. In alchemy, the *massa confusa* (confused mass) excavated from the deep mountain (the subconscious) must undergo a long process of treatment and purification; it is repeatedly dissolved and coagulated, and from this process emanates the raw material for making alchemical gold.

Thus the Great Work of the occultist implies dying to the old personality and being reborn as a new person. This procedure is explained in the Hermetic *Emerald Tablet*, a short alchemical treatise that reveals in cryptic words the secret of the *prima materia* (first matter) and its transmutations. Furthermore, ancient esoteric treatises indicate that the one who completes the Great Work comes to possess the Universal Medicine and the Elixir of Life of the alchemist.

In closing, it should be mentioned that there is a great resemblance between Jung's analytical psychology and the therapy performed by the Pathwork Center. The Pathwork Center is an American spiritual organization created by Eva B. Pierrakos and her husband, psychiatrist John Pierrakos; it is based on the teachings of a disembodied entity called "the Guide." The basic premise of the Pathwork Center is that the subconscious is the main factor in determining the character of an individual and in dictating human destiny; therefore the organization encourages the exploration and liberation of the dark, destructive elements from the subconscious in order to reclaim humankind's original creative, divine being. As the Guide states, "When man speaks of his fate, the fateful happenings and non-happenings, the truth of the matter is that it is really nothing else but the governing force of unconscious factors."[15]

Like Jung's individuation, this work is a lengthy process of self-analysis and self-exploration, identifying and confronting the dark side of the soul, accepting our lower nature, and transforming and purifying negative elements, so as to attain wholeness through the integration of unconscious forces.[16]

PART FOUR

Fundamentals of Mind Healing

Chapter 17

New Thought and the Law of Attraction

Thought is a force—a manifestation of energy—having a magnet-like power of attraction.
—William Walker Atkinson

The essence of the Law of Attraction is encapsulated in the biblical statement "For as he thinketh in his heart, so is he" (Proverbs 23:7, King James Version). Contrary to common assumption, I postulate *that an individual attracts according to his "state of being" rather than what he wants.* For the sake of clarification, this "state of being" is different from one's deepest nature, which is the Self or the "I Am." The state of being can be regarded as the summation of a person's core beliefs plus her habitual state of feeling; this is, as it were, her "state of vibration." Therefore, whether a person constantly focuses on what she desires or on what she wants to avoid, she will experience these things according to her state of being. *The state of being is the point of attraction.*

Ordinarily, people are not aware of the beliefs that dwell in the subconscious mind. For instance, a person with a tendency to be judgmental, critical, and cynical will most likely also nurse feelings of insecurity, inadequacy, and unworthiness. This in accord with the Law of Correspondence: "As within, so without." An individual may put out his desires for success, love, and happiness into the universe, but the universe will respond to his state of being rather than to his desires.

There must therefore be a congruence or attunement between one's inner desires and one's state of being.

Thoughts and feelings, which are automatic ways of reacting to certain situations, are real forces of attraction and repulsion. Belief systems, however, can play a selective role in their operation. Individuals make decisions according to their core beliefs and will interpret their experiences and observations in ways that reinforce these beliefs. At the same time they will automatically discount or ignore experiences that are in conflict with these beliefs. Events in one's life will unfold according to these predominant beliefs, although most of the time one may be unaware of it.

Those beliefs that are so ingrained and rationalized in our mind constitute our "normal" outlook of life. They are hidden beliefs that most of the time control our lives and create our external conditions. A man is literally what "he thinks in his heart." His character is the sum of all his thoughts and attitudes whether correct or incorrect. Some are willing to improve their circumstances but unwilling to explore honestly their core beliefs. Therefore they remain bound to these false beliefs, and consequently perpetuate and replicate the same circumstances and situations over and over again.

The metaphysical concept of the Law of Attraction has been intrinsically associated with the New Thought movement since its onset. The term was coined by William Walker Atkinson, who was the first to use it to describe the phenomenon that "thoughts attract circumstances," in his book *Thought Vibration or the Law of Attraction in the Thought World*, published in 1906. By introducing this concept, Atkinson revealed to the general public what was deemed an occult teaching at that time. He asserted that *thoughts are things* in the mental realm, and man attracts people and circumstances according to his predominant thoughts.

Another early American proponent of the Law of Attraction was Wallace D. Wattles (1860–1911). In his book *The Science of Getting Rich* (1910), Wattles claimed to have used the Law of Attraction to rise from extreme poverty to a comfortable life. Wattles's book was extremely influential for many motivational speakers and writers in America. Ernest Holmes devotes a subchapter to the Law of Attraction in *The Science of Mind*. But the practical application of the Law of Attraction to all areas of life was popularized by Napoleon Hill (1883–1970) in his masterpiece, *Think and Grow Rich*, originally published in 1937. This is a pioneering work in the area of personal development and in the motivational field.

It is worth describing how Napoleon Hill became acquainted with this kind of knowledge. At the turn of the twentieth century, Hill, who was a reporter by profession, was given the assignment of writing a series of success stories of famous men of the time. The turning point in his life was when he interviewed the American multimillionaire Andrew Carnegie, who later became his mentor. Carnegie helped Hill formulate a philosophy of success. He commissioned Hill to interview over 500 millionaires in order to discover a success formula that could be used by average people. Hill undertook that assignment as a mission for his entire life.

Hill interviewed the most affluent people of the time and arrived at the conclusion that *"every human being has the power to use his mind and direct it to whatever he wants to achieve in life."* He summarized the success formula in one sentence that can be used by anybody: *"Whatever your mind can conceive and believe, your mind can achieve, regardless how many times you have failed in the past."*[1] In other words, the predominant beliefs and thoughts held in your mind, consciously or unconsciously, shape your success or failure in life. That is the essence of the Law of Attraction.

It is important to further elaborate on the Law of Attraction to remove the cloud of secrecy that has surrounded it in the past. It is through the subconscious mind that an individual is able to reach goals in life, whether material or spiritual. The basic principle is that the astral plane is inhabited with vitalized thought-forms and images (positive and negative) created by the collective consciousness. They are hovering and ready to be attracted by a human mind in tune with their vibratory levels in order to become crystallized in the physical realm. People attract the thought-forms that resonate with their own idiosyncrasies. Most of the ones that are floating in the astral plane are irrational and destructive, and they are drawn to people with similar tendencies. Positive imagery, supported by the emotions, attracts positive events and people, while negative imagery attracts negative ones. In some cases, a desired goal can be prevented from manifesting by a lack of emotional resonance.

The Law of Attraction has its basis in the Law of Affinity. The idea is that an individual is surrounded by an electromagnetic field, which is magnetized by her thoughts and emotions. This field pulls toward the individual events and situations that are akin to her predominant thoughts and state of being. Having conscious awareness of this principle, an individual can exert control over her external circumstances through right thinking, right feeling, and right action—that is, through self-mastery. A person's thoughts and emotions (conscious and unconscious) will attract the corresponding positive and negative experiences. In general terms, the Law of Attraction states that whatever one focuses one's attention on will come to manifest into one's experience sooner or later. In layman's parlance, this law can be expressed as "You get what you habitually think about." Quantum physics seems to be in agreement, suggesting that our environment is a projection of our mind.

The Law of Attraction is also based on the metaphysical notion that *thought* is the primary element of creation. The ensuing notion is that nothing happens by chance; everything occurs according to the Hermetic principle of *cause and effect,* or *action and reaction.* "Everything happens according to Law; Chance is but a name for Law not recognized; there are many planes of causation, but nothing escapes the Law."[2] In fact the initial element in the world of causation is a thought/emotion: "thought" and "emotion" are the head and tail of the same coin. One cannot be separated from the other; for instance, emotions make events memorable, that is, when a person recalls an event, the emotion attached to that memory is stirred up on the spot. Somehow, man is attached to his emotions, and when he has no control of his emotions, they drive his thoughts, and his thoughts drive his actions.

One characteristic of a law is that it guarantees a predictable outcome given a specific input. By analogy, in the mental realm, we can infer that a deliberate *intention* sets direction and maneuvers circumstances in advance so that the desired intention can be manifested. This idea is not as far-fetched as may appear; medical professionals are embracing the influence of intention in the healing system. Gary E. Schwartz, professor of psychology, medicine, neurology, and psychiatry at the University of Arizona, has written a book entitled *The Energy Healing Experiments*, in which he describes "intentions" as a means of healing.[3]

Moreover, Dr. Jeanne Achterberg, in her book *Intentional Healing*, has demonstrated the power of positive intention in the healing process: focused thoughts and intentions can affect our bodies for better or worse.[4] In this sense, conscious intention and purpose are a means to influence events that otherwise would happen randomly and unpredictably. Any creation, whether physical or mental, has a starting point, and this starting point is a definite intention. In other words, no creation or event in the physical or spiritual world can happen without an initial intention or desire. The metaphysical principle states that in order to manifest our intention in the physical realm, we have to be attuned to or in vibrational harmony with that desired intention. We live in a universe of pure energy, which is an aspect or extension of the energy of the Infinite Source. Our conscious intentions purposely direct the course of this energy.

Hence the initial step in a deliberate cocreation with the Infinite Intelligence is to put forward a conscious intention with confidence in the expected outcome. What is often seen as external reality is the manifestation of multiple mental creations of the collective consciousness. These creations appear to us in an apparently chaotic condition, and events seem to happen circumstantially or accidentally, but that is not the case. Those who set a firm intention and stick to it will, most of the time, get what they aim for. When a person chooses from the onset to entertain uplifting thoughts in her mind, she will attract events accordingly. Collective intention is a powerful means for creation, because it is an energy emitted by a group of people with a common purpose.

Thus there are higher probabilities of making things happen when an intention is set beforehand. This is a major downside of divination and fortune-telling. The querent, the person wanting to foresee his future, will often manifest the "predictions" given by the fortune-teller because those predictions are very powerful suggestions for a receptive querent.[5] Susceptible people tend to internalize suggestions given by individuals who are considered to have special psychic faculties; hence they are also prone to attract and manifest the suggestions given by the fortune-teller. In these cases, the fortune-teller's "predictions" become self-fulfilling prophecies.

According to the Law of Attraction, one's external reality and circumstances are nothing but the reflection of one's inner world. As the adage says, "The soul attracts that which it secretly harbors." In general, New Thought adherents regard the Law of Attraction as a guide for right thinking and right living; in addition, they practice affirmative prayer as a way to attract favorable conditions.

The assertion that *thoughts are energy* is complementary to the metaphysical viewpoint that *energy follows thought*. Nowadays, these assertions have been confirmed by quantum mechanics. According to this theory, everything in the universe is a flow of energy; physical reality is fluidic energy in nature. Before something is observed by conscious awareness, it exists in a formless state of probabilities, because the universe is mental.[6] Again, one directs this energy through one's thinking and emotions.

The nonphysical being called Abraham, channeled by Esther Hicks, recommends the following procedure in his recorded talks entitled *The Law of Attraction*: (1) determine a specific desire, (2) focus on the thing desired with strong emotion, (3) feel and behave as if the object of your desire is already yours, and finally, (4) be open to receiving it.

This last step is designated by Abraham as the "Law of Allowing," which is the key to manifestation. The Law of Allowing is the unwavering expectancy that the object of your desire is on its way, and it should not be contradicted with negative emotions or doubts. In other words, you should confidently rely on the universe eventually manifesting your constructive desires, as long as they are in accordance with the morals and ethics of the society in which you live. When people do not get what they want, most of the time it is because their desires are contradicted by hidden beliefs, which lie deep in their subconscious minds, preventing the materialization of the outcome.

Chapter 18

The Concept of the Egregore

The highest form of ignorance is when you reject something you don't know anything about.

—Wayne Dyer

At this point, it is important to introduce the metaphysical notion of the *egregore* (sometimes spelled *egregor*). The word is derived from a Greek word meaning "to be aware of" or "to watch over."[1] This concept can explain incidents of group healing such as the adherents of Christian Science experienced in its first years, the cures that happen in evangelical crusades, healings in shrines and holy places, and so on. Likewise this term can help us understand sociological phenomena such as political fanaticism (for example, Nazism, Fascism, and Stalinism) and extreme supporters of sports teams and musical groups, as well as the rationale behind dogmatic religious organizations.

From the metaphysical point of view, an egregore may be seen as a composite thought-form charged with psychic energy. It is an "astral entity" usually generated by a collective *group mind* when people come together for a common purpose or espouse collective aspirations and ideals. In this way, shared thoughts and ideals receive an amplified response. The egregore sets a mood and tone that indirectly influence the thoughts and feelings of a person or a group connected with it. The leaders of the group mind usually manipulate this energy, directing it to the group's intentions and desires or to their personal advantage.

An egregore can also be created by a single person with strong willpower. A magician or a sorcerer, through active imagination and rituals, creates mental images, and when these images are fed with emotional energy such as hate, jealousy, and vengeance, or love, compassion, and understanding, they become egregores floating in the astral world.

Concentrated thought and strong emotions are potent psychic energy for creating thought-forms. In the astral plane, although they are artificial creatures generated by the human mind and vitalized by emotions and beliefs, they are nonetheless real entities. As long as an egregore is fed by emotional human responses, it can survive in the astral plane. This is the case with supporters of groups who share common thoughts and feelings, such as members of religious organizations, fans of sport teams, or fans of celebrities or musical groups: they generate amplified quantities of emotional energy that nourish the egregore. This entity can be nurtured for years by human mental projections as people synchronize their vibratory levels to the icon or image representing it.

The concept of the egregore was developed by the members of the Hermetic Order of the Golden Dawn. A former associate of this organization, Dion Fortune, wrote an interesting article on this subject entitled "The Group Mind." She called the egregore an "artificial elemental" and described it as a thought-form energized by an elemental essence. That essence may be drawn directly from the elemental kingdom, or it may be derived from the magician's own aura or from a group of people. It is built up through continued visualization and concentration, and vitalized with strong emotion. An egregore is also capable of existing independently outside the consciousness of its creator. Fortune writes:

> Exactly the same process that leads to the formation of an artificial Elemental by a magician takes place when a number of people concentrate with emotion on a single object. They make an artificial Elemental, vast and potent in proportion to the size of the crowd and the intensity of its feelings. This elemental has a very marked mental

atmosphere of its own, and this atmosphere influences most powerfully the feelings of every person participating in the crowd emotion. It gives them *telepathic suggestion*, sounding the note of its own being in their ears and thereby reinforcing the emotional vibration which originally gave it birth; there is action and reaction, mutual stimulus and intensification, between the Elemental and its makers. The more the crowd concentrates upon its object of emotion, the vaster the Elemental becomes; the vaster it becomes, the stronger the *mass suggestion* it gives to the individuals composing the crowd that created it; and they, receiving this *suggestion*, find their feelings intensified. Thus it is that mobs are capable of deeds of passion from which each individual member would shrink with horror.[2] (Italics are mine.)

Occasionally an egregore can be created unintentionally, by a strong desire or strong tide of emotions, such as in a political campaign, by fanatical groups at a sporting event, and in religious organizations, where there is a charismatic leader who stirs up the emotions of the members for common purposes and ideals. Likewise a number of people working to accomplish a common idea, even though they are not aware of it, will create an egregore as they pour mental energy into the goal, symbol, or emblem. In this case an egregore will take on a life on its own. When any social organization soars in popularity, its egregore becomes powerful and influential. This in turn creates a symbiotic relationship or an "energy loop" within the group, feeding the egregore further.

In some cases, egregores have been vitalized over many centuries. Clear examples can be found in old temples, medieval Catholic churches, cathedrals, shrines, and other sacred centers of energy where healings and miracles happen. These places are infused by an egregore that exalts the soul of the individual, activating his inner mechanism so that his desire can be fulfilled.

Carl Jung experienced these psychic forms when he was undergoing his individuation process. He named one of them Philemon. He wrote:

> Philemon and other figures of my fantasies brought home to me the crucial insight that there are things in the psyche which I do

not produce, but which produce themselves and have their own life. Philemon represented a force which was not myself. In my fantasies I held conversations with him, and he said things which I had not consciously thought.[3]

Mircea Eliade, a renowned religious historian, made an interesting observation regarding archaic humanity in his masterpiece *The Myth of the Eternal Return*, which can help us to understand how an egregore is formed. Studying ancient Near Eastern mythology, he concluded that ancient humans gave religious meaning to particular objects such as stones, rocks, mountains, and so forth on the basis of their shape, location, or appearance. Eliade wrote:

> If we observe the general behavior of archaic man, we are struck by the following fact: neither the objects of the external world nor human acts, properly speaking, have any autonomous intrinsic value. Objects or acts acquire a value, and in so doing become real. . . . Among countless stones, one stone becomes sacred—and hence instantly becomes saturated with being—because it constitutes a hierophany [revelation], or possesses mana, or again because it commemorates a mythical act, and so on. *The object appears as the receptacle of an exterior force* that differentiates it from its milieu and gives it meaning and value.[4] (Italics are mine.)

Even modern people still have the tendency to assign value to inert things. Eliade observes that any selected object can becomes a receptacle of an exterior force, that is, the collective psychic energy from believers, and can form the basis of an egregore. To take another example, the Incas used to venerate mountains called "*apus*" (a word meaning "Andean spirit"). Each of the most important mountains had its own apu, such as the Apu Pachatusan, one of the guardian mountains of the city of Cusco, Peru, which, with its partner mountain, Apu Huanacaure, was honored with sacrifices. Some rocks and caves were also believed to have their own apu and were venerated.[5]

The following example illustrates how people can manifest a collective egregore spontaneously and inadvertently. Marie-Bernarde Soubirous (1844–1879), now Saint Bernadette, was a naive teenage peasant, the daughter of a miller from the town of Lourdes in southern France. Her impoverished family lived in a tiny room shared by the whole family. When Bernadette began to attend school, she displayed serious learning disabilities. On February 11, 1858, when Bernadette was fourteen years old, she was out with her sister and another friend gathering firewood by the grotto of Massabielle, outside the town of Lourdes. Bernadette suddenly claimed to see "a small young lady" (*una petita damisela*) at the top of a grotto; however, her sister and her friend, who were next to her, did not observe anything.[6]

Subsequently, Bernadette reported seeing eighteen apparitions of the "small young lady" at the top of the grotto; she was the only one who was able to see this phantasm. It should be kept in mind that she never claimed to have seen the Virgin Mary; she always identified the apparition simply as a small young lady.[7] Nevertheless, Bernadette's story caused a sensation among the townspeople, who were divided about whether or not she was telling the truth. Some believed her to have a mental illness and demanded that she be put in an asylum.[8] Others, motivated by their spiritual needs, thought Bernadette was having visions of the Virgin Mary. They followed her on her daily journey to the grotto. But she was still the only person who saw this lady.

On the ninth visitation, the lady told Bernadette to drink from the spring that flowed under the rock and eat the plants that grew there freely; however, there was no spring, and the ground was muddy. Bernadette did as she was told by first digging a muddy patch with her bare hands and then attempting to drink the brackish water. She tried three times, failing each time. On the fourth try, the droplets were clearer and she drank them. Some people followed her example, drinking and washing their faces with the water from the spring, which reportedly had healing properties. A commission from the town of Lourdes examined the quality of the water and found that it was highly contaminated and did not have any curative attributes.

Many assumed that the "small young lady" was the Virgin Mary, because Bernadette described her as wearing a white veil, a blue girdle, and a golden rose on each foot and holding a rosary of pearls. Soon the rumor spread that the apparition was the Virgin Mary, initially to the towns nearby, and later to other countries. As the number of believers in these apparitions rapidly grew, the Catholic Church, in order to satisfy the increasing demand of devotees, decided to build a grotto over the rock, which became known as the Grotto of Our Lady of Lourdes. This was also an excellent opportunity to strengthen faith in the archetype of the Virgin Mary.

As time passed, some cures were examined by the Lourdes medical bureau and declared "inexplicable." The Catholic Church claimed the healings were verified by "rigorous scientific and medical examinations." However, Bernadette herself had said that it was faith and prayer that cured the sick. In fact, when she was questioned by a visitor about miraculous healing at the shrine, she denied it, stating she had not witnessed any.[9] On this Bernadette was absolutely certain; the people were cured through their own faith and belief and not by any deity. Nonetheless, the beliefs and ideals of the devotees, poured onto the image of a Virgin on top of the grotto, created an egregore of the Virgin Mary, turning the grotto into a shrine of healing and a spiritual place. The devotees who earnestly prayed and expressed their higher feelings made this place vibrant as they fed the egregore with energy coming from their devotions. Other like-minded people coming to this grotto can benefit from this exchange of energy.

These considerations lead us to infer that some human beings need a "mental support," similar to a cane or a crutch, to satisfy their inner thirst for spiritual meaning. Jung would say that people need a myth that can give meaning and spiritual satisfaction to their lives. In this case, the water, the grotto, and the place did not have any healing or magical attributes in themselves; the devotees made them holy. And those who regained their health did so because of their own faith and belief. They needed mental or spiritual crutches represented by the "holy" water, the mud, or the grotto to awaken the inner mechanism that cured them. These incidents verify our postulate, "Man heals himself."

The irony is that the alleged "holy water" that Bernadette found at the grotto did not cure her or her family members from many illnesses. Bernadette was a sick child; she suffered from cholera in infancy and had asthma most of her life; she later contracted tuberculosis and died of it at the age of thirty-five on April 16, 1879. Nevertheless, she was canonized as a saint by the Catholic Church on December 8, 1933, and named a patron saint of sick persons, the family, and poverty.

The story of Bernadette is a clear example of how people can collectively create an egregore that serves their inner purposes; in Lourdes, they built an image based on information given by an illiterate teenager with emotional problems. Peasants identified the phantom lady with the archetype of the Virgin Mary. This egregore was invigorated by believers who came to visit this "sacred place" from all over the world, who in turn were seeking something that could satisfy their spiritual needs. Nowadays, the place where the Virgin of Lourdes supposedly came into view has become the source of a very lucrative enterprise. Currently, millions of visitors make pilgrimages to this place every year.[10] This has created an excellent opportunity for the development of tourism and businesses that sell stamps, amulets, thousands of gallons of "miracle water," and other souvenirs such as religious statues and booklets.

The debunker James Randi made an interesting comment regarding this "holy water":

> Bathing in the mineral springs of Lourdes and drinking of the spring water have been confused with the healing stories. The church has never made any claim that the spring water from the Lourdes grotto is curative in any way, yet every year the souvenir shops sell thousands of gallons to the faithful in tiny vials, as amulets. Those who attend Lourdes in person have consumed millions of gallons more.[11]

The egregore created around this story has in time become strong enough to benefit some faithful visitors to this grotto, as they established a symbiotic exchange of energy. Like an old cathedral such as Notre Dame or other spiritual temple, the grotto awakens a sense of awe and wonder.

This example shows the creation of an egregore for altruistic purposes, but the same principle can be used to create a negative egregore, as in the case of mobs and in the spontaneous responses of multitudes to the fanatical appeals of political leaders such Adolf Hitler in Germany, Benito Mussolini in Italy, and Joseph Stalin in the Soviet Union. In these cases, an egregore was generated by a leader who stirred up repressed feelings of resentment and hate within some segment of the society that became politically predominant. Once the creation is made, this astral entity functions as if by its own will.

To take the example of Nazism, Hitler and his confederates mesmerized the German people, creating an egregore of racism and hatred under the guise of the ideals of patriotism and nationalism. This was the Germany of highly educated people, the land of great philosophers such as Immanuel Kant, Georg Wilhelm Friedrich Hegel, Johann Fichte, Friedrich Schelling, Karl Marx, Friedrich Engels, and famous writers such as Johann Wolfgang von Goethe. This was the place where the original Rosicrucian order was born. Furthermore, at the time, Germany was the world's leading nation in science and culture.

Nevertheless, the strong thought-forms of Hitler and his political associates found resonance within a social segment of the nation. Hitler was a master of manipulation and sold his racist ideas to the people under the pretext of patriotism and territorial expansion. These ideas were vitalized by a group of followers and were reinforced by collective acceptance, creating a mass thought-form of immense proportions that took on a life of its own. This can be seen in films of Nazi military parades and demonstrations where Hitler was present. It is amazing to see the fervor of the masses and their identification both with Hitler's pronouncements and with the swastika symbol. The masses seem completely hypnotized.

In this case, the Nazi swastika served as a powerful symbolic focus of the egregore of Nazi Germany while Hitler was in power because it was fed with strong patriotic sentiments. After Germany was defeated, the Nazi egregore gradually faded away because there were no more masses feeding it. Thus, in time, when the emotions and feelings that were feeding an egregore disappear, the egregore slowly dissolves.

Another example will show how an egregore can change people's attitudes. At sporting events, a spectator who is known to be shy can be transformed into a demanding and aggressive fellow when his emotions are aroused by the fervor of the game. This is because the supporters of his team share common emotions that create an amplified response. Identifying with his team and his fellow supporters, he will say and do things that he would never even think of doing under normal circumstances. If the referee makes a call that the group considers unfair, he will respond at the emotional level of the group; there will be a *resonance* between the individual and the group's feelings. Some psychologists regard this phenomenon as an emotional discharge of repressed instinctual emotions.

As a general rule, the thought-form is built around some person or group of persons. As the number of adherents increases, so do the power and range of the egregore, and a peculiar reciprocal action takes place. Each member of the group pours energy into the thought-form, but each member of the group is also influenced by the pressure of the collective idea.

The above considerations lead us to another aspect of collective beliefs: generally the beliefs imposed by the leading social class of a society set the mental tone of the society's egregore. This is a subtle form of coercion, since ordinary people tend to feel safe when embracing the values and beliefs held by the predominant social, religious, or political institutions. In the Middle Ages, for example, the Catholic Church with its Inquisition was a powerful influence in spiritual, social, and political life. People felt secure and protected when they embraced the dogmas of the Catholic hierarchy. Otherwise, they would feel unsafe and distressed, living in an environment that was hostile to them and their families. Indeed some people seek out association with a specific group in order to have a sense of belonging; they may feel that they are somehow protected by being part of a group.

A more recent example is the Christian Science egregore. When Mary Baker Eddy was alive, her strong will and determination evolved an egregore that was amplified by her followers, who blindly believed her teachings. It was further vitalized by the strict rules that she imposed, by the Wednesday testimonial meetings and Sunday services, and by the bond established between Christian Science practitioners and church members. Every member had to have a personal practitioner, who served as a powerful means of indoctrination. In this environment, thousands of healings of all kinds of maladies were reported. The egregore generated by Eddy and her followers had created a climate of suggestibility among the organization's members.

Every social structure, whether political, religious, or metaphysical, has its own egregore, a composite thought-form that serves as a focus of identification for the members of the group. A newcomer will enter into the group atmosphere and will either accept it or leave.

Chapter 19

Spontaneous Healing and the Placebo Effect

The placebo effect offers dramatic proof that all healing is essentially self-healing.

—Dr. Rick Ingrasci

To better understand the power of the mind to heal the body, it is important to examine the concepts of spontaneous remission, suggestion, and the placebo effect. A *placebo* is an inert but harmless material (such as a sugar pill) given to a patient to provide mental relief. The change in the patient's symptoms as a result of getting a placebo is called the *placebo effect*. This means that the person taking the placebo may experience what she expects to happen. If a person expects to feel better, that may happen. If she believes that she is getting a strong medicine with side effects, these may appear. The effect occurs because the patient believes in the substance, the treatment, or the doctor. This does not mean the person's illness or symptoms were not real.

A placebo bypasses the conscious mind and puts into action the subconscious mind, which in turn can result in a "miraculous" healing. The basic premise is that the human body is designed to heal itself and stay well; it has a tremendous capacity to heal itself under normal circumstances. The body's recuperative abilities can handle an entire variety of physical illnesses and emotional disorders and promote an optimum level of wellness. The aim of all healing therapies is to tap the body's natural resources. The automatic functions of the body in turn

177

are under the care of the subconscious mind, and the subconscious is affected by the kinds of suggestions given to it. Thus, when the body falls ill, it is appropriate to reinforce its recuperative process with uplifting and optimistic thinking, in addition to taking corrective measures such as cleansing the body of toxins.

Émile Coué developed a therapeutic system based on oral suggestion through affirmations; reportedly this method rendered positive effects and cured thousands of people from minor illnesses. Although Coué was successful in performing healing through this method, he was honest enough to attribute the healing to the patient himself. His therapeutic system was based on two principles: (1) the mind can think one thought at a time, and (2) a consistent focused thought over a period of time will be internalized in the subconscious mind. Hence Coué developed the theory of conscious autosuggestion.

Psychologically a placebo works because of a suggestion produced by an operator (that is, the person performing the role of a healer). The placebo may be a sugar pill, an herbal tea, or any other substance. When a patient is given, say, a sugar pill and told that it is a real medicine, the operator has given a subtle suggestion, symbolically represented by the pill. The cure will follow according to the effectiveness of the suggestion and patient's desire to be healed. Placebos are highly effective in curing psychosomatic disorders such as stress- and anxiety-related maladies as well as pain and other minor symptoms. This makes sense because a psychosomatic illness is created by the mind, and the agent of healing is the mind, not the medicine. In such cases even a real medicine would serve only as a placebo.

The Latin word *placebo* means "I shall please." This would imply that the placebo effect may in some cases be the result of the patient wishing to please the doctor. This principle is also at work when a patient feels better as soon as the doctor enters the treatment room. The harmonious participation of both doctor and patient is vital for the healing to take place. Furthermore, the *expectation* of the patient and the doctor is of paramount importance in the outcome. It will work as long as the patient has internalized a belief in health and *expects* a favorable outcome.

The key to the effectiveness of a placebo is to make the patient believe in it; once this is done, the patient's subconscious will act according to this belief. As we have seen, the subconscious has no capacity to distinguish between a factual or imaginary thing—in this case, between the real medicine or a fake one. When the patient takes a sugar pill, the subconscious is under the impression that the pill will render the result promised, and this belief in turn will activate the imagination toward healing. Then, *voilà*: "According to your belief it will be done unto you" (Matthew 9:29, New International Version). The placebo tricks the subconscious mind into action that can result in "miraculous" or spontaneous healing.

Every human being has a psychological predisposition to respond positively to different kinds of placebos. Because of this principle, many devices can be used to influence the subconscious. In metaphysical, esoteric, and religious organizations it is common to employ special pictures, mandalas, alchemical and esoteric symbols (such as Tarot keys), bones, stones, relics, etc., to stimulate a sense of awe. Carl Jung's individuation process, in addition to self-analysis, incorporates the interpretation of dreams, symbols, mandalas, and other devices. Shamanistic rituals, as well as the ceremonial rituals performed in esoteric organizations, also have it as their objective to affect the individual subconscious. These rituals use symbols and actions rather than chemicals or placebos to activate inner mechanisms in the subconscious mind.

The power of suggestion and the placebo effect explain cases of healing by faith healers, quacks, and charlatans, who accomplish their purposes even though they are using false methods. They may claim to restore the health of an individual using special paraphernalia as a placebo, or they resort to a saint, a personal influence, or a higher power. These charlatans have the ability to create expectations in naive people. The object of evangelical camp healings, for example, is to raise the emotional level of people and so create an atmosphere favorable to activating the individuals' imagination and inner resources. This in turn will facilitate their healing from psychosomatic distresses. In any case, the real credit should be given to the Inner Self of the sick person.

One excellent book that addresses these issues is entitled *Snake Oil Science: The Truth about Complementary and Alternative Therapy*, by R. Barker Bausell, a retired University of Maryland professor and research director of a National Institutes of Health–funded program to evaluate complementary and alternative medicine (CAM). The author claims that he penned it after he had enough scientific evidence to permit a rigorous evaluation of CAM. He concludes that all complementary and alternative therapies are only placebos. He closes his book with the following statement: "CAM therapies are nothing more than cleverly packaged placebos. And that is almost all there is to say about the science of CAM."[1]

While Bausell's book is well-documented with years of research and is written at a rigorous academic level, he does not explain the psychological process of healing. How does healing with placebos take place? How does the placebo work? What is the psychological factor that activates the body to get well? Bausell does not give much importance to the role of the mind in regaining wellness, as he does not mention the key word *suggestion*, which plays a primary role in the placebo effect. He also neglects to consider the tremendous ability of the human body to regain its health, which medical scientists regard as "spontaneous healing" or "spontaneous remission."

Placebos work because they make the patient believe that something has been done. They are a form of suggestion that bypasses the conscious, rational mind to influence the subconscious mind. Once the subconscious accepts the suggestion, the healing process will occur as long as the patient has an authentic desire to get well. Thus all *placebos are hidden suggestions*; they change the expectation of the subject from a mind-set of illness toward one of getting well.

The human body is a marvelous biological machine that has tremendous recuperative power as long as it is not hampered by negative thoughts, unhealthy food, or harmful medicine. Drugs and medicine usually have side effects and damage other parts of the body. James H. Young, a medical doctor, gives more credit to the body's recuperative capacity than to the intervention of any outside agent. He emphasizes that people do not usually realize that most ailments can improve with time *regardless of treatment*. He writes:

> Our body has incredible powers of recovery by itself from illnesses, whether it follows self-medication, treatment by a scientific practitioner, or treatment by an unscientific practitioner. This fact may lead individuals to conclude that the treatment received was the cause of the return to good health. . . .
>
> When a symptom goes away after he doses himself with a remedy, he is likely to credit the remedy with curing him. He does not realize that he would have gotten better just as quickly if he had done nothing! He may also fail to distinguish between cure and temporary symptom relief. Thousands of well-meaning people have boosted the fame of folk remedies and have signed sincere testimonials for patent medicines, crediting them, instead of the body's recuperative powers, for a return to well-being.[2]

Young further indicates that even when someone feels better after using a medicinal product or any alternative procedure, people usually give credit to the practitioner and the product or procedure, dismissing the body's own restorative power. According to Young, medical history has demonstrated that *most illnesses, even incurable conditions, can have natural remission*. In this way, the theory of self-healing, under certain conditions, has been endorsed by the medical profession.

The conclusive proof of the body's recuperative power is being provided by new scientific disciplines such as neuroscience, new biology (epigenetics), quantum physics, and psychoneuroimmunology (PNI). In the past, it was thought that genes and DNA determine the biology of a human being, but new discoveries have demonstrated that the truth is the other way around. Dr. Bruce H. Lipton, a renowned cell biologist, has advanced the theory that thoughts and the environment have a direct influence over genes.[3] In an article entitled "Mind over Genes," Lipton offers a scientific explanation for the mechanism of spontaneous remission:

> Environment controls gene activity through a process known as epigenetic control. This new perspective of human biology does not view the body as just a mechanical device, but rather incorporates the *role of a mind and spirit.* The breakthrough in biology is *fundamental in all healing* for it recognizes that when *we change our perception or beliefs* we send totally different messages to our cells and reprogram their expression. The new biology reveals why people can have spontaneous remissions or recover from injuries deemed to be permanent disabilities.[4] (Italics are mine.)

It has already been indicated that charismatic and persuasive personalities can play a suggestive influence in spontaneous healing. Mesmer and Quimby exerted a considerable positive influence on their patients. They had the ability to create confidence in their mental treatment, and this in turn enhanced the degree of suggestibility of their patients, as we see in the cases of Julius and Annetta Dresser. A remark by Dr. Stephen Barrett confirms this idea: "Confidence in the treatment by the patient and the practitioner make it more likely that a placebo effect will occur."[5]

An osteopathic physician named Irving Oyle agrees about the importance of belief by both the practitioner and the patient in the magic of healing. This is understandable because when two people believe in the same goal there is a collective power of mental energy that is favorable to the cure. He writes:

> All healing is magic. The Indian healer and western healer have a common denominator. The trust and confidence of both the patient and the healer. They must both believe in the magic or it doesn't work. Western doctors make secret markings on paper and instruct the

patient to give it to the oracle in the drug store, make an offering in return for which they will receive a magic potion. Neither understands exactly how the medicine works, but if they both believe, it often does.[6]

The placebo, which is a hidden suggestion, may cause even a nonbeliever to respond favorably to the therapy. *The necessary requirement for the effectiveness of a placebo is the belief that a procedure or anything done or given to the patient will create the cure.* For example, a simple prescription of a tonic or a vitamin will be enough for a large percentage of patients to get well, although the substance prescribed does not have any curative attributes. The simple fact that it was prescribed by a medical doctor, an authority in the medical field, in itself produces a powerful suggestion. The effect is usually reinforced by the reputation of the doctor, the medical setting and procedures, and sophisticated devices and machines; all these have a significant psychological impact on the sick person. Furthermore, the fact that a patient is required to undergo several tests, through often complicated medical machinery, undoubtedly activates imagery that favors recuperation.

Although placebos and suggestion can be considered similar in many ways, they involve a subtle difference. A suggestion is usually an implied oral message given by another person, for instance, the suggestions giving during a hypnotic session. Suggestion can be defined as an act of conveying, in a skillful way, certain images into the mind of the subject. On the other hand, a placebo usually works with a tangible object, such as a sugar pill, to induce the patient into believing that something will work to alleviate his problem. A placebo could be defined as a tangible substitute for a suggestion. Both techniques seek the same result: bypassing the critical conscious mind and activating curative imagery in the patient. The essential condition is receptiveness and willingness to be healed.

The following case will further illustrate how placebos work. There was a man who had a serious scalp disease for many years that conventional medicine could not alleviate. A relative on his wife's side of the family was Catholic; she made a pilgrimage to the grotto of Lourdes and brought back a bottle of water from the fountain. The family, which was Jewish, did not know anything about this trip. One day, she visited the sick person and gave him the bottle of "blessed water," telling him that it was a powerful medicine for his condition. She recommended rubbing his scalp every morning and night with some drops of the water and she assured him that he would be cured. The man did not have anything to lose and decided to follow her recommendation. After a few weeks, to the amazement of his family, his scalp condition gradually improved and eventually was completely healed. The question here is, was this case the result of a spontaneous remission or a placebo effect? The most plausible answer is that he was healed by the suggestion given, and the "blessed water" acted as the placebo. Interestingly, the man never learned that the "miracle water" was from the grotto of Lourdes: this may or may not have made any difference to his recovery.

Divine Science Church minister Joseph Murphy cites the case of a Frenchwoman named Madame Bire, who was blind, with optic nerves that were atrophied and useless. However, after visiting the grotto of Lourdes and drinking its water, she regained her sight. Murphy asserts that she was not cured by the water but by "her own subconscious mind, which responded to her belief."[7] Her subconscious was activated by her blind faith and her firm expectancy that something would happen. The water from the grotto acted as a placebo.

Young indirectly confirms the "talking cure" technique as follows: "A sympathetic ear from a doctor and reassurance that no serious disease is involved may trigger the patient's recuperative mechanism."[8] The words of reassurance that "no serious disease is involved" coming from the treating physician serve as an extremely powerful suggestion. It is well documented since the time of Breuer and Freud that some patients get well after they vent their problems to an attentive doctor in a medical setting. For a suggestible person who comes to the therapist's office seeking mitigation of her suffering, a verbal release of her troubles and a pep talk will often do the job. Therefore therapists can do much good or harm with merely their words and attitude. Young expresses his honest concern about the medical profession, arguing that some physicians have forgotten the basic meaning of the Hippocratic Oath:

> Scientific physicians, moreover, have a problem because of their power and status. Many laypersons feel ill at ease in the presence of an expert. Perceiving the physician as busy and under pressure, the patient may feel like an intruder. Doctors may be brusque, fail to take the time to listen, or neglect to explain; their prognoses may be discouraging, their therapy prolonged and unpleasant. They charge immense fees, earn more money, and live better than the patient, perhaps causing irritation and envy. Some patients are just plain frightened away from reputable doctors whose amiability falls below that which quacks are able to muster. Even patients who think well of their own doctors may think ill of doctors as a group. The power side of establishment medicine has alienated many people. Organized medicine, they have felt, works for its own economic and political self-interest more than for the common good.[9]

Young and Barrett, who are open adversaries of all complementary therapies and alternative methods of healing, consider anyone who practices healing without medical credentials to be a quack. In this category they include faith healers, mental healers, Christian Science practitioners, herbal healers, crystal healers, energy healers, Reiki practitioners, and so forth. They advocate for drastic laws and regulations governing healing and for prosecuting "unprofessional healers" and putting them behind bars.[10] But other medical doctors are advocating complementary and alternative methods of healing, as we will see in the chapter below entitled "The Healing Power of Love and Forgiveness."

Chapter 20

The Role of Imagery in Healing

Imagination is more important than knowledge.
—Albert Einstein

Individuals who have been harboring feelings of hate and bitterness for many years may manifest those negative emotions in emotional and physical disturbances. Complementary and alternative methods of healing, such as prayer, meditation, forgiveness, offering unconditional love, practicing awareness of the divine presence, relaxation, yoga exercise, journal writing, dancing, singing, painting, music, drawing mandalas, etc., have the purpose of leading the imagination of the sick person toward wellness. In some instances, they generate the emotional discharge known as catharsis. This in turn allows the free flow of the healing powers of the body and helps it to recuperate.

The significance of the imagination in the healing process was scientifically determined in the late eighteenth century by the French royal commission appointed by King Louis XVI to examine Mesmer's claims of the existence of a magnetic fluid. The members of the commission concluded that they could not verify the existence of a magnetic fluid. They asserted that Mesmer's healings were the product of the power of the imagination and the fantasy of the individual. "Imagination is everything, magnetism nothing."[1]

Joseph Murphy has indicated the importance of imagination in the healing process. He mentions the case of a South African Methodist minister who recovered his health from an advanced case of lung cancer using his power of imagination. He advises the reader, "Imagine the end desired and feel its reality; then the infinite life-principle will respond to your conscious choice and your conscious request."[2]

The importance of imagery in the recovery of health and improving of human potential abilities cannot be stressed enough. Imagery uses a symbolic language to communicate with the subconscious mind. It must be understood that the subconscious mind recognizes only symbols and images; thus the most effective suggestion is the one that elicits some specific image in the mind of the individual. Carl Jung resorted to active imagination for his process of individuation. The use of active imagination is also extremely indispensable in metaphysical endeavors to enter into another realm, such as in the system known as pathworking or treading the Path of Return in the Qabalistic Tree of Life. Along these lines, Paul Foster Case has recommended meditation on the Tarot cards and the use of creative imagination for spiritual transformation. Reportedly, meditation on the Major Arcana of the Tarot can melt away all the negative patterns petrified in the subconscious mind.[3]

These techniques often involve the right side of the brain, which governs the symbolic, metaphorical, and nonverbal part of the mind. It is theorized that the right side of the brain is the agent of communication with the subconscious mind. That is why guided imagery has powerful physiological consequences. Through active visualization an individual can imagine a desired therapeutic outcome and can actively participate in his own healing. Currently active imagery is employed in professional settings to alleviate a variety of symptoms and stimulate healing responses. A healing approach through imagery evokes the patient's own inner resources for self-help.

Since early childhood, mental images have been ingrained in our psyches, and they are at the core of our belief systems. These images strongly influence our outlook on life. A mental image can be defined as a thought-form with sensory qualities, such as seeing, hearing, tasting, smelling, touching, and feeling. The term "guided imagery" refers to a wide variety of techniques, including visualization, storytelling, fantasy exploration, dream interpretation, and drawing. In this way subconscious elements surface as images and provide important information to the conscious mind.

Historically, the practice of healing through rituals and ceremonies can be found in many cultures throughout the world. Guided imagery can be considered one of the oldest and most ubiquitous forms of healing. Currently it is finding widespread acceptance in professional therapeutic settings.

Mental imagery can influence the autonomic nervous system and stimulate untapped healing resources of the body. The autonomic nervous system controls many involuntary functions of the vital organs that operate below the level of consciousness, such as the heartbeat, digestion, breathing, salivation, perspiration, and conversion of food into tissue. Imagination can promote the healthy function of these processes.

One technique currently used to influence the autonomic nervous system is *autogenic training*, a method developed by the German psychiatrist Johannes H. Schultz. This technique incorporates progressive relaxation, meditation, and visualization to overcome any psychological or physiological problem as well as to alleviate many stress-induced psychosomatic disorders. In addition, many studies indicate that certain imagery techniques (self-hypnosis, creative visualization, meditation) may stimulate the immune system and endocrine responses that are necessary for optimum health.

The following example will demonstrate how imagination can create our reality. A ten-year-old child who is left home alone and told that there is a monster somewhere in the house will create the conditions for being scared. If he believes that the monster exists, he will excite his imagination and will not be able to sleep at night without thinking or feeling the presence of the monster. He may think that the monster is hiding in the closet or below his bed. If the night is stormy, any noise made by the wind through the window or any shadow cast into the room will appear to him as the monster, and he will think that it is ready to attack him. So the child, by the power of his imagination, "creates" the existence of the monster, and he might even feel its presence. The following day, he will tell his friends at school that he saw the monster in the shadows reflected in the room and heard the monster in the noises made by the wind blowing through the windows of the house.

Over the years, it has been demonstrated in clinical settings that imagery activates an individual's latent, innate healing abilities to promote recovery and physical wellness. The efficacy of imagery, as we have already seen, is based on the principle that the subconscious mind does not distinguish between what is real and what is fantasy, as long as the images are clearly fashioned; all that matters to the subconscious is that the conscious mind is submitting a specific image to work on. The body will respond to the imagery given. As the subconscious has no notion of time and space—a feature noted both by Freud in *The Interpretation of Dreams* and by Troward in his Edinburgh lectures—it cannot differentiate between past, present, and future. That is why it is important to formulate precise images in the present time as if the desired goal is already obtained.

Nowadays mainstream medicine is ascribing increased importance to the employment of imagery. The Academy for Guided Imagery (AGI) teaches the "uses of imagery and imagery related approaches to therapy and healing."[4] The Simonton Cancer Center, founded by oncologist Dr. O. Carl Simonton, teaches people meditation and mental imagery in order to boost their immune systems and fight cancer.[5] The practice of meditation and mental imagery gives the patients a sense of control over their illness, and allows them to actively participate in their healing process.

It should be noted that any diagnosis or treatment in a medical office creates certain images and expectations in the patient. These kinds of images (or suggestions) can affect the course of the patient's health for better or for worse.[6]

The use of imagery in New Age healing systems is known as *creative imagination* or *creative visualization*. In either case, the process is to mentally fashion clear-cut images, including color, sound, and taste, as realistically as possible. Psychologist Jeanne Achterberg, in the introduction to her groundbreaking book *Imagery in Healing: Shamanism and Modern Medicine*, defines imagery as "the thought process that invokes and uses the senses: vision, audition, smell, taste, and the senses of movement, position, and touch. It is the communication mechanism between perception, emotion and bodily change. A major cause of both health and sickness, the image is the world's oldest and greatest healing resource."[7]

This description implies that a vivid imagination stirs up specific emotions. Achterberg's characterization is similar to the definition of emotions given by author Daniel Reid, which leads one to consider the close relationship between emotions and imagery:

> Emotions are triggered by sensory contact with the outside world, based upon the input of the five senses. Since humans relate to the phenomenal world and to each other through the five sensory organs, they remain in a constant emotional response. . . . Therefore, the initial stimulant for each and every emotional response is external sensory contact, which at the primary stage is a physiological function of the nervous system, not a psychological process.[8]

The remarkable difference is that emotions are physiological responses while imagery is a psychological function. In any type of healing, the patient directly or indirectly activates his or her inner mechanism of creating images for getting well.

Achterberg observes that in the past the traditional healer was known under different names, such as "shaman," "sorcerer," and "witch."[9] They have also been known as "witch doctors" or "medicine men." For the purpose of this study, I will classify all of them under the name *shaman*. Throughout most of human history shamans were both magicians and healers. They were believed to be endowed by the gods or the spirits with powers to invoke and expel evil spirits and to restore health. The shaman works by *activating the imagination* of the patient in order to restore health. To do this, the shaman enters into an altered state of consciousness, in which he perform dances and conjures and "expels evil spirits."[10] This ritual has the aim of affecting the subconscious mind of the sick person, enchanting her imagination and putting her into a state of receptiveness to the shaman's pronouncement of healing.

Traditionally, successful healers have been masters of using imagery in curing. A healing treatment without medicine usually involves two basic components: a strong desire to be healed, fueled by emotion, and the use of active imagination. Achterberg observes that shamanic healing is conducted in the realm of the imagination: "Shamanism is the medicine of the imagination. The shaman's ritual work has a direct therapeutic effect on the patient by creating vivid images, and by inducing altered states of consciousness conducive to self-healing."[11] This is confirmed by scientific studies that show the brain responds to an imagined scene much as it would to something it actually sees.

The basic principle of the above practice is that imagery and emotions affect the biochemistry of the body. This is similar to the placebo effect: when a sick person is given a placebo, her biochemistry undergoes a subtle transformation because she subconsciously creates images of getting well. Some scientific evidence suggests that the placebo effect may be partly due to the release of endorphins in the brain. Endorphins are the body's natural painkillers. Ordinary people are unaware of the great power they possess. As simple as it sounds, this power resides in the correct use of the mind, emotion, and creative imagination.

Achterberg regards the physical location of the healing as important. She indicates that the shaman's setting and a church setting are somewhat similar: the purpose of both is to prepare a special environmental condition for something to occur. Moreover, a person who goes to a shaman for help is like a person who goes to a religious setting. The shaman's place may be replete with archaic symbolism or artifacts, such as skulls, bones, and other paraphernalia, all of which will exert a powerful impact on the imagination of the patient. Similar features can be observed at a religious shrine such as the grotto of Lourdes or an old cathedral. The same is true even of a medical office, which is furnished with therapeutic devices and sophisticated equipment. All of these therapeutic settings have been decorated with the appropriate elements to inculcate a sense of receptiveness to the ensuing treatment.

The power of the mind over the body is easily and conclusively demonstrated by Indian fakirs, who have attained perfect control over their body and emotions. They can walk barefoot on red-hot coals or over broken glass or sleep on a bed of nails, and they will not experience any injury whatsoever.

Achterberg has also investigated the power of imagination over human immunology. She posits that trained imagery can keep the body's defense system working to keep an individual in perfect health. According to her, many diseases result from a sluggish or malfunctioning immune system. The prevalent medical opinion is that stress is one of the primary factors in weakening the immune system; this in turn facilitates the formation of many illnesses. Consequently, major diseases could be conquered if the immune system is trained to function effectively. The use of creative imagination during sessions of meditation and hypnosis has been proven useful in mitigating anxiety-provoking events and in helping the body in its recuperative process.

Chapter 21

The Healing Power of the Subconscious Mind

The Healing Power is in your subconscious mind.
—Joseph Murphy

As we have seen, the subconscious mind, as the seat of the imagination, the storehouse of memory and of human creative powers, plays an important role in recovering and maintaining good health. The placebo effect is a conclusive proof that the subconscious mind is the healer of the body. A placebo could be a sugar pill, a harmless injection, any kind of medical or nonmedical procedure, or any type of therapy that doesn't directly affect the illness being treated. The placebo does not act on the disease but on the subconscious mind.

The teachings of nonphysical beings such as the Guide, Seth, Abraham, and others, have been supported by modern psychologists and mental scientists such as Thomson Jay Hudson, Thomas Troward, Sigmund Freud, and Carl Jung, all of whom have acknowledged that *the most powerful feature of in a human being is the subconscious mind*. No healing was ever accomplished, or can be achieved by mental means or other methods until the subconscious mind of the patient is impressed with an image of wellness. *This is the fundamental key to understanding mental and spiritual healing in general.*

An individual has two minds: the conscious and the subconscious mind; these are two aspects of one Self. The conscious mind is expressed in the awareness of physical reality, while the subconscious works below the conscious level, having control over the vital functions of the body. These two aspects of the mind can be verified in a hypnotized person or somnambulist: in the first case a person carries out tasks given under hypnosis, while in the second case the individual performs certain actions in a state of slumber. In both cases, the logical inference is that these actions were directed by the subconscious mind without conscious intervention. In metaphysics, in addition to these two parts of the mind, there is another level, the superconscious, which is equivalent to Universal Mind or Infinite Mind.

Before the studies conducted by the Nancy school and the interpretation of those investigations by Thomson Jay Hudson, the subconscious and its role in the human personality were unknown entities. The common belief was that the unconscious, as its name implied, was inert and dormant, a mental attic without any influence over a person's life. However, the truth is the reverse. Depth psychologists such as Jung found that in the subconscious mind dwell primitive instinctual forces, primeval energy, and universal human experiences. These are usually dormant, repressed by the conscious ego, but when the censorship of the ego is somehow removed, these forces can emerge from the depths of the mind, sometimes in a creative and constructive way, sometimes violently. This could explain brutal crimes and homicides committed by people who were considered honorable and inoffensive citizens, such as some of the recent school shootings, which were committed by apparently quiet and pacific students.

The subconscious thus plays a very important role in molding our thoughts, feelings, and emotions; in fact it is the most active and influential factor in our daily lives. As Stefan Zweig wrote:

> Our life does not move freely in the domain of the rational, but is continually exposed to the working of unconscious forces. Out of the subconscious emerge positive and negative emotions, habitual thoughts, hunches, the elements of our decisions, the automatic reaction to specific situations, the lightning flashes of inspiration, etc.[1]

Depth psychologists hold that traumatic events and unmet desires from childhood live actively in the subconscious realm, and that from its depths come fears and anxieties, as well as compulsive behavior, that do not have any rational basis or explanation. This could help explain addictions and relapses from recovery. Although a person may have decided not to do something, she slips and does it anyway; the subconscious will always win. One cannot fight against it; one has to make it an ally. This was the secret of secrets in the authentic ancient mystery schools.

Furthermore, communication between the conscious and the universal or collective mind is only possible by way of the subconscious. This contact commonly occurs in special circumstances, such as deep sleep or meditation, and can be expressed through intuition, hunches, inspiration, and so forth. On the other hand, by impressing one's desires on the personal subconscious, one can communicate with the collective mind. A person who has a burning desire charged with emotional energy will bring the desired object into vibrational harmony with himself, causing it to manifest eventually in physical or experiential reality. As the channeled entity known as Abraham teaches, you cannot experience anything unless you are in vibrational harmony with what you want to get or to experience. This principle works equally well for positive and negative experiences.

Because the personal subconscious is intimately connected to the collective subconscious, there is no separation among people; all human beings are linked to the Universal Mind. This explains telepathic communication as well as sympathy or antipathy between people who are strangers. Therefore, everyone is connected at the subconscious level, as illustrated below:

Collective Unconscious (Universal Mind)

↑↓↑↓

Individual Subconscious

↑↓↓↑

Individual Conscious (Self-Conscious Ego)

This interconnectedness of the conscious, the subconscious, and the collective subconscious is accurately described by Dr. C. George Boeree, who has drawn an interesting parallel between Jung's theory of the collective unconscious and the concept of *Atman*. Atman is a term used within Hinduism to identify the soul, whether in the universal sense (the world soul) or in the individual sense (personal soul). Dr. Boeree explains that the outer world belongs to what is called *maya* (illusion). The self-conscious mind (or ego) is called *jivatman*, the perception of outer illusion regarded as reality. This self-conscious mind sees other individuals as disconnected entities, each with a separate subconscious, but the separation is illusory. "We are united in the ocean of life [collective subconscious] or Atman."[2] This metaphysical concept of the oneness of life is the cornerstone of Vedanta, the Hermetic Qabalah, and other metaphysical doctrines.

The self-conscious mind is the part that plans, thinks, and takes initiative, but the agent that will carry out these plans and bring them into fruition is the subconscious mind. Therefore the role of the self-conscious mind is limited to reasoning, initiating, and setting goals. It can discriminate and decide what kind of information to focus upon; it also has the power to reprogram the "software" of the subconscious mind. Once the "program" is submitted to the subconscious, it becomes automatic or second nature. The subconscious mind has been compared to a powerful server mechanism, an uncritical, nonjudgmental computer. It accepts as true any suggestion that bypasses the critical part of the conscious mind. The good news is that this biological "computer" can be reprogrammed for optimum health, both emotional and physical, through autosuggestion, self-hypnosis, autogenic training, positive affirmations, and creative visualization.

The mere selection of a definite goal with the determination to carry it out will put hidden mechanisms into action that will provide an individual with the necessary resources and connect him to the persons and circumstances needed to attain that goal. This is the Law of Attraction. Something below conscious awareness makes the connections with whatever the individual needs in order to attain the goal. Emerson summarized this point by saying, "Once you make a decision, the universe conspires to make it happen."[3] The key is to impress our goals upon the subconscious mind and then adopt an attitude of determination and confidence without contradicting them with adverse thoughts, words, and feelings.

Various writers have given different names to the universal subconscious. Carl Jung referred to it as the collective unconscious, while Ralph Waldo Emerson called it the "oversoul" and wrote that "we live in the lap of an immense intelligence that, when we are in its presence, we realize that it is far beyond our human mind."[4] Hermetic Qabalists call it Universal Consciousness or Infinite Intelligence; quantum mechanics refers to it as the "mental universe" or as "zero point energy."[5] The genius and extraordinary talents expressed by some people are the manifestations of their ability to tap into this Universal Consciousness. Masters in all fields of life have confirmed that their outstanding skills and talents are demonstrations of something beyond their understanding. This is the real source of all invention and discovery made by human minds.

At the personal level, the subconscious controls every function of our bodies from birth. It regulates the heartbeat, glucose levels, and the transformation of food into living cells, among other things. Paul Foster Case remarked in his private lessons that the subconscious cures every disease. According to him, medicine merely sets up a chemical action to which the real healing power of the subconscious acts in response. He further stated that "surgery does not heal; neither do the mechanical adjustments; they simple remove obstacles for the free manifestation of the curative power."[6] Thus, provided there is no interference from the conscious mind, *the role of the subconscious is to restore our bodies to good health and maintain them in good health*. This could explain why some methods of mind and spiritual healing have succeeded where conventional medicine has failed.

Wellness depends on the predominant suggestions given to the subconscious. People ordinarily do not realize that they are constantly submitting suggestions to their subconscious; they are also unaware that the life force that pervades the universe is responsive to their thoughts and feelings. In fact we have been using this energy unwittingly in every activity, including thinking and feeling. Therefore the first step in maintaining a healthy body is to become consciously aware of the vast energetic reservoir in the universe that is available to everybody. Indeed this life force that pervades the whole universe is the only energy there is. It has been called by different names, such as the Great Magical Agent, Fohat, Hidden Power, and Spirit.

The Bible states that God bestowed upon humanity the power to have dominion over creation. The universal life force is included in this creation; consequently, human beings can employ it for their own wellness and the welfare of others. This energy is always subject to human command; it is always docile and always obedient to our thinking and feeling. Remember the adage "Energy follows thoughts."

Conventional wisdom holds that the art of bringing subconscious activities under conscious direction is extremely difficult or impossible. Nothing could be further from the truth. In fact the subconscious has always been under the direction of the conscious mind. The problem is that we have been programmed to view the subconscious as elusive, intangible, and out of our control. Since the subconscious mind is very docile, it will act according to those beliefs. It is said that the subconscious is easy to direct and never resists our efforts to manage it. Paul Foster Case indicates that the subconscious is so submissive that whenever we think of it as being defiant, it immediately plays up to the suggestion given and will continue to do so until it is given a strong, definitive counter-suggestion.

Control of the subconscious by the conscious does not, however, mean constant interference. Once a suggestion has been given to the subconscious, it should be left to carry out its directions with full confidence. The job of the conscious mind ends when it has formulated a clear-cut image of the desired outcome and turned it over to the subconscious. Case contends that it is important to stay completely confident in the powers of the subconscious.

Metaphysical teaching holds that everything we think and feel is recorded in the subconscious. Likewise, every single thought and emotion from one individual has some repercussion on others, because everyone is interconnected. If one dislikes a person to whom one was just introduced, the other person will pick up on the feeling of aversion. Likewise, if one feels misunderstood by friends and business associates, it will be perceived and responded to accordingly. Motivational and prosperity speakers recommend that one "magnetize" oneself with ideas of goodwill, love, peace, and success; as a result, the world will change for the better. In the same manner, self-help author Dr. Wayne Dyer has popularized the saying "If you change the way you look at things, the things you look at will change." That is, everything depends on attitude: when one has a positive and friendly attitude and shows genuine care for others, one's whole world will transform itself for the better.

The subconscious can be our ally, or it can be our enemy if we don't know how to deal with it. When its contents are not examined and the conflicts therein are not resolved, the results can be harmful. On the other hand, if we eliminate negative emotions and harmonize conflicting desires in a constructive manner, the subconscious will maintain a healthy body as well as harmonious social relationships.

The influence of the subconscious becomes evident in situations where we are only partly aware of our surroundings. For instance, when one is driving a car through a daily route, such as to and from work, over time the subconscious mind memorizes the way. In the moments when the conscious mind is preoccupied with personal business or we are deep in thought with work or family problems, we find that we have driven some distance without being aware of it; we have automatically stopped at traffic lights and turned corners. In this case, the subconscious mind did some part of the driving.

In general, then, the personal subconscious has been programmed without the conscious participation of the individual. In most cases, this automatic programming consists of conventional wisdom and mass media that are neither necessary, positive, nor constructive for our success and well-being. If we have internalized harmful ideas and beliefs, the subconscious will sabotage our efforts to achieve whatever we want in life: the more we endeavor, the more we will keep failing. For instance, if we have instilled in our subconscious the belief that we don't have a good memory, the harder we try to remember the name of a person, the more it eludes us. Other examples are, "I do not want to smoke cigarettes, but I cannot help it," or "I want to be a public speaker, but I am afraid to."

In all these situations, the subconscious ironically wins, because *it has been programmed to fail*. The subconscious is always the victor over personal will. An addict may sincerely want to give up his compulsion but be unable to do so because his will has been weakened to the point where the person acknowledges that the addiction has power over him. He feels frustrated and unable to do anything to remedy his situation. In that sense, the subconscious can be our worst enemy if we don't come to terms with it. The addict or alcoholic may have an honest desire to become sober, but he is irresistibly compelled to relapse in spite of the harmful consequences, of which he is fully aware. In certain cases, criminals have committed felonies in spite of their desire not to do so. When they were questioned why they acted so, they replied that they were powerless and could not control themselves; something stronger than they were compelled them to do such things.

Thus people are ordinarily conditioned to dress, eat, drink, and enjoy life according to what is imposed on them by mass media, social pressure, and conventional wisdom. If an individual is not aware of this situation, she has no free will. Authentic free will lies in an individual's capacity for genuine self-awareness, self-determination, and "self-reliance." That is, her decisions should be free of any influence from social and cultural conditioning. Free will is in directly proportional to one's capacity for self-awareness and self-control.

This discussion takes us to the issue of alienation in contemporary society: people have lost their identities as spiritual beings and as a result feel estranged from themselves. To counteract the influence of a negative environment, some people withdraw from society and retire to the countryside; others avoid being exposed to the mass media, so they cannot be affected by human opinion and worldly fears. But this apparent state of the external world is "the liar" and "the tempter." We should remain steadfast in the belief that the Infinite Intelligence is taking care of the welfare of humanity, although we cannot explain many apparent injustices and miseries that are happening around the world. The negativity broadcast by the mass media is psychic energy that is feeding an egregore. Our task as light bearers is to keep our minds oriented toward peace, understanding, and love for humankind. In this way, we counteract the negativity spread by common opinion and mass communication. Focused thought is condensed energy.

As long as individuals manage to have control over the quality of their thoughts, they will exercise dominion over themselves and the circumstances of their lives. The only way to counteract the negative predispositions of the social environment is to issue a strong opposite suggestion. Paradoxically, an intention tends to manifest at a time when consciousness is unaware of it, perhaps because the subconscious works behind the curtains of awareness. The secret, if there is any, is setting a clear goal and then detaching conscious awareness from it in order to allow the subconscious to do its job.

A person who lacks purpose in life leaves her destiny in the hands of uncertainty and lives at the mercy of other people's thoughts. The subconscious mind in its natural condition can be compared to an untamed horse full of life and energy, without bridle and reins. The rider can attempt to take it in one direction, but ultimately the horse will take the rider wherever it wishes. If, however, the rider succeeds in putting a bridle and reins on the horse and skillfully subjugates the animal, the horse will become a helpful and loyal ally.

In passing, it should be mentioned that the subconscious does not understand negatives such as the word *no*; for the subconscious, every statement is neutral. Finally, the subconscious will never accept forceful commands or orders; we cannot oblige it to do something. It responds only to subtle suggestions.

The above statements are not an esoteric secret anymore; the most successful American entrepreneurs, such as Andrew Carnegie, Napoleon Hill, and Henry Ford were aware of their effectiveness. Unfortunately, people who lack understanding of these principles do not have control over this creative aspect of the mind and create their circumstances by default, or are at the mercy of other people's creations.

The characteristics of the subconscious mind can be summarized thus:

1. The fundamental function of the subconscious is to maintain the well-being of the body. It has the power to heal the body of any form of disease.
2. The subconscious is amenable to being controlled by suggestions. We should be mindful of the kinds of suggestions we submit to the subconscious mind.
3. The subconscious possesses the capacity for deductive reasoning.
4. The subconscious stores all recollections of our past experiences; therefore it has perfect memory. It also has access to universal human experiences and memories. This is one source of our intuitions and premonitions.
5. The subconscious has the power to attract things that resonate with our main beliefs, prejudices, and personal idiosyncrasies. This is the basis of the Law of Attraction.
6. The subconscious has a perfect connection with all points in the universe. This law is the basis of telepathic communication. It is also the law that puts us in touch with whatever we need in

order to achieve our goals. It sends information to, and receives information from, other subconscious minds.

7. The subconscious is "propulsive," according to Paul Foster Case; "it is the driving force in human personality."[7]

Case's notion that the subconscious is a propulsive force is similar to the concept of libido in psychology and suggests the enormous power of the subconscious mind. At the universal level it is the driving energy for human evolution; at the personal level, it is the engine that provides the energy to carry out one's goals in life. How do we control this torrent of energy? The answer resides in two key words: *suggestion* and *autosuggestion*.

Chapter 22

Suggestion and Autosuggestion

These two words are the most important concepts in the science of mind. The entire life of man is the result of continuous suggestions and autosuggestions. We have been receiving and giving them directly or indirectly, through words, deeds, gestures, and behaviors. Our state of mind and well-being are influenced by suggestion. There are many cases in which healings have occurred after the patients have read inspirational books such as biographies of saints, the Bible, or other sacred scriptures. Such spontaneous remissions can also result from listening to or reading testimonies of other healings. For instance, when the Christian Science egregore was powerful, people from all walks of life were reportedly experiencing spontaneous healing just by reading the Christian Science textbook. A monthly magazine entitled *Healing Thoughts*, published by the Plainfield Christian Science Church, Independent, in New Jersey, devotes an entire page of each issue to the first edition of the textbook, *Science and Health*. The article starts with these words: "This was *the book which healed many thousands at first reading* and helped inspire the phenomenal growth of the early Christian Science movement" (italics are mine).

This validates the thesis that, at least in some cases, healing is the result of suggestion and autosuggestion. These lead the imagination of the sick person toward a spontaneous remission. In other words, *we heal ourselves*. Otherwise how could the reading of a book based on faulty premises cure people? People have an enormous capacity for self-healing, and the key to unlocking this healing power is different for different people. What may work for one individual may be ineffective or harmful to another.

The fundamental metaphysical premise taught by New Thought is that the subconscious mind is the agent that carries out the healing process. Ernest Holmes says, "The thing that makes us sick is the thing which heals us. We need not look for a law of sickness and a law of health. There is only One Law."[1] Joseph Murphy emphasized, "this healing power is in the subconscious mind of every person, a changed mental attitude on the part of the sick person releases this healing power."[2] The royal road to the subconscious mind is a mental image—a suggestion. Only when a mental image is impressed upon the subconscious mind will the healing process be initiated.

If this is so, why are many people resistant to healing either by conventional medicine or by mental treatment, even though they apparently want to be cured? I have discussed this issue in my essay "The Concepts of Psychological Resistance and Psychological Reversal" in my book *Beyond Conventional Wisdom*. It suggests that some people are subconsciously determined to sabotage their own healing because they harbor self-defeating beliefs. Some of these self-defeating ideas are so well rationalized and ingrained in their minds that they appear normal, or at any rate it is difficult to detect them. In these cases, the subconscious mind is controlled by those self-defeating beliefs.

Under these conditions, the possibilities of healing are minimal. A person may consciously want to be healed or be successful in life, but if she holds negative patterns or beliefs of self-punishment or self-victimization or unworthiness in her subconscious mind, she will disrupt the healing process and the achievement of her goals. The remedy is to identify and remove all stumbling blocks from the subconscious mind that are hindering her from attaining wholeness.

In some instances, becoming sick could be a way to call attention to oneself, or it could be a coping skill to avoid facing difficult situations in life. It can also be a subconscious way of asking for love and compassion.

To eradicate these negative patterns requires great courage as well as a rigorous analysis and review of one's most cherished beliefs. It also entails the detection of self-punishing ideas that are harbored in the mind. This process can result in a temporary period of personal crisis because one's erroneous beliefs are being questioned at their very roots.

The mechanism of sabotaging the process of healing or the attainment of goals in life has been called *psychological resistance*, a phrase coined by Dr. Roger Callahan, founder of the system of healing known as Thought Field Therapy. The operations of resistance are quite subtle and can manifest in different ways. There may be an unknown fear of the fulfillment of a goal and, consequently, a subtle attitude of rejection or avoidance of what is required to attain it. One can also have a feeling of not deserving to be happy because of a guilt complex.

It has been theorized that the mechanism of psychological resistance works somewhat like Newton's third law of physics: a certain amount of physical pressure creates an equal amount of resistance. In psychological terms, mental pressure generates an equal amount of subconscious resistance. When there is an imposition of pressure from without, there is equal or greater resistance from within. When the subconscious mind feels it is being coerced by external imperatives such as "you must be successful," "you should become somebody," or "you must be a winner," a subconscious reaction may arise that will oppose the achievement of these goals. For a person who is subconsciously determined to fail, any pressure for success or personal improvement will create inner conflict and anxiety.

The same thing can be observed in interpersonal relationships: people react adversely to doing something when it is imposed on them by somebody else. For instance, in a work environment, if someone orders another person to do something in an authoritarian manner, the resistance mechanism immediately arises. People usually oppose something when they feel obligated to do it. That is why a kind and indirect request is a way of gaining cooperation: it seems to come from inside the person rather than from outside.

To explain this, Callahan has also developed the concept of *psychological reversal,* which is defined as a subconscious determination to defeat or sabotage opportunities for success and healing.[3] Some men and women appear to have strong commitments to happiness, health, and prosperity, and yet they fail to reach their goals. This is because in their subconscious minds they foster unfounded misconceptions, ideas of unworthiness, guilt, and other destructive thoughts. The irony is that they are not aware of these things. Similarly, the presence of psychological reversal or resistance can block the natural process of self-healing.

It should be remembered that whatever idea or impression the conscious mind accepts as true—whether it is so or not—will act as a powerful suggestion for the subconscious mind. This statement is in perfect agreement with Hudson's second premise: the subjective mind is amenable to control by suggestion. Therefore, it follows that whatever the predominant belief of an individual may be, the subjective mind will try to accomplish it. Both Hudson and Troward considered faith to be the *power of the soul,* and they equated the soul with the subconscious mind. As Troward writes:

> The subjective mind [subconscious] is the soul, or spirit, and is itself an organized entity, possessing independent powers and functions; while the objective mind [conscious mind] is merely the function of the physical brain, and possesses no powers whatever independently of the physical organization. The one possesses dynamic force independently of the body; the other does not. The one is capable of sustaining an existence independently of the body; the other dies with it.[4]

My essay "All Is Faith or Fear" in *Beyond Conventional Wisdom* extensively discusses faith and its importance in healing. As it indicates, Jesus Christ required his apostles to have faith as a prerequisite to emulating his miracles. Therefore one of the essential conditions for success in every mental treatment is the belief of the patient in the operator. Before performing a healing, Jesus Christ asked the sick person if he believed that he, Jesus, could carry out the healing. When the answer was positive, he would say: "Your faith has healed you" (Mark 5:22, 10:52; Luke 8:48; Matthew 9:22); "Let it be done just as you believed it" (Matthew 8:13); "According to your faith let it be done to you" (Matthew 9:29; all from the New International Version).

A skeptic, on the other hand, is one who believes the opposite: "No healing can be done by mental means." In reality, the disbeliever holds a negative belief—but it is still a belief. Individuals who think that no one will be able to heal them are absolutely right, for three reasons:

1. Every healing needs active participation from the sick person.
2. The unbeliever has consciously blocked the possibility of any healing.
3. The individual may be subconsciously determined to be unwell.

The Qabalistic master Paul Foster Case has warned that we should be mindful about what we think, say, and do all day long, because these are powerful suggestions to our subconscious minds. If we want to maintain perfect health, we should be careful in our thinking and actions concerning our physical condition. We should avoid giving pejorative names to parts of our bodies, and we should keep in mind that every cell is a conscious unit. Furthermore, we should provide our bodies with the right food, pure water, abundant air, sunlight, and proper hygiene. By doing these things, we give our subconscious mind powerful suggestions that we want perfect health.

Thomson Jay Hudson describes suggestion as "the act of indirectly imposing an idea on the mind of another." That is, an idea is imparted to another person without argument, command, or coercion. The subconscious mind more readily responds to what is *implied* rather than to what is explicitly stated. The *Emerald Tablet*, an ancient alchemical text ascribed to Hermes Trismegistus, says that the work of controlling our hidden powers must be done "suavely, and with great ingenuity."

Subtle influences come from different fronts. The subconscious is constantly bombarded by multiple suggestions coming from such sources as conventional wisdom, the mass media, words spoken by a prominent person or an intimate friend, the physical environment, physical gestures that have specific implications, advertising, and so forth. All these factors can influence the subconscious mind without the individual's awareness.

Thus it is important to be mindful of what is happening in our daily lives. The subconscious, in perfect obedience to our suggestions, can create contradictory situations. For instance, an individual may have been using affirmations for attaining perfect health. At the same time, however, the person may be eating junk food or failing to provide the body with the appropriate food, water, air, and sunlight. Therefore, the goal of maintaining perfect health has been counteracted by the suggestive power of habitual behavior. Even a well-crafted suggestion of health will be unsuccessful under these circumstances, because there is no congruence between the goal and the deed. We cannot deceive the subconscious mind; it knows our most intimate thoughts and feelings. Hence *the most effective suggestions are our deeds.* And the most potent suggestion is one that is in harmony with the individual's natural instincts.

These considerations lead to the concept of *personal congruence.* Personal congruence means that our thoughts, actions, and words are in harmony with one another. Otherwise we will be giving our subconscious mind contradictory suggestions, imparting one idea with our thoughts and a different one with our actions. This is exemplified by the popular saying "Do as I say, not as I do." Unfortunately, incongruence between intentions and actions appears to be a common trait.

Autosuggestion can also be employed to great advantage for therapeutic purposes. It can enable one to resist disease, prevent illness, strengthen the immune system, and facilitate the healing power of the body. Positive attitudes and congruent actions are the heart of good health. They enable one to boost the immune system and resist the intrusion of any disease.

Now it is clear how Quimby and the other New Thought leaders healed themselves by means of suggestion and autosuggestion. Quimby came to the conclusion that the medical diagnoses of the time were, in most cases, wrong. In his diary he affirmed that he had created his own illness because he had believed his medical diagnoses. When he began to practice, people came to him for help after they had unsuccessfully sought alternative ways of healing. Quimby was the last resort. He gave them new hope: he was able to persuade them that they can be healed by changing their frame of mind. This was a powerful suggestion, considering they had already tried all means of conventional and nonconventional medicine of the time.

Quimby's patients were healed by means of his constructive suggestions. Following his "explanation" of the unreal nature of the illnesses, the patients changed their mental imagery from images of disease to those of health and well-being; consequently, at least in some cases, their health was restored. Quimby himself stated that the secret of his achievements was that he was able to persuade patients that their maladies were only in their minds. This was reinforced by his magnetic personality and his assurance in providing hope and relief to the patients.

One cannot deny the immense benefits of New Thought philosophy and organizations for millions of people throughout the world. This is not an empty statement. Although it may be difficult to believe, the evidence for healing without medicine is overwhelming, and in some cases has been corroborated by the medical profession. There are also conclusive testimonials and evidence from people who have been healed from incurable diseases without medicine. In most cases, these healings were carried out after conventional medicine failed to cure the patients. Some of them not only improved their health but lengthened their life spans; others became successful in their personal business and relationships by applying the prosperity principles of New Thought.

For example, Joe Dispenza, a student of neuroscience and ex-member of Ramtha's School of Enlightenment (an esoteric school based on the teaching, channeled by J. Z. Knight, of a disembodied entity identified as Ramtha), has written a book called *Evolve Your Brain*. This book, which is over 510 pages long, summarizes most of the modern scientific strides toward proving the power of mind over matter and showing how healing occurs by changing an individual's frame of mind. Although Dispenza does not seem to be aware of Quimby or New Thought, the book substantiates the basic ideas of the movement, as is confirmed by its subtitle: *The Science of Changing your Mind.*

Chapter 23

Self-Help and
Self-Empowerment

Physician, heal thyself.
—Luke 4:23 (King James Version)

This chapter may be one of the most important in this book. Without the metaphysical components of self-help and self-empowerment, the principles described in the foregoing chapters are much less significant. Personal initiative and action are vital elements in self-healing.

The guiding hypothesis that led to the development of this book was the idea that ultimately *people heal themselves*. In the modalities of healing that we have examined, we have found that the subconscious mind is the driving force in restoring health. The key objective is to make the patient's subconscious mind believe in the placebo or suggestion. Diverse methods of healing work for different people. For some, it may be worshipping a favorite saint; for others, making a pilgrimage to the Lourdes grotto; and for still others, believing in a relic, a stone, a special tree, a mountain, a crystal, magnets, or some other object. One thing should be kept in mind. The individual is the one who gives power to the selected object; the object in itself has no power at all. However, it can serve as a symbolic mental support for his belief. Once the sense of wonder activates the imagination by means of one of these symbols, the subconscious mind will work accordingly, provided the individual has a strong desire to be healed. Without this desire, no method will work.

215

Ultimately, all healing is self-healing. Every human being creates her own reality according to her needs for self-development, and illness may be part of this. A disease (dis-ease) can be a blessing for one and a curse for another. Sickness and healing respond to the Law of Attraction. We can attract the malady through our inner or unstated thoughts; conversely, we can redirect and refocus our minds to wholeness and attract it accordingly. The purpose of hypnosis and suggestive therapies, as well as the other methods of treatment, is to impress the healing image into the subconscious mind of the patient.

Taking into account the ancient occult aphorism "Nature unaided fails," and considering the premise that health is a natural condition of man, we can conclude that sickness is unnatural. The concept of *self-help* is important; the individual has to set the initial intention—a desire to get well—to trigger the inner mechanisms that will lead to recovery. Without this preliminary intention, nothing will happen. Let's remember the famous adage attributed to Benjamin Franklin, "God helps those who help themselves."

Western mystical schools regard the devil—which can be equated with the external, sensorial world—as an illusion that tempts us through our senses. Some have even surrendered to this illusion and have become worshippers of this "devil." But this illusory world, which Hindu philosophy calls *maya*, is the collective creation of humankind. In addition, today the negative messages given by the mass media, including movies, TV, radio, and newspapers, keep people mesmerized and alienated by selling an ideology of consumerism, individualism, and materialistic values. The media create superficial needs, making people believe they require material things to be happy and fulfilled. There is nothing wrong with advancement of technology and the mass media, as long as they are used as means of entertainment, education, and information. The problem arises when people become slaves to such inventions and have no time to spend with their families. Instead of uniting families, these technologies are separating them. The illness of modern humanity is loneliness, and its consequence is depression.

A person can feel alone and isolated even when millions of people are nearby. Moreover, modern materialistic society has alienated humans; modern man and modern woman feel estranged to themselves; they lack meaning in life and have lost their real identities. In other words, man has become a slave of the sensory world, forgetting his spiritual dimension and his real role in the arena of life as cocreator with God. Some pursue money and fame or become addicted to drugs or alcohol as means of finding happiness or compensation for their loneliness, but in the end, they find only more emptiness.

Historically, human beings have created many healing techniques as ways of curing themselves. Sometimes they appeal to unusual techniques, such as the exotic method of curing using human secretions—urine therapy. The first time I heard about this was in Cusco, Peru, about seven years ago. At that time I thought this was a folkloric method used by native people. Further research proved me wrong; it is not a technique restricted to local people in Peru but is widespread around the world and practiced by intelligent and highly educated individuals who consider human urine as a natural elixir for healing. See, for example, the book entitled *Urine Therapy: Nature's Elixir for Good Health*, by Flora Peschek-Böhmer and Gisela Schreiber. They run a naturopathic healing center in Hamburg, Germany. The Internet also shows centers in America propounding urine therapy. One of the most prominent is Omaha's Heartland Healing Center, whose website has an interesting article with a flamboyant subtitle: "Welcome aboard. Coffee, tea or pee?"[1]

It would be folly to deny the effectiveness of medicine and the tremendous advances of technology in the treatment and relief of many diseases, such as malaria, smallpox, and cholera, as well as a variety of congenital illnesses. The downside is that extreme reliance on medicine and technology can take away people's capacities to heal themselves. Mind treatment can play a complementary role in disease prevention and in keeping optimum health. There needs to be a symbiotic relationship between the two. Our minds and spirits need to be nourished with positive, constructive, and inspirational ideas. As Jesus Christ stated, "Man does not live by bread alone." We need spiritual food as well.

Mystics, religious thinkers, and some segments of the medical profession consider prayer to be an important factor in the restoration of health because it acts as a powerful affirmation impressed upon the subconscious mind. There are many books that verify the effectiveness of prayer in regaining health, establishing harmonious relationships, and repairing finances. Medical doctor Gabriel Weiss has authored a book entitled *The Healing Power of Meditation*. His main postulate is that our bodies have a tremendous capacity for self-healing through prayer and meditation. He further claims that meditation can unlock the natural healing power of the body and "activate genuine and long-lasting well-being," among other benefits.

Indeed prayer, meditation, and creative visualization can achieve what are seen as miracles. The development of human potential during the coming Age of Aquarius is unlimited; there are scientists who claim that the human lifespan could be extended up to one thousand years, like those of the antediluvian patriarchs in the Bible. This may be hard to believe, but scientists such as biologist Aubrey de Grey consider aging to be an illness and believe future medicine should be able to cure that illness. He further argues that long-lasting youth will become reality in a few decades.[2]

Metaphysical considerations go far beyond these possibilities. The quest of authentic students of the Western mystery tradition is the completion of the Magnum Opus or the Great Work, which could be interpreted as perfect self-knowledge and the reinventing of oneself in order to become a new human being.

Human beings have access to a force of incalculable power that permeates everything in the world. Conscious awareness of this fact is indispensable if we want to direct this energy toward fulfilling our undertakings. Spiritual writer Marianne Williamson expresses this idea in these words: "Our greatest fear is not that we are inadequate. Our deepest fear is that we are powerful beyond measure. It is our light, not our darkness, that most frightens us."[3]

The main ideas that we have arrived at during this study can be summarized as follows:

1. People's miseries have been created by themselves, so only they have the power to undo them.

2. People have the capacity to heal themselves through creative imagination, positive determination, and positive expectations.

3. The body has the ability to recuperate as long as there is no interference from the mind or the environment.

4. The body can go through periods of cleansing or adjustment that can manifest in discomfort that could be interpreted as dis-ease. The ingestion of harmful medicine to alleviate this condition may hinder the body's recuperative process.

5. Mental disturbances, including anxiety, depression, and post-traumatic stress disorder (PTSD), can be manifested in bodily dysfunctions. Once the origin of these disturbances is removed, the body will return to wellness.

6. Suggestion and autosuggestion can create illnesses as well as cure them.

7. The influence of healthy, magnetic personalities is contagious and has a positive influence on sick people as they orient their imaginations toward wellness.

PART FIVE

Modern Trends in
Healing without Medicine

Chapter 24

The Healing Power of Love and Forgiveness

Behold, the kingdom of God is within you.
—Luke 17:21 (King James Version)

During the last half of the twentieth century a shift in the healing paradigm took place in America. Mainstream medicine is now heading toward a more comprehensive and integral system. Some scientists in the field of neuroscience, new biology, and psychology believe that we are on the verge of a medical transformation that is bridging the current view of the spirit, mind, and body as separate entities. More medical doctors now are advancing more humanistic and spiritual ways of healing rather than adhering to old materialistic concepts based heavily on technology and harmful chemicals. This is exemplified by the introduction of healing through unconditional love and forgiveness, writing journals, drawing mandalas, painting, dancing, meditation, walking in the wilderness or forest, and yoga exercise.

In the past, traditional Western medical care neglected the incorporation of the mind and spirituality in healing matters. In modern times medical and allied health practitioners are actively seeking the reintegration of religion, spirituality, praying, intention, and imagery into the healing equation. A prominent example is the establishment of the Duke Center for Spirituality, Theology, and Health. This center, established by Dr. Harold G. Koenig and a team of health professionals, has been studying the impact of spirituality on mental and physical health. They postulate that spirituality can affect physical outcomes including immune functioning and the well-being of a person.[1]

Using the power of love as an agent of healing has also been advanced by Bernie Siegel, M.D., who believes that love is the most potent stimulant of the immune system. Dr. Siegel pioneered alternative modalities of healing in his bestselling book *Love, Medicine and Miracles*. He has advocated practicing love, meditation, imagery, relaxation, and journal writing in overcoming some types of cancer. Siegel is also the author of *Faith, Hope and Healing*, in which he presents cases of patients with cancer who have been healed by following the above recommendations.

Dr. Deepak Chopra advocates the ayurvedic method, an ancient Indian system of healing that includes a vegetarian diet, yoga exercises, and classical yogic meditation as ways of improving health. According to this view, through the practice of regular meditation one can control the mind, the senses, and the body, promoting a sense of inner peace and personal security.

Many physicians and nurses have written books recommending healing through prayer, laying on of hands, Therapeutic Touch, art therapy, drawing pictures and mandalas, and other methods. Michael Samuels, M.D., and Mary Rockwood Lane, R.N., authors of *Creative Healing: How to Heal Yourself by Tapping Your Hidden Creativity*, advocate painting, writing, music, and dance as ways of healing and claim that many people have been healed through these methods. The practice of these techniques may stimulate endorphin secretion in the brain, furthering the recuperative processes of the body. In addition, excitement, pain, love, and orgasm can increase the secretion of endorphins in the body.[2]

At last medical opinion is beginning to endorse New Thought tenets regarding the influence of the mind in the healing process. Larry Dossey, M.D., an eminent physician, for example, "advocates the role of the mind in health and the role of spirituality in healthcare." In his 1989 book *Recovering the Soul*, Dossey introduced the medical profession to the old metaphysical concept of nonlocal mind—the idea "that the mind is not confined to the brain, but surpasses the limits of time and space."[3] Dossey's breakthrough book, *Healing Words* (1993), has been a seminal work for medical schools, having set the precedent for courses devoted to exploring the role of religious practice and prayer in health.

Then there is the old proverb, "Laughter is the best medicine." This assertion has been tested by several studies. The positive benefits of humor and laughter as a therapeutic method for the body and spirit are unquestionable. A good laugh keeps the mind and body in balance and helps a person stay emotionally healthy. Thoughts produce chemical reactions in the brain, and a good laugh triggers release of endorphins that the body needs to promote a sense of well-being. Moreover, laughter relaxes the whole body, boosts the immune system, improves the function of blood vessels, and increases blood flow. All these are powerful antidotes for stress and depression. Laughter makes a person feel good and helps one keep an optimistic outlook in complicated circumstances. It is said that when Abraham Lincoln was facing difficult times during the Civil War, he used to tell funny stories to his cabinet as way of shifting attention from their problems for a moment.

Laughter as a therapeutic component was popularized by Norman Cousins (1915–1990), an American author, political journalist, and professor who regained his health by watching funny movies and TV shows. He was diagnosed with a terminal disease, and when his doctors told him had little chance of surviving, Cousins developed a recovery program incorporating vitamin C along with a positive attitude, love, faith, hope, and laughter. He reported, "I made the joyous discovery that ten minutes of genuine belly laughter had an anesthetic effect and would give me at least two hours of pain-free sleep." He healed himself, lived another sixteen years, and pioneered the use of laughter and humor in healing.[4]

The key, then, is to identify the activity that one's *inner core* most responds to, that is, what one enjoys doing most and makes one feel good when doing it. Writing journals and poems, dancing, gardening, hiking in the mountains, praying, meditation, contemplation, spiritual retreats, and reading biographies of saints and sages are different modalities that can be used to heal. In other cases, getting out of stressful situations, choosing healthy food, fasting, practicing rhythmic breathing, withdrawing to the countryside or the forest, and living a quiet life will facilitate healing as well.

The goal is to redirect the mind from negative conditioning to uplifting and constructive thoughts, and to attune oneself with the infinite. Finding enjoyment in the chosen activity can stimulate the endorphins needed and allow the life force to flow through the body. As author and mythologist Joseph Campbell said, "Follow your bliss." One has to gain access to the inner world, which is often overshadowed by the influence of the material world and the demands of the physical senses. The practices suggested above can help one balance the relationship between the inner nature and the physical body.

Finally, the most important and natural way to let go of negative emotions is to *forgive and forget*. First, one should forgive oneself honestly and unconditionally, then forgive others who may have harmed you directly or indirectly, including your worst enemies. Grudges are forms of negative energy that harm you. The best approach is to accept that you have attracted everything that has happened to you for the purpose of your spiritual unfoldment.

Chapter 25

The Qabalistic Method of Treatment

One modern esoteric system of healing without medicine comes from the Qabalistic tradition. Paul Foster Case, founder of the esoteric school known as Builders of the Adytum (BOTA), an American offshoot of the Hermetic Order of the Golden Dawn, wrote extensively on Qabalah, esoteric Tarot, alchemy, and Rosicrucianism. He is not well-known because most of his writings are imparted solely by correspondence lessons to BOTA members. Case delineated a system of healing through sound, color, and meditation on the Tarot keys. The principle behind this system is that sound and color are vibrations, each operating at different rates; thus each color and sound is associated with different parts of the body according to their astrological correspondences. Once the part of the body is identified, one meditates on the corresponding Tarot key utilizing the associated sound and color. Unfortunately, very little information can be disclosed about this method because these teachings are restricted to BOTA affiliates, who are bound by oath not to reveal them publicly. (People who want information about BOTA's teachings should visit its website, www.bota.org).

The late Israel Regardie was the leader of the revival of the Golden Dawn in America. Despite the opposition of members, he was not reluctant to publish the rituals and writings of this esoteric order, which had been entrusted to him under severe oaths of secrecy under the title *The Golden Dawn*.

As the reader may recall, Israel Regardie was cited previously in this book in the chapter on Mary Baker Eddy. Regardie wrote extensively on the early pioneers of the New Thought movement and was knowledgeable about mind healing and suggestive therapies, as we can see from his book *The Romance of Metaphysics*, published in 1946.

Although Regardie thought highly of Eddy as a mind healer, he proposed a different method of therapy from hers, based on the Hermetic Qabalah. Eddy, for her part, would have condemned Regardie's method. She detested all occult, esoteric, Qabalistic, and other teachings that differed from or were opposed to her Christian Science, which she considered to be the result of divine inspiration; all other ways of healing were false. She would have deemed these things to be forms of *malicious malpractice* (her favorite term for labeling ideas or methods that contradicted or differed from her own).

Later in his life, Regardie, a Jungian psychotherapist, published an essay entitled "The Art of True Healing," based on the teachings received from the Golden Dawn. The kind of therapeutic treatment he described is quite different from those described in previous chapters. It can be seen as a form of energy medicine.

This method is based on the Qabalistic Tree of the Sefirot (stages of emanation of the life power or Cosmic Consciousness), also known as the Tree of Life. The technique makes use of rhythmic breathing, meditation, and visualization of the Sefirot of the Middle Pillar of the Tree. The Middle Pillar corresponds to the spinal column, where the seven chakras, or psychic energy centers, are supposedly located. Meditation on and visualization of the chakras activate the flow of the universal life force through these psychic centers; this in turn releases negative emotions trapped in the body. This technique also utilizes the visualization of color and the use of sound to stimulate the energy centers of the body and, finally, includes prayer and the use of religious mantras.

In "The Art of True Healing," which is part of his book *Foundations of Practical Magic*, Regardie describes the principle behind his method:

Within every man and woman is a force which directs and controls the entire course of life. Properly used, it can heal every affliction and ailment to which mankind is heir. Every single religion affirms this fact. All forms of mental or spiritual healing, no matter under what name they travel, promise the same thing. Even psychoanalysis employs this power, though indirectly, using the now popular word *libido*.[1] (Italics Regardie's.)

This is a departure from the concept of healing that Regardie portrayed in *The Romance of Metaphysics*. At that time he flirted intellectually with New Thought and believed that illness arose from a negative frame of mind. Now sickness was seen as arising from the depletion and incorrect use of the life force energy. Regardie said that a lack of proper breathing and a failure to understand the fact that we are surrounded by the life force is the reason we become ill. Nevertheless, this theory can be seen as complementary to New Thought, since we direct this life force by means of our thoughts and emotions. Regardie further states:

> In the ambient atmosphere surrounding us and pervading the structure of each minute body-cell is a spiritual force. This force is omnipresent and infinite. It is present in the most infinitesimal object as it is in the most proportion-staggering nebula or island universe. It is this force which is life itself.[2]

The root of this concept is found in the Hindu school of philosophy known as Vedanta, with which Regardie was well acquainted. Vedanta holds that there is one indestructible substance pervading the whole universe, from the remotest star to the most minuscule atomic particle. Regardie equates this universal life force, known in the yogic philosophy as prana, with God. "This Spiritual force constitutes man's higher self; it is his link with God in man. Every cell in the body should be soaked with its universal energy." Disease, Regardie concluded, is fundamentally due to a depletion of the life force.

According to Regardie, the ordinary individual puts up so much resistance to the free flow of this universal energy in his body that he becomes tired and ill. Regardie contends that man has "surrounded himself with a crystallized shell of prejudices and ill-conceived fantasies," which act as a shield preventing the free flow of the life force. Therefore, man should practice honest self-examination of his value system. Regardie also recommends conscious relaxation as a preliminary step, then loosening up the neuromuscular tensions of the body to the degree that all the cells and muscles are brought within the scope of awareness.

Regardie lays out two basic principles for well-being. First, we should consciously realize that we live in this vast spiritual reservoir of life force energy. Second, we should employ regulated or rhythmic breathing, similar to the breathing exercises of yoga, in order to vitalize the body.

These ideas are in accord with Hermetic and yogic philosophies, which hold that the entire universe is a living organism and moves according to an immutable of law of rhythm and cycle. Therefore, rhythmic breathing keeps our bodies in a healthy condition. In every breath, we inhale prana, the life force that vitalizes the body and mind. Regardie argues that an inability to grasp this principle is the reason for the failure of many mental and spiritual healing systems.

Regardie further recommends meditation on the psychospiritual centers that are located along the spinal cord. These centers of energy are known in yogic philosophy as chakras and in the Qabalah as the Sefirot of the Middle Pillar (which is associated with the spinal column). They are vortices of energy through which the life force flows. Although the yogic philosophy says there are seven of these centers, Regardie uses only five.

Regardie recommends concentrating the mind on these centers. Then one should intone and vibrate the names of God associated with them in the Qabalah. "Finally, each center is to be visualized as having a particular color and shape. Slowly, they become stimulated into

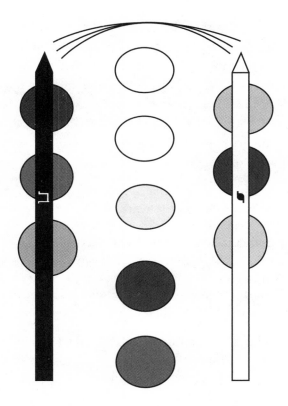

The Middle Pillar of the Tree of Life.

functioning, each according to its own nature, pouring forth a stream of highly spiritualized energy and power into the body and mind."[3] At this point the individual can direct the resulting spiritual power to heal various ailments and diseases of both a psychological and a physical nature.

This energy can also be transmitted by the laying on of hands. Thus Regardie, like Mesmer, believes in the transmission of energy from one person to another. Moreover, Regardie agrees with Hudson and Troward that healing energy can be sent telepathically to another person who is miles away. This is known as *absent treatment* or *distant healing*.

Like Case, who said that the subconscious is the propulsive factor in the individual, Regardie argues that this method of healing can cure even psychogenic eruptions, because the "currents of force arise from the deepest strata of the unconscious, where these psychoneuroses have their origin and where the nervous energy is confined, preventing spontaneous restoration of health."[4] Unlike Christian Science, which prohibits its members from receiving medical assistance, Regardie does not exclude the use of a physician:

> Where organic disease is the problem to be attacked, the procedure to be followed is slightly different. (One should still be under the care of a competent physician). In this instance a considerably stronger current of force is required such as will dissolve the lesion and be sufficient to set in motion those systemic and metabolic activities to construct new tissue and cellular structure. To fulfill these conditions in an ideal sense a second person may be requisite so that his vitality added to that of the sufferer may overcome the condition.[5]

As with any kind of healing, conventional or unconventional, the participation of the individual is extremely important. For a successful treatment with this method, the patient has to be totally receptive and must maintain an attitude of acceptance toward the incoming force.

Regardie recommends prayer or contemplation as the final step of his healing method, because they also activate these psychospiritual centers. Indeed, most genuine esoteric schools and religious organizations strongly advocate meditation and prayer as a means of attaining a higher state of mind as well as of stimulating emotional fervor toward the awakening of the spiritual centers. From time immemorial, mystics have given such injunctions as "Inflame thyself in praying." Ceremonial rituals can also be used to awaken the inner mechanism of healing.

Regardie contends that his system of treatment can be used not only for healing but also for solving a variety of problems in life, such as enhancing human potential, eliminating negative aspects of our personalities, improving relationships, and resolving marital difficulties.

Chapter 26

Rational and Cognitive Behavioral Therapies

A new psychological trend of healing without medicine appeared in United States during the 1950s and 1960s: rational emotive behavioral therapy (REBT) and cognitive behavioral therapy (CBT). These types of healing emerged as a reaction to the costly psychoanalytical method, which can take many years to yield results. About this approach, author Daniel Reid has observed:

> Conventional Western medical practice attributes emotional disturbances exclusively to the mind and usually refers emotionally disturbed patients to psychiatrists for treatment. The typical Freudian explanation for neuroses and emotional trauma is that they are a result of childhood fixations and unresolved psychological conflicts, and the Freudian approach to treating such problems is to lie the patient down on a couch and get to the root of the disturbance through endless hours of meandering conversation. As often as not, psychoanalysis turns out to be a colossal waste of time and money that provides no lasting relief from mental and emotional disturbances.[1]

In the 1950s, Albert Ellis developed REBT as a short-term therapy. It changed the course of psychotherapy in America. This school adopted the slogan "Short-term therapy, long-term results." The basic principle is that people in the course of their lives have adopted irrational beliefs and behaviors that stand in the way of achieving their most cherished goals. Often these irrational attitudes or ideas take the form of extreme or dogmatic attitudes that conflict with their desires. The rationale is that when we become upset, it is not because of the event; rather, the beliefs that we hold in our minds are what make us feel depressed, anxious, or enraged. Ellis held that our feelings don't control our thoughts; on the contrary, *our thoughts control our feelings*. Consequently, negative emotions are the result of patterns of thinking that we have acquired over the years. (This notion appears to be the opposite of the theory of emotions held by Troward and William James, for whom emotions are prior to thoughts.)

Following this trend, in the 1960s, psychiatrist Aaron T. Beck developed CBT, which emphasizes the importance of thinking in determining our feelings and dictating our behavior. Again, our thoughts are seen as causing our feelings and behaviors and not the other way around. In this paradigm, external factors such as people and events are neutral. Beck claimed that most of our emotional and behavioral reactions are learned; thus the goal of treatment is to help clients *unlearn* their unwanted reactions and be trained in new ways of reacting and coping with external situations. Consequently, therapy should focus on changing one's attitudes by concentrating on one's thoughts, images, and beliefs, and how these relate to one's behavior when dealing with life's daily problems.

The common denominator between these modalities is that they emphasize the importance of thoughts over feelings; they are short-term and goal-oriented therapies. They hold that whenever a person has a psychological problem, it is the result of distorted thinking: the thinking process is the problem and should be the target of treatment. At this point, the reader will recognize a similarity to Quimby's philosophy. Quimby's major tenet was that individuals inflict maladies upon themselves with the thoughts they hold in their minds. Changing these negative thoughts will result in the healing of the person.

Likewise, the fundamental idea in the cognitive therapies is that individuals should change their distorted ways of thinking and eliminate self-defeating and harmful self-talk, which may be constantly running in their minds. They should replace these patterns with uplifting and constructive ways of thinking. If they do this, their lives will change for the better. (As we have seen, this viewpoint has been held by New Thought since at least the turn of the twentieth century.) The role of the therapist is to assist the patient in identifying the quality of past thinking and reactions to events that have generated problems, and in reinterpreting and reframing these events in a positive way. It is interesting to note that the basic idea of the cognitive modalities was first articulated by the Greek philosopher Epictetus about two thousand years ago, when he stated, "Men are disturbed not by events, but by the views which they take of them."[2]

In reality, thoughts and emotions are intimately connected. A thought is a form of psychic energy and has an emotional component to it; likewise, an emotion is a form of psychic energy as well and has a component of thought. Thoughts and feelings cannot exist independently. A thought usually generates an immediate emotion; for instance, the thought of speaking in public for the first time often generates the emotion of apprehension. The nature of an emotion depends on the quality of the thought: the emotion that arises when someone thinks about an abusive boss is different from the one that is generated when one thinks about a loving father who lives far away.

The personal interpretation of an external event is what causes a specific emotion, and that emotion is manifested in a specific behavioral response. This interpretation of reality is shaped by a "personal screen" composed of biological predispositions, personal beliefs, prejudices, and outlook on life. The idea in essence is similar to what the Stoic philosophers pointed out: "People give their worlds the colors of their own thoughts." But philosophers, psychologists, and other behavioral scientists still do not agree about which comes first, the emotion or the thought—a point about which they have argued throughout history.

Chapter 27

Energy Psychology and Energy Healing

All healing involves energy and conscious intention.
—Gary E. Schwartz, Ph.D.

The development of short-term therapies without medicine has continued in America; one of the latest types is called energy psychology or energy healing. A new form of healing that has appeared during the last three decades, energy psychology (a term coined by psychologist Fred Gallo) is a psychotherapeutic technique that combines Eastern medicine and Western psychological approaches. It entails a shift in the paradigm of healing from changing the frame of thinking, as in cognitive therapy, to releasing negative emotions trapped in the body. Psychotherapy attempts to release negative emotions from the subconscious mind, while energy psychology releases energy from the nervous system. Chiropractor George J. Goodheart, one of the pioneers of this new perspective, explains: "If you do not correct the disturbance in the nervous system, there will be adverse effects in the physical, chemical and emotional sides of health."[1]

The scientific basis for this viewpoint is that, like everything in the world, the human body is made up of energy. In the chapter on Qabalistic therapy, we encountered the idea that there is a life force energy that permeates and maintains everything in the universe, and which flows through the chakras. Unfortunately, conventional medicine is mainly focused on the physical manifestation of the malady, disregarding the mental and emotional levels of life. Nor does it recognize this vibrational energy, even though it encompasses the whole universe and serves as the underlying basis of life. In Hermetic philosophy this concept is not new; in fact this energy is mental energy, according to the first Hermetic principle of Mentalism, a subject discussed in *The Kybalion*.

Energy psychology, or energy medicine, attempts to correct the imbalances in the body's energy patterns. It addresses the free flow of energy through the body, and in so doing corrects disturbances in the energy field, enabling the body to heal itself. Since everything is composed of energy patterns, working directly with these influences makes sense.

Metaphysics teaches that in addition to the corporeal body, we have subtle bodies, which are sometimes referred to as the emotional, mental, and spiritual bodies. We also have an energy field, which is commonly known as the *etheric body* or *aura*. The energy field surrounds and permeates the physical body. In physics, matter is condensed energy; thus the physical body is also an expression of that energy. This etheric body, and not the brain, is the shell that contains our thoughts and emotions; it is the energy that never dies or disappears, even though the brain will disintegrate and vanish once a person passes away.

Energy psychology borrows the concepts of meridians, acupoints, and acupressure from Chinese medicine. According to Chinese medicine, the universal life force, called *chi* or *ki*, flows through the meridians in the body. The meridians are subtle energy channels that interconnect and regulate the flow of this life force energy. This idea has been used for thousands of years to treat physical and mental diseases through practices such as acupuncture.

From a psychological point of view, when a person is subject to traumatic events, psychic energy appears to become trapped in some parts of the meridians, creating a disruption in the flow of the subtle energies. This disturbance can be manifested in physical or emotional illnesses. The fundamental aim of the therapy is to identify the energetic or emotional disruption and then to free the flow of energy.

Author Daniel Reid describes the importance of emotions in healing as follows:

> The emotion leaves the realm of mind and enters the body's meridian system as a form of energy. Like all forms of human energy, emotions exert profound physiological effects on the internal organs, glands, and other tissues to which they travel through the energy channels. The word "emotion" is best understood as a contraction of "energy in motion," or "e-motion." In other words, the mind attaches a value to a physical or cerebral sensory stimulus, then sets a powerful current of emotional energy into motion through the body's energy channels. Once the energy is in motion, it takes on a life of its own.
>
> Each emotion we generate triggers physiological reactions throughout the system, including secretions of various hormones, release of neurotransmitters in the brain and nervous system, changes in pulse and blood pressure, adjustment in breathing and respiration, and stimulation and suppression of digestion and peristalsis.[2]

This quotation is nicely complemented by a statement from Wilhelm Reich (1897–1957), an influential Austrian psychoanalyst, who said that "fixation and conflicts cause fundamental disturbances of the bioelectric system and so get anchored somatically and that it is impossible to separate the psychic from the somatic process."[3]

The treatment is based on the premise that our traumatic experiences in life have been recorded in the nervous system. Our cellular system is like a recording machine that stores all emotional problems. Hence Dr. James V. Durlacher, author of *Freedom From Fear Forever*, states: "Because your body knows exactly what the problem is and will share this secret if asked, there is a way to handle all fears. The key to understanding and treating phobias is balancing the energies in your body with a very simple stimulation of specific acupuncture points."[4] In this kind of therapy, the healing process begins with diagnosing the specific disruptions in the energy system of the patient, which is done using *applied kinesiology*, a muscle testing system developed by Goodheart. Applied kinesiology has been defined as a form of diagnosis using muscle testing to examine how a person's body has been conditioned by specific emotional situations; the body provides information about psychological disturbances. The idea behind this approach is that when a person thinks about a trauma, there is a reaction in a specific muscle which strengthens or weakens that muscle. Goodheart also demonstrated that the acupuncture meridians are connected with specific emotions. According to Durlacher, "Dr. Goodheart found that the same muscles associated with the organs were also associated with the corresponding energy organ meridians."[5]

Psychiatrist John Diamond was the first to diagnose psychological and emotional problems by means of the meridian system. Diamond pioneered in applying this technique to his patients and discovered that he could reach the core of emotional problems faster than by using orthodox methods of treatment such as psychoanalysis.

It was the psychologist Roger Callahan, using the work of Goodheart and Diamond, who formulated the final component of Energy Psychology. In the early 1980s Callahan proposed a scientific method for treatment of psychological and physical maladies known as Thought Field Therapy, or the Callahan technique. The underlying principle is that tapping acupuncture points while thinking about an anxiety-producing event can cure anxieties and phobias, as well as other mental and emotional disturbances, in a short time.

This process of treatment can be summarized in the following steps; first, the therapist detects an energy disruption in the body applying the muscle test technique. Then she diagnoses the meridian involved in the disruption and finally, she has the patient tap specific acupuncture points on his body. Using this method, the therapist is able to heal several psychological problems and traumatic events on the spot.

Callahan recounts how he developed this method of healing. In 1980, he was working with a patient named Mary, who had an intense water phobia. As a result of this phobia, she suffered from constant headaches and terrifying migraines. Mary sought help for her maladies with many different therapists for several years without any success. Finally, she came to Callahan, who also initially tried to help her with conventional psychotherapy for a year and a half without much success. One day during a session, as Mary was complaining of a stomachache, Callahan was impelled to tap with his fingertips under Mary's eyes. (In the Chinese healing system, the point under the eye is the end of the stomach meridian.) To his astonishment, after he tapped this point, she exclaimed immediately that her phobia was gone, and she ran to a nearby swimming pool and began throwing water on her face. After that, all her emotional maladies went away, including her fears, headaches, and nightmares. Surprisingly, she was completely freed of her troubles with a treatment that lasted a couple of minutes.

From these experiences Callahan postulated his theory, which actually lies at the core of all methods of energy healing. Recall that in the eighteenth century, Mesmer had already articulated the view that the cause of all illness is a disruption in the energy system of the patient. It appears that Mesmer had anticipated energy psychology. In fact, Mesmer posited that illness was a "disturbance of the harmony which would be present in the human organism; it is a pernicious interruption of the rhythmic tide of ebb and flow of energy."[6] The proponents of energy psychology, probably unaware of Mesmer's ideas, credited only the Chinese method of healing.

After Callahan developed his system of treatment, known as Thought Field Therapy (TFT), many other approaches evolved that are based on the same principles. All these modalities have been subsumed under the category of energy psychology. Other versions have arisen; perhaps the most successful version is the Emotional Freedom Technique (EFT), developed by engineer Gary Craig. Craig describes his therapy as "an emotional version of acupuncture wherein we stimulate certain meridian points by tapping on them with our fingertips."

Other forms include Energy Diagnostic and Treatment Methods (EDxTM), developed by Fred Gallo. David Feinstein, Ph.D., uses the same technique under the name of Energy Psychology. Other innovators adopting Callahan's method have given it different names such as Body Talks, Energy Tapping, Be Set Free Fast (BSFF), and Hypnotapping, the last being a treatment that combines hypnosis with TFT. But the core of the method is the same as the one outlined by Callahan in his works such as *Five Minute Phobia Cure, A Rapid Treatment of Phobias*, and *Psychological Reversal*.

Energy healing seems to validate the metaphysical notion that an electromagnetic energy surrounds the human body. The human body is composed of about fifty trillion cells, and each of these cells is a unit of consciousness, an energy center; therefore the human body is the sum of all these trillions of conscious energy units. The cell's consciousness apparently records all emotional traumas and problems in our lives. When a person confronts a traumatic situation, his or her energy system is disrupted and consequently creates psychological and emotional problems such as post-traumatic stress disorder, phobias, panic attacks, anxieties, and addictions. The individual may not have any memory of these traumatic situations, because remembering all of them would be unbearable for anyone. But from time to time, a cell-thought-memory somehow causes a disruption to the energy system, generating a negative emotion.

Consequently, the approach to emotional and psychological problems has been gradually changing during the last three decades. As recounted in previous pages, the healing approach without medicine began by changing the patient's frame of mind, evolved toward a more behavioral approach, then to cognitive therapies, and finally to the energy psychology model. In the near future, it is likely that the paradigm of psychotherapy will be reformulated and the psychological approach to healing in academia and scientific circles will change.

Energy psychology claims to heal a wide variety of physical and emotional disturbances, including phobias, fears, grief, addictions, physical pain, sexual abuse, guilt, conditions such as asthma and constipation, post-traumatic stress disorder, and most physical illnesses, in a short period of time. On his website Stanford engineer Gary Craig, creator of EFT, has documented the healing of a multitude of ailments, physical and psychological, including different kinds of cancer and long-standing physical illnesses, where medicine has failed. (The reader interested in using this technique, which is quite simple, would do well to visit the EFT website, www.emofree.com.)

Energy psychology therapy has been extended to many other part of human life. It is used for the enhancement of human potential in sports performance, public speaking, weight loss, and many other areas. Its applications seem unlimited.

Stubborn illnesses that do not respond to any method of treatment could be due to a psychological factor that needs to be corrected. The concept of *psychological reversal*, discussed above in the chapter entitled "Suggestion and Autosuggestion," can explain why and how many people unwittingly sabotage their own healing. The theory is that some patients are subconsciously determined to fail and resist any healing processes, even though they may consciously want to regain their health. Callahan explains that psychological reversal is a hindrance to the healing process, and healing will not take place until it is corrected. This psychological impasse can be identified and corrected through examination of the meridian system.

Currently, energy psychology techniques are being used for many psychological disturbances with enormous success, especially in posttraumatic stress disorder (PTSD). The promoters of energy psychology claim that a person can be cured of most physical and psychological disturbances in a relatively short period of time without medicine. The reader interested in verifying these assertions would do well to visit the websites of these healing methods, where they can read and hear live testimonies.

A similar approach to energy psychology is the technique known as Eye Movement Desensitization and Reprocessing (EMDR), developed by Francine Shapiro. This technique is intended to address unresolved disorders resulting from exposure to traumatic or distressing events. This apparently simple technique, which consists of moving the eyes in different directions while thinking about the anxiety producing event, has proved to be very effective. The EMDR website claims success in treating PTSD in combat veterans. This technique is currently receiving acceptance in academic circles, and some therapists consider this method to be equivalent to cognitive behavioral therapy.

The fundamental difference between rational or cognitive behavioral therapies and energy psychology is that the first stresses the mind, reason, and thoughts in its model of treatment while the second emphasizes the body, emotions, and feelings. The first attempts to provide freedom from negative thoughts and the second freedom from negative emotions. Cognitive therapy says that whenever a person has a psychological problem, it is because of disordered thinking. Thinking is the problem; consequently it should be the target of treatment. If it is corrected, the problem will fade away. On the other hand, energy psychology says that the cause of negative emotions is a disruption in the body's energy system. Correcting the disruption of the energy will eliminate the emotional disturbances. We can see that these two models are complementary. Thoughts and emotions are inseparable, and both involve psychic energy. Therefore the combined application of these approaches according to the needs of specific cases could result in a comprehensive healing system.

Energy psychology promises to become one of the leading methods of healing in America and throughout the world. These healing modalities will gradually supplant psychoanalysis and traditional psychotherapies as models of treatment. The advantage of energy psychology is that it can be self-administered. Ordinary people can learn to treat themselves for their traumas, fears, anxieties, etc. According to psychologist Fred Gallo, the future of healing will be prevention and self-healing.[7] People will be able to resolve their own psychological disturbances with beneficial impact on their physical health and social environment.

In this sense, energy psychology provides a perfect paradigm for self-help and self-healing in the Age of Aquarius (Water-Carrier). It is an easy and straightforward formula for getting well just by tapping specific meridian-points of the body. It is a therapy that is affordable, is not invasive, does not need a second party, and has no negative secondary effects.

One of the latest modalities of healing without medicine is Therapeutic Touch (TT), which was developed by Dora Kunz and Dolores Krieger at Pumpkin Hollow Retreat Center in Craryville, New York. This modality also falls into the category of energy healing, as it is based on the principle that human beings consist of energy fields. Reportedly, the treatment enhances healing and promotes the flow of subtle energies. It is gradually being accepted in the medical field to alleviate minor illnesses.

One common denominator of all these modern therapeutic modalities, including New Thought, cognitive psychology, energy psychology, and Therapeutic Touch, is that they all have been developed in America.

Chapter 28

Faith Healing and Fake Healers

Many false prophets will appear and
deceive many people.
—Matthew 24:11, NIV

Much has written about faith healing. (For further discussion, see the chapter "All Is Faith or Fear" in my book *Beyond Conventional Wisdom*.) Throughout history, many faith healings have been recorded, mostly in religious contexts. The Bible recounts remarkable healings performed by Jesus Christ, and Christ is said to have endowed his disciples with the faculty of healing and commanded them to go into the world, heal the sick, and alleviate human suffering.

The natural law of life is *belief*; thus faith healing can do wonders as long as the patient firmly believes in the operator as an agent for the healing. Jesus Christ regarded faith as indispensable for his healing. He said such things as "It will be done to you as you believe," "according to your belief it is done unto you," and so on. When the sixteenth-century physician Paracelsus asserts, "Whether the object of your faith be real or false, you will nevertheless obtain the same results," he is aptly ascribing the healing power to the believer and no one else. Unwavering faith is the most potent agent for triggering the healing process of the subconscious mind.

New Thought proponents recommend the use of scientific prayer as a means of reinforcing the healing treatment. Regular prayer is the reiteration of our deepest desire endorsed by a firm belief. Thus the key to effective prayer is to imbue the subconscious mind with the image of the desired outcome. Prayer and faith go together. The ancient occult injunction "Inflame thyself with prayer" is the secret to bringing a person in harmonious attunement with his or her subconscious mind.

Joseph Murphy believed that healing is the result of a harmonious relationship between the conscious and the subconscious minds. He described faith healing as follows:

> A faith healer is one who heals without any real scientific understanding of the powers and forces involved. He or she may claim a special gift of healing, and the sick person's blind belief in him or her or in his or her powers may bring results.
>
> In many parts of the world, traditional healers treat their patients by dances, incantations, and invocations of spirits. A person may be healed by touching the relics of a saint, wearing special ritual garb, lighting a holy incense stick or a candle, or drinking a mixture of brewed herbs. Anything that leads the patient to honestly believe in the method or process will make a healing more likely.
>
> Any method that causes you to move from fear and worry to faith and expectancy will heal.[1]

In the healing arena, the practitioner's role is to stimulate the sick person's subconscious mind to generate recuperation. If the patient believes in the healer and has strong expectations of his or her own recovery, the healing will manifest accordingly. Faith is a powerful device for activating the imagination and impressing images on the subconscious mind. They work by instilling a powerful autosuggestion toward regaining health. Of course, neither the patient nor the practitioner will be able to understand exactly how the cure occurs, because it is accomplished through the silent work of the subconscious.

Some people need a psychological crutch, an "external agent," such as the picture of a saint, a totem, or a relic. They need these because deep inside, they feel powerless and unable to regain their health by themselves. But these things serve only to arouse their own capacities for inner healing. Again, the truth is that people cure themselves through their own beliefs and faith.

Nevertheless, a healthy skepticism is always necessary, especially in our modern society, where charlatans, quacks, and false prophets abound. They claim to have special occult powers or to have been entrusted by the divine source with exclusive faculties for healing. But this is wrong: in the ultimate analysis, every healing is self-healing. Metaphysical knowledge is reached only through systematic examination of evidence and rigorous tests. Using a process similar to that of "Cartesian doubt," one should question any spiritual revelation, healing by divine powers, or practitioners who pretend to have spiritual powers. Methodic doubt and healthy skepticism are tools of scientific and spiritual discernment.

In the late part of the twentieth century, the stage magician James Randi came forward as the merciless debunker of all false faith healers. At age sixty, after his retirement as a stage conjurer, Randi began devoting his time and effort to investigating and unmasking false faith healers as well as paranormal and supernatural practitioners. As a conjurer, Randi knows the techniques of stage magic, so he is adept at unmasking fakes.

Randi has gone so far as to found an organization named the James Randi Educational Foundation (JREF), which offers a prize of one million dollars (the "One Million Dollar Paranormal Challenge") to anyone who can demonstrate evidence of healing faculties or paranormal, supernatural, or occult powers, under test conditions agreed to by both parties. Nobody yet has managed to claim this prize.[2] He has also challenged renowned psychics who have written books on the paranormal, including Uri Geller. Randi has repeatedly accused Geller of trying to pass off magical tricks as displays of paranormal ability. Randi has also published books about the false claims of charlatans, prophets, diviners, and visionaries such as Nostradamus throughout history.

In his book *The Faith Healers*, Randi unmercifully unmasks evangelists who do public demonstrations of healing on TV and in church settings. One of Randi's victims was the evangelical minister

Peter Popoff. Randi found that Popoff used an earpiece to receive information from his confederates about attendees who asked for healing. Popoff made people believe that this personal information had been revealed to him by the Holy Spirit, when in reality it had been given by his associates over the earpiece. Randi has also criticized other well-known faith healers, such as Pat Robertson, V. A. Grant, and Oral Roberts, among others. Nevertheless, Randi believes that faith healing might actually work on occasion because of the placebo effect.[3]

In passing we can note the claims of false prophets such as evangelical ministers Ronald Weinland and Harold Camping, who claimed to be biblically inspired and predicted, with absolute certainty, the end of the world in 2012. Apparently the purpose of false healers and prophets is to gain power and control.

The fact that these figures have appeared does not mean that religion per se is wrong. The senior editor of the magazine *ODE*, Tijn Touber, has written an article that can shed some light on this impasse. In his article "How I Lost Faith: How the End of Religion Can Be the Beginning of God,"[4] Touber relates how he came to realize that most of the time, supposed intermediaries distort and obstruct the direct connection between God and human beings. This criticism seems applicable to many forms of organized religion led by fundamentalists and orthodox clergy.

Sometimes even highly educated people believe in evangelical healings. For instance, New Thought minister Jack E. Addington is the author of a number of books, including an interesting and well-written work entitled *The Secret of Healing*. Addington attended healing meetings given by the evangelist Kathryn Kuhlman. When he was asked if he believed in her public performances, he wrote:

> Do I believe that healing takes place at Miss Kuhlman's meeting? I was there. I saw it with my own eyes. I heard it with my own ears. Yes, I believe that many were healed.

I used to watch Oral Roberts conduct his televised tent meetings. To me, the healings were most convincing. I consider Oral Roberts a man of deep conviction and strong faith.

Addington knows better than that. In previous pages of the same book, he states that the "omnipotent Power," and not any personality, is the source of the healing. He goes on to ask, "What part do Oral Roberts and Kathryn Kuhlman play in the healing?"[5] He does not answer.

Chapter 29

The Power of the Mind to Heal

The role of a healer is to assist the
patient to heal himself or herself.
—Albert Amao

The major premise of this book has been that mind has power over matter. The corollary is that people have the capacity to heal themselves. These principles have been corroborated by recent revolutionary discoveries made in epigenetics (new biology), neuroplasticity (brain plasticity), and psychoneuroimmunology (PNI). These findings are confirming the power of thought over the wiring and functioning of our brains and over DNA and genes. In other words, the power of the mind over the body is being conclusively demonstrated by science. These discoveries are fulfilling the dreams of the medieval alchemists and magicians, who wanted to prolong the human life span and help the body regenerate itself.

Modern investigations into the nervous system have led to the belief that injured brains have the power to heal themselves. Dr. Daniel G. Amen's book *Change Your Brain and Change Your Life* and Dr. Norman Doidge's *The Brain That Changes Itself* have been pioneering works in this endeavor. Regarding Doidge's book, *The New York Times* commented, "The power of positive thinking finally gains scientific credibility."

Nevertheless, it is not the brain that changes by itself or heals itself, as the titles of these books suggest; it is the *thought* or *consciousness* that heals and changes the brain. The brain is an organ of the body that is subject to thought or consciousness. The *brain is the epiphenomenon of consciousness;* it is the *result* of the mind. The universal life force, or consciousness, creates the means—in this case the brain—to apprehend reality and express itself in the physical world. Indeed, according to the philosophies of the occidental Qabalah and the oriental Vedanta, the only thing that exists is this Universal Consciousness.

Even so, these findings indicate that the scientific world and academia have made great strides in acknowledging the influence of the mind and thoughts over the physical body. The most significant breakthrough in modern times is the realization that our thoughts can change the structure and functions of our brains *even into old age.* Is this not amazing? This is one indication that individuals may be able to reinvent themselves through their minds in this coming Age of Aquarius.

The old paradigm of healing is inexorably changing from the idea that thought and consciousness are products of the brain to the realization that consciousness shapes and rewires the physical brain to meet its own needs. Hence consciousness creates the physical means to express itself. The brain can reorganize itself according to its needs by forming new neural connections throughout life. Neuroplasticity also demonstrates that the neurons (nerve cells) in the brain rewire themselves in cases of injury and disease. They also adjust their activities in response to new situations, changes in the environment, or new learning experiences.

The idea that thought and consciousness change the structure and functioning of the brain is indeed a revolutionary concept in the scientific paradigm. A few decades ago, scientists considered some parts of the brain to be fixed and immutable once adulthood was reached. They also deemed most cases of brain damage to be incurable. But neuroplasticity is demonstrating that the brain continues reshaping itself and new neurons are continually born even in advanced adulthood. The brain is not, as was previously thought, a type of fixed hardware. Rather it keeps changing itself in response to the quality of thoughts, mental activity, and social environment. Thus thinking and learning—that is, keeping this wonderful organ active—are essential for maintaining its vitality. The old adage holds: "If you don't use it, you lose it." This scientific understanding offers new hope for those born with mental limitations, learning disabilities, and brain damage. In *The Brain That Changes Itself*, Doidge recounts stories of people whose conditions were diagnosed as hopeless but who recovered through the power of thought.[1]

Amen, a neuropsychiatrist and clinical neuroscientist, goes further, embracing the idea that by changing the brain, one can change one's life and destiny. In his book he presents scientific evidence that anxiety, depression, anger, and obsession are related to the way specific structures in our brains work; he suggests that it is possible for an individual to modify his or her brain structure.[2] This is a breakthrough concept that shatters the old deterministic beliefs regarding the brain's limitations. Scientific investigations are demonstrating that imagination produces changes in the structure of the brain, as does mental rehearsal. That is, an individual who in his imagination consistently practices tossing a basketball into the basket develops the same brain circuits as someone who physically practices tossing the ball. This confirms that a human being is a *bio-psychic-energy system*. Science is now saying that thoughts generate electrochemical discharges in the brain, and feelings and emotions release chemicals in the body. This could explain how by exchanging a negative mind-set for a positive one, an individual can regain health.

Human beings are surrounded by an energy field, which is in essence electromagnetic. This consists of thoughts (which can be seen as electrical) and feelings (which can be seen as magnetic). The ancient metaphysical teaching was that thoughts are electrical energy, and now neurologists are saying that "thoughts fire the wires of the brain," thus confirming the ancient notion.

The Ageless Wisdom teaches that the life force is a flow of energy permeating the entire universe. It exists in a formless state of possibilities until it is shaped by consciousness. Consciousness captures this fluid and converts it into thoughts and emotions. These thought-forms are in turn the blueprints for manifesting the emotional energy in physical reality. Therefore *consciousness transforms the universal life force into mental forms, and emotional energy will tend to crystallize them into a potential reality.* Thus the free flow of the universal energy is channeled into a mental structure (thought-form) by consciousness.

These statements are in accord with modern quantum physics, which says that concentrated thought shapes quantum energy. Without the focus of attention, the quanta are only "quantum potential." When something is observed, the quanta come together to form subatomic particles, then atoms, then molecules, until they finally manifest in the physical realm in accordance with the thought-form of the observer. Furthermore, quantum mechanics says that atoms are made from spinning immaterial energy vortices; consequently the physical universe is indeed immaterial.[3] In addition, *external circumstances are susceptible to being changed by the observer.* Using this postulate, Wayne Dyer asserts, "If you change the way you look at things, the things you look at change."[4] Everything resides in the individual's attitude, and each person experiences a unique reality, different from that of anyone else.

In biology, Dr. Francis Collins, director of the Human Genome Project, and Dr. Bruce Lipton, a former medical professor and research biologist, contend that the environment and the mind play an important role in changing the structure of DNA, which is the code of life. Previously, biology had asserted that genes determine the structure of the physical body as well as predispositions to certain illnesses. Mental and physical limitations were regarded as hereditary: an individual could do nothing about them. In other words, the genetic code was seen as immutable and predetermining the fate of the physical body. This idea, as Lipton observes, "is ingrained in the biological sciences as a consensual truth, a belief by which we frame our reference for health and disease."[5]

The new paradigm is that one's beliefs and perception of the environment have a powerful influence on genes and on the organization of the DNA; therefore an individual can modify adverse predispositions. This statement is confirmed by the new discipline known as noetic biology, of which Lipton is a prominent representative. He has written:

It is now recognized that the environment, and more specifically, our perception (interpretation) of the environment, directly controls the activity of our genes. Environment controls gene activity through a process known as epigenetic control.[6]

In another scientific article, Lipton emphasizes the influence of the environment and human perception over genetic conditions.

We perceived that the action of genes and neurochemicals, the hardware of the central nervous system, were responsible for the behaviors and our dysfunctions. The foundation of quantum mechanics, vibrational chemistry, and epigenetic control mechanisms, however, provide for a profound new understanding of psychology. The environment along with the perceptions of the mind controls behavior and the genetics of biology.[7]

Hence the new understanding in biology is that the mind and environment influence DNA. Lipton indicates that the new discipline called epigenetics explains cases of spontaneous recovery from serious injuries or disabilities.[8] Epigenetics is the study of changes in gene expression that take place apart from changes in the underlying DNA sequence. Under certain circumstances, these changes can be inherited. This fact gives scientific validation to the metaphysical statement that led Myrtle Fillmore to her healing from a long-standing disease: "I am a child of God, and I do not inherit sickness." This will be the mantra of the future. Individuals should hold steadfast to this affirmation until it becomes ingrained. The idea is to change our minds by changing our habitual thoughts and feelings, and our brains will be rewired accordingly.

However—and there is always a *however*—we should not fall into a sightless optimism and deny human limitations. In this world, we are bound by universal physical laws; they are inexorable whether we believe in them or not. For instance, the law of gravity and the law of cycles in nature will make themselves felt no matter how spiritual a person may be. The power of the human mind cannot override these universal laws. The same holds true for the law of aging. One can extend the span of life, enhance the human body for optimum efficiency, and live free of sickness and misery, but in the long run, the unstoppable law of aging will be manifested in our physical bodies.

Moreover, since the brain has a dual structure, there are two basic ways of apprehending reality: one is symbolic, and the other is analytical. This division corresponds to the right and left hemispheres of the brain respectively; each has its specific function and processes information in a different way. The left hemisphere is verbal and analytical, while the right side is symbolic and global. Individuals tend to process information using their dominant hemispheres. This limits human potential. The learning and thinking processes are enhanced when the less dominant hemisphere of the brain is strengthened and both sides of the brain participate in a balanced manner.

The power of the mind is extraordinary. One example will illustrate this statement. Two men who exerted a profound influence on the lives of millions were Phineas P. Quimby and José Silva (1914–99). The first, as we have seen, was the discoverer of mind healing and the father of New Thought; the second was the founder of the renowned Silva Method, a technique to optimize the use of the mind that is taught throughout America and abroad. The two men have similarities in their upbringing. They were born into modest families. Quimby had little formal education, while Silva had none. Quimby had to work from the time he was very young; Silva started working since he was six years old, shining shoes and selling newspapers to help his impoverished family. From early life, both showed inventiveness and creativity. Without formal education, they excelled in their particular fields. Moreover, these two great men never lost the ability to use the right side of their brains. This is apparent from the fact that they retained their creativity and inventiveness, which are attributes of the right side of the brain. They actively maintained the capacities of their symbolic, nonverbal, and metaphorical right brains, where mental power and creativity are virtually unlimited.

Chapter 30

Spiritual Mind Healing

All things are possible to him who believes.
— Mark 9:23 (New King James Version)

In this book, I have used the terms *mental healing, mind healing*, and *spiritual mind healing* interchangeably. However, there are slight differences among these terms. For instance, *mental healing* can be regarded as the exertion of mental force or transmission of personal energy. Mesmer thought he performed his healings by means of his magnetic personality and by transmitting a universal fluid energy to the sick. In this case, the healer believes he is performing the healing by means of his imposing personality and mental power; he also considers the patient a separate human being. In the case of *mind healing*, the practitioner attempts to instill healing suggestions in the mind of the individual. This approach uses the methods known as the *suggestive therapies*. Finally, *spiritual mind healing* regards the sick person as a spiritual entity endowed with a perfect divine spark that is encased by a physical "shell" that has become ill. Spiritual mind healing has lifelong effects. It empowers the individual and awakens his or her inner resources so that healing can take place.

In psychological terms, changing the mind implies persuading the individual to replace negative beliefs and ideas with positive ones. According to metaphysics, in order for something to be expressed in the physical realm, it first has to be formulated in the mind. That is, all causation is mental. Spiritual mind healing takes place when we acknowledge that behind the personal mask, behind the physical being, there is a spiritual being, which is always whole and perfect. The Inner Self and the mind have to be in agreement in order for the healing to take place in the physical realm. Recognition of this fact dispels the notion that one is bonded to physical causation.

Spiritual mind healing often involves the use of prayer, which New Thought adherents call *scientific prayer* or *spiritual mind treatment*. Scientific prayer is completely different from what is usually understood as prayer. Conventional wisdom regards prayer as supplication or requesting the intercession of a Higher Power to solve our problems or grant our wishes. In New Thought, the act of praying is a way of reminding the individual that she has the inner means to resolve her situation and obtain her goals as long as they are in accordance with spiritual laws. In the case of healing, the purpose of prayer is to redirect the focus of the mind to images of wellness rather than illness. Addington defines scientific prayer or spiritual mind treatment based on the Science of Mind philosophy:

> It is an individual thought process whereby man's thinking is directed away from the need or problem and put in direct alignment with the Divine Mind, thereby enabling him to express his highest good. Spiritual mind treatment, whether for the self or another, is a clarification of the mind so that the divine perfect action of Universal Mind Power can come through.[1]

As we grow in our understanding of the true nature of reality, the distinction between energy healing and spiritual mind healing is being bridged. The lines of distinction between spirituality and science are also disappearing, because science is demonstrating that there is no difference between what is called solid matter and what is called psychic energy. Scientists from around the globe are currently beginning to acknowledge the interconnectedness and oneness of the whole universe.

According to metaphysics, outward appearances are merely disguises of the One Spirit. The physical world is the manifestation of the spiritual realm. Our bodies respond not only to the way we think, feel, and act, but also to the social and physical environment of which we are a part. Human beings are not isolated islands; they are interconnected in a universal web. Thus our attitudes and patterns of thinking influence our families and associates and also have a ripple effect on the social environment. Every choice we make affects not only the future of our lives but that of others as well.

Spiritual mind healing has been sometimes thought to be limited to curing emotional and psychosomatic disorders caused primarily by stress and anxiety. It also used to be believed that psychosomatic disease existed only in the mind of the patient. However, modern medical science regards psychosomatic illness as real. The University of Michigan Health System has defined psychosomatic illness as "a disorder that involves both mind and body." In other words, the illness may be emotional or mental in origin, but it has physical symptoms. Psychosomatic illnesses are not imaginary; they are physical disorders in which both emotions *and* thought patterns play a fundamental role. These illnesses usually develop when the person's disease-fighting ability—that is, the immune system—has been weakened by anxiety and stress.[2]

The New Thought concept of healing is based on the idea that the causes of an illness are thoughts and emotions. These causes are invisible and cannot be seen by the physical senses, but we do perceive the manifestations. Conventional medicine views the situation in exactly the opposite way, regarding the effect (the external conditions—in this case, the illness) as the cause. Thus their efforts are directed to eliminating the result, not the cause. The solution is to reverse this paradigm, seeing thoughts and emotions as the source of illness. The mind affects the physical body and its circumstances according to the individual's belief system. This in turn produces chemical changes which, over time, are manifested in the body as an illness.

Thoughts and emotions are invisible. To cure is to detect and eradicate those causes that are creating the trouble. The findings of current medicine and biology are offering evidence to support the notion that our minds can really promote healing and recovery. Along these lines are the investigations performed by Drs. Bruce Lipton, Francis Collins, Jeanne Achterberg, Daniel Amen, and Norman Doidge, among other leading scientists. Their investigations are showing how focused thoughts and intentions affect our bodies for better or for worse. They overwhelmingly substantiate the power of positive thought and intention in the recovery of health.

Contemporary New Thought holds that positive thinking and good intention can be a sound course of treatment as complementary components to healing. Since the boom of the New Age in the 1960s, techniques of holistic healing such as guided imagery, relaxation, positive thinking, and releasing of negative emotions have been considered alternative means of reducing stress and anxiety and promoting physical and mental health. Achterberg offers convincing evidence that certain guided techniques can harness the power of the mind to maintain physical and emotional fitness. Furthermore, modern mainstream medicine is now using healing techniques such as guided imagery, prayer, meditation, intention, positive thinking, and Therapeutic Touch as complementary modalities.

These ideas are based on the metaphysical principle that the entire universe and everything in it are the manifestation of One Mind (Universal Consciousness), which is the First Cause. This Infinite Mind is a conscious, intelligent energy, also called life force energy or *spiritus*. Paul Foster Case has stated that this Infinite Consciousness creates human beings as a means of experiencing the physical world. According to him, the universe is in a perpetual state of expansion and evolution. Although we are "individuations" of the universal life source, we are part of it. There is no real separateness in the universe; everything is one.

Scientific tools for apprehending reality are constantly evolving. A scientific theory that today is seen as unshakable truth may in the near future be proven wrong, as happened to the geocentric theory and many other theories that in time became obsolete as new discoveries were made. Since the time of Thomson Jay Hudson and Thomas Troward, science has made extraordinary strides, some of which corroborate metaphysical principles. For instance, quantum physics questions the existence of a physical reality as conventional wisdom understands it. Indeed there are some scientists who hold the viewpoint that the universe is immaterial, that is, mental.[3] This theory confirms an ancient postulate of the Hermetic philosophy known as the principle of Mentalism.[4] The Hermetic Qabalah asserts that the universe is pure consciousness. When Albert Einstein revealed his theory of relativity to the scientific world and demonstrated that matter is only condensed energy, he was also confirming the occult idea that everything in the universe is thought energy, and this energy is in a perpetual state of vibration. This was a long-established concept in the Hermetic doctrine—that everything in the universe is mental substance. We live in the mind of God, not outside it. As the evangelist Paul put it, "For in him we live, and move, and have our being" (Acts 17:28; King James Version).

Jesus Christ, the first faith healer of whom we have an account in the Western world, commanded his apostles to heal the sick in order to alleviate suffering. This task was taken as a primary obligation by the Rosicrucian order. Its manifesto, the *Fama fraternitatis*, describes the mission of its members. Their first agreement was "that none of them should profess any other thing than to cure the sick, and that gratis."

This is the hallmark of real and authentic spiritual healers: they do not seek recognition or publicity and do not undertake this profession seeking to amass money, prestige, or power. Their labor is silent and humble. They do not need to boast about their accomplishments; their only goal is to alleviate suffering. True spiritual healers never advertise themselves, because, strictly speaking, the only real healer is the Christ who dwells in each individual. One cannot practice healing to accumulate money, because as soon as a person uses this art for business purposes, he will lose his healing abilities. In fact, the Rosicrucian order commanded its members to hold a different profession as a means of earning a living. In modern times, this might seem difficult, but the truth is that true Rosicrucians work for the welfare of humanity without expecting recognition or material compensation.

In the past, this kind of healing was considered by scientific and academic circles to be magic, superstition, a nonsensical fallacy for quack practitioners.[5] When Quimby began his healing work, "educated" individuals of the time called him an impostor, a charlatan, and a "snake oil" salesman. This last epithet is interesting, because in the past, charlatans used to give public demonstrations selling snake oil as the panacea, the universal medicine for all maladies. Ironically, spiritual mind healing has been proven to be the "magical potion" to cure maladies where conventional medicine sometimes fails. That is why the idea of curing disease without medicine is being gradually endorsed and accepted by increasing segments of the educated public.

Scientific discoveries are enabling us to reject limiting beliefs about human potential. For instance, new advances are gradually disproving the old assertion that genes determine the life of an individual. The new biology tells us that cells are controlled by thoughts and the physical environment, not by genes. This new understanding of biology, expressed by Dr. Bruce Lipton, is refreshing:

> Scientists who follow Darwin continue to make the same error. The problem with this underemphasis on the environment is that it led to an overemphasis on "nature" in the form of genetic determinism—the belief that genes "control" biology.[6]

The healing paradigm of the future is a psychospiritual one. It regards human beings as having three aspects: biological, mental, and spiritual. This in turn implies an integral healing of the human being, not only the body but the emotional and spiritual dimensions as well.

As spiritual beings, we need the physical instrument, the body, to manipulate physical reality. The interactions between the spiritual and the physical realms generate emotional responses. Problems arise when we give power to the external world (sensory reality), thereby allowing negative thoughts to intrude into our minds. Spiritual mind treatment enables us to regain our power in order to counteract the effects of harmful agents (illnesses) and eventually eliminate them.

The major factor hindering the effectiveness of spiritual mind healing is the failure to understand that we are surrounded by the infinite life force, which is available to everyone, and the idea that we do not have any power over apparently solid physical reality. Actually the reverse is true. As we have seen, the theories of relativity and quantum mechanics have revealed that physical objects do not have the solidity that our senses lead us to believe. Science says that the apparent density of solid physical objects is shaped by tiny electromagnetic elements, which are in a state of fluidity and constant vibration. Indeed Hermetic philosophy (for example, in the work known as *The Kybalion*) and quantum mechanics affirm the same thing. Both hold that *there is no difference between the energy which takes form as thought and that which takes form as physical matter.* Therefore the mind exerts influence, knowingly or unknowingly, for good or for ill, over the corporeal body.

Contemporary physics has also given us a completely new concept of the nature of reality by saying that matter is eternally creating itself, apparently out of nothing. From this emptiness, photons unexpectedly appear and disappear. From this "nothing" an atom is formed, and then the molecule, and finally the structure of apparently solid matter. In other words, consciousness is continuously creating atoms out of nothing. This means that the universe is in a constant course of self-creation, and everything in the universe is in a continuous process of self-development. Along the same lines, Qabalistic philosophy says that the Universal Mind is continuously expressing itself in myriad forms in the physical dimension. Thus the teachings of Hermetic philosophy, esotericism, and Qabalah are in perfect agreement with the latest scientific theories of how the universe comes into being. All physical manifestation is ultimately the result of light vibrating and manifesting as energy, and this vibrating light can be controlled by mental means.

Epilogue

Know yourself and you will know that you are the son of God.
                                                    —Albert Amao

We have undertaken a long journey exploring the history and rationale of mental and spiritual healing. The common denominator of these approaches is that all of them have the purpose of changing the mind, impressing a healing suggestion, and correcting the flow of the life force through the person. Healing suggestions can be delivered in multiple modalities and will work for different people according to their personal makeup. The crux of the matter is that the sick person must regain his or her inner power as a spiritual being and take charge of his or her mental and physical wellness.

There are three fundamental premises in metaphysical and esoteric philosophy: first, the universe is one; second, the universe and everything within it are interconnected; and third, everything is a manifestation of a supreme Mind or Consciousness. This Universal Consciousness is manifested as energy that pervades the entire universe and is known as life force, *ruach* in Hebrew, *pneuma* in Greek, or *spiritus* in Latin. According to metaphysical philosophy, there is no separateness; everything is part of the One Identity. In Vedic philosophy this is known as *satchitananda*, the Universal Mind that is omniscient, omnipresent, and omnipotent and dwells in a blissful state. The entire universe is in a perpetual state of expansion, evolution, and becoming. As human beings, we are individual manifestations of the Universal Source.

Conventional wisdom of the past held that man was bound by several limitations that were imposed on him in a fatalistic fashion. For instance, people believed in astrological determinism, whereby destiny is ruled by faraway stars and not much can be done about it. Religious determinism held that a man's life and his destiny are dictated by a faraway God, and human suffering is due to the "original sin" committed by Adam and Eve. The economic determinism of Karl Marx and Friedrich Engels holds that the economic structure of a society determines the nature of all other aspects of life; that is, individuals' lives are determined by their position in the mode of production and their relationship with social classes in a capitalist society. Psychological determinism, exemplified by Freud's psychoanalytic theory, states that human behavior and mental health are dictated by repressed desires and sexual drives. Freud also held the fatalistic view that we are bound to the Oedipus complex. Biological or genetic determinism embraced the viewpoint that the human body and behavior are determined by genetic and hereditary information contained in DNA.

Given the tremendous strides science and technology have been making recently, it has become clear that all these deterministic theories have flawed foundations. But they will influence us as long as we believe in them. The greatest gift that God has given to humanity is free will. This free will can be exerted according to our level of conscious awareness and discernment. We have to be aware that we possess the power of self-determination and self-mastery. Only then are we able to shape our destiny as we wish.

The Gospel of the Age of Aquarius is one of the brotherhood of humanity and of universal enlightenment.[1] The deterministic theories that have been predominant in past centuries are falling apart to give room to new, holistic paradigms. Quantum physics is now confirming the teachings of the Ageless Wisdom that we are the cocreators of our lives and destinies. Epigenetics is showing the error of genetic determinism. Neuroplasticity of the brain and discoveries in genetic engineering will allow human beings to reinvent themselves.

Gradually, the problem of human relationships characterized by the dichotomy of dominion and submission will disappear. Historically, in human relations, someone plays the role of leader and another plays the role of follower; sometimes this scheme is not obvious because the control is very subtle, and the parties do not realize it. The same thing happens in social groups. Sociological theories have demonstrated that the development of humanity has been characterized by the struggle for power and control. This struggle is clearly manifested in all kinds of social organizations, such as religious, political, and economic groups. Some use religion, politics, or economics as a way to subjugate and take advantage of other people.

Hunger for power is due to the fact that inside humans, there is a deep-rooted fear of loneliness and sense of inferiority, of which they are not aware. Psychologist Alfred Adler held that the origin of neurosis was man's sense of inferiority. This destructive feeling is the driving force behind our destiny. Some seek major achievements in life as a way to compensate for this sense of inadequacy. In other cases, this deep-rooted subconscious fear compels people to gain power over others through many different means. Conventional wisdom, religious organizations, and political groups in our society have instilled this fear through education and mass media, making people believe they are powerless and therefore need leaders or organizations to think and make decisions for them.

As a result we have lost our inner power of self-determination. Consequently, we ordinarily act from a place of fear rather than from a place of love and security. Since our childhoods, we have been programmed to be followers; we usually seek something or somebody on whom to rely. Here the concept of self-reliance propounded by Ralph Waldo Emerson is extremely important.

No matter what the theory or treatment method is, the principle is always the same. By means of words, actions, or other devices, the healer conveys a suggestion to the patient, changing his mind from a *place of fear* to a *place of empowerment*. Thus she makes the sick person expect the healing, and the image of health is impressed into the subconscious. As a consequence, the body's natural capacity for healing is activated. The cases of suggestive healing and spontaneous remission have been confirmed by the cures in sacred shrines and old churches, such as the ones that took place at the grotto of the Virgin of Lourdes. They can also be the result of collective suggestion and autosuggestion, like the healings that occur at evangelical camp meetings.

Jesus Christ taught that the Father that is within Jesus is the father that is within you (John 14:9-11; 17:21). He showed us the way, the direction where to go, but we are the ones who have to walk the path of return. For this reason, honest spiritual leaders such as Jiddu Krishnamurti consistently rejected any "personality worship" and encouraged their followers to think and act independently and search for the truth on their own. Krishnamurti said, "Truth is a pathless land," implying that there is no royal road to reach union with the One.

René Descartes's famous statement *Cogito ergo sum*, the cornerstone of Western metaphysics, is commonly misunderstood. It is translated as "I think, therefore I am." My understanding of this statement is that Descartes is referring to the act of thought or consciousness as an expression of the "I Am." "I Am" is a form of the verb "to be," which is synonymous with existence.

Interestingly enough, we find the same intimation in the names of God given to Moses in the Bible. The first name was "*Ehyeh asher ehyeh*" ("I am who I am")—again a form of the verb "to be." The second name was the Tetragrammaton or Yod-Heh-Vav-Heh, wrongly rendered in some translations of the Bible as "Yahweh" or "Jehovah." Authoritative interpretations of the Tetragrammaton are "That which was, is, and shall be" or "I will be what I will be"—again, forms of the verb "to be."[2]

Finally, John the evangelist expressed a similar idea when he solemnly opened his gospel with "In the beginning was the Verb." The translation from the Greek into Latin is "*In principio erat verbum et verbum erat apud Deum et Deus erat verbum*." (John 1:1, Latin Vulgate). The *verbum* (from which we get our word "verb") represents God (that is, Consciousness): the "Verb" is the universal Consciousness. (Rabbi David A. Copper encapsulates this idea in his book entitled *God Is a Verb*.) Hermetic Qabalah holds that in the beginning was the "Thought." Stated in other words, the Verb (God or Consciousness) in the beginning was expressed in a *thought*, which in turn manifested in a sound (thought in vibration), and the sound in turn is the beginning of creation. This expresses the true relation to which Descartes alluded—thought is the consequence of being—and that is why in Hindu philosophy it is said that the universe is maintained by the sacred sound "AUM."

An ancient occult proverb states, "Restore the king to his throne." This statement is nicely complemented by the well-known biblical verse "Behold, the kingdom of God is within you" (Luke 17:21, King James Version). The practical application of these statements is the essence of spiritual mind healing: it is the acknowledgement of the Inner Self in every human being, which is similar to Jesus Christ's concept of the "kingdom within." It is also known as the Inner Consciousness. In that kingdom dwells the Inner Christ (or Consciousness), that is, the King who creates his "personal universe" according to his needs for further unfoldment. We live in our own creation according to the laws and regulations that we ourselves have instituted. The problem comes when we ascribe power to the external manifestation of our creation that we call physical reality.

In fact, we have been indoctrinated since early childhood with the materialistic belief that physical sensation is the only reality. But as Paul Foster Case has stated, we become devil worshippers when we give power to externals and to material causation.[3] The solution to this impasse was provided by the great metaphysician Jesus Christ when he said "the kingdom of heaven is within you." And the King is the Christ within you.

Notes

Introduction

1. Micki McGee, *Self-Help, Inc.: Makeover Culture in American Life* (New York: Oxford University Press, 2005), 11.

2. Marco R. della Cava, "The Secret History of *The Secret*," *USA Today*, March 29, 2006; usatoday30.usatoday.com/life/books/news/2007-03-28-the-secret-churches_N.htm.

3. Albert Amao, *Beyond Conventional Wisdom* (Bloomington, IN: AuthorHouse, 2006).

4. James Allen, *As a Man Thinketh* (New York: Barnes & Noble, 1992), 10.

Chapter 1. Franz Anton Mesmer: The Father of Mesmerism

1. "Franz Anton Mesmer," http://www.anton-mesmer.com/index.htm.

2. "Great Theosophists: Anton [*sic*] Mesmer," *Theosophy* 26:10 (August 1938), 434–40, http://www.wisdomworld.org/setting/mesmer.html.

3. Stefan Zweig, *Mental Healers* (New York: Ungar, 1932), 31.

4. "Franz Anton Mesmer," http://www.knowledgerush.com/kr/encyclopedia/Franz_Anton_Mesmer/.

Chapter 2. The Metaphysical Phenomenon of New England

1. "New Thought: What It Is and How It Can Help YOU!", Calgary New Thought Centre, http://cornerstone.wwwhubs.com/history2.htm.

2. Ibid.

Chapter 3. Phineas Parkhurst Quimby: The Father of New Thought

Epigraph: Quoted in Julius W. Dresser, *The True History of Mental Science*, Boston: Alfred Mudge, 1887, 27.

1. Willa Cather and Georgine Milmine, *The Life of Mary Baker G. Eddy and the History of Christian Science* (Lincoln: University of Nebraska Press, 1993 [1909]), 45.

2. Horatio W. Dresser, ed., *The Quimby Manuscripts, Showing the Discovery of Spiritual Healing and the Origin of Christian Science* (New York: Thomas Crowell, 1921), 28.

3. "Mercury(I) Chloride"; http://en.wikipedia.org/wiki/Mercury%28I%29 _chloride. See also "Heavy Metal Medicine" at http://pubs.acs.org/subscribe /journals/tcaw/10/i01/html/01chemch.html.

4. Horatio W. Dresser, ed., *Quimby Manuscripts*, 28.

5. See Annetta G. Dresser, *The Philosophy of P. P. Quimby* (Boston: Builders Press, 1895), http://jadresser.wwwhubs.com/quimby1.htm.; and Horatio W. Dresser, *A History of the New Thought Movement* (New York: Thomas Crowell, 1919).

6. Horatio W. Dresser, *New Thought Movement*, 31–32.

7. Horatio W. Dresser, ed., *Quimby Manuscripts*, 33–34.

8. Ibid., 34.

9. Ibid., 35

10. Ibid., 36.

11. Julius W. Dresser, *True History of Mental Science*, 8; and Annetta G. Dresser, *Philosophy of P. P. Quimby*, 19–20.

12. Annetta G. Dresser, *Philosophy of P. P. Quimby*, 46.

13. Ibid., 13.

14. See Horatoio W. Dresser, *New Thought Movement* and *Quimby Manuscripts*.

15. Horatio W. Dresser, *New Thought Movement*, 52.

16. Ibid.

17. Annetta G. Dresser, *Philosophy of P. P. Quimby*, 41.

18. Horatio W. Dresser, *New Thought Movement*, 24.

19. Annetta G. Dresser, *Philosophy of P. P. Quimby*, 103–4.

20. "Andrew Jackson Davis: The First American Prophet and Clairvoyant," http://www.andrewjacksondavis.com.

21. "Andrew Jackson Davis," http://www.fst.org/ajdavis.htm.

22. "Andrew Jackson Davis: The First American Prophet and Clairvoyant," http://www.andrewjacksondavis.com.

Chapter 4. Warren Felt Evans and Julius and Annetta Dresser: Pioneers of New Thought

1. Julius A. Dresser, *True History of Mental Science*, 8 (see note for chap. 3, *epigraph*).

2. Annetta G. Dresser, *Philosophy of P. P. Quimby*, 19 (see chap. 3, n. 5).

3. Ibid., 43–44.

4. "Annetta and Julius Dresser: Early Practitioners of the Quimby System of Mental Treatment of Diseases," http:// jadresser.wwwhubs.com/.

5. C. Alan Anderson and Deborah G. Whitehouse, *New Thought: A Practical American Spirituality* (New York: Crossroad, 1995), 21–22.

6. Quoted in Horatio W. Dresser, *New Thought Movement*, 74 (see chap. 3, n. 5).

7. Anderson and Whitehouse, *New Thought*, 22.

8. Harry Gaze, *Thomas Troward: An Intimate Memoir of the Teacher and the Man* (Los Angeles, CA: DeVorss, 1992), 4.

9. "Horatio Dresser," http://en.wikipedia.org/wiki/Horatio_Dresser.

Chapter 5. Mary Baker Eddy: Founder of Christian Science

Epigraph: Mary Baker Eddy, *Miscellaneous Writings, 1883–1896* (Boston: First Church of Christ, Scientist, 1896 [1924]), 348.

1. Quoted in Israel Regardie, *Romance of Metaphysics* (Chicago: Aries, 1946), 75.

2. Cather and Milmine, *Life of Mary Baker Eddy*, 42–43 (see chap. 3, n. 1).

3. Regardie, *Romance of Metaphysics*, 72.

4. Annetta G. Dresser, *Philosophy of P. P. Quimby*, 50 (see chap. 3, n. 5).

5. Regardie, *Romance of Metaphysics*, 72.

6. There are several letters of Mary Baker Eddy written to Quimby as well as poems and articles about him published in the local newspapers. Copies of those documents can be found in Annetta G. Dresser, *Philosophy of P. P. Quimby*; Horatio W. Dresser, *New Thought Movement* (see chap. 3, n. 5); and Cather and Milmine, *Life of Mary Baker Eddy*, among others.

7. *Portland Courier*, Nov. 7, 1862. The entire text of this letter can be found in Cather and Milmine, *Life of Mary Baker Eddy*, 58–59.

8. "Mary Baker Eddy (1821–1910): Founder of Christian Science," http://mary bakereddy.wwwhubs.com/.

9. Quoted in Horatio W. Dresser, *New Thought Movement*, 108.

10. Regardie, *Romance of Metaphysics*, 77.

11. Ibid.

12. "People: The Universal Friend," http://www.yatescounty.org/upload/12 /historian/friend.html.

13. Isaac Woodbridge Riley, "The Faith, The Falsity, and the Failure of Christian Science," *Journal of the American Medical Association*, 1925; 85(12): 924; http://jama.jamanetwork.com/article.aspx?articleid=237520#qundefined.

14. Viktor E. Frankl, *Man's Search for Ultimate Meaning* (New York: Plenum, 1997), 15.

15. Mary Baker Glover (Mary Baker Eddy), *Science and Health with Key to the Scriptures* (Boston: Christian Science Publishing, 1875), 4. According to Eddy's biographers, she gave three different dates for her "great discovery," going back to 1853: Cather and Milmine, *Life of Mary Baker Eddy*, 77.

16. Julius W. Dresser, *True History of Mental Science*, 26 (see note for chap. 3, *epigraph*). See also Cather and Milmine, *Life of Mary Baker Eddy*, 70, where the poem is reprinted in full.

17. Mary Baker Eddy, *Retrospection and Introspection* (Boston: Trustees under the Will of Mary Baker Eddy, 1891), 24.

18. Cather and Milmine, *Life of Mary Baker Eddy*, 86.

19. Ibid., 73–74.

20. Zweig, *Mental Healers*, 162–63 (see chap. 1, n. 3). See also Cather and Milmine, *Life of Mary Baker Eddy*, chapter 5.

21. Cather and Milmine, *Life of Mary Baker Eddy*, 135.

22. Ibid., 129.

23. "Mary Baker Eddy," http:// en.wikipedia.org/wiki/Mary_Baker_Eddy.

24. Regardie, *Romance of Metaphysics*, 10.

25. Eddy, *Science and Health with Key to the Scriptures*, 468.

26. "Mary Baker Eddy," http:// marybakereddy.wwwhubs.com/.

27. Quoted in Regardie, *Romance of Metaphysics*, 9.

28. "Mary Baker Eddy," http:// marybakereddy.wwwhubs.com/.

29. Eddy, *Retrospection and Introspection*, 76.

30. Cather and Milmine, *Life of Mary Baker Eddy*, 87.

31. "In all the relations of life, Quimby seems to have been loyal and upright. Outside of his theory he lived only for his family and was the constant playmate of his children. His only interest in his patients was to make them well. He treated all who came, whether they could pay or not. For several years Quimby kept no accounts and made no definite charges. The patients, when they saw fit, sent him such remuneration as they wished" (Cather and Milmine, *Life of Mary Baker Eddy*, 50).

32. Regardie, *Romance of Metaphysics*, 13.

33. Zweig, *Mental Healers*, 123.

34. Eddy, *Science and Health with Key to the Scriptures*, 584.

35. Mary Baker Eddy, *Unity of Good* (Boston: The Trustees under the Will of Mary Baker Eddy, 1908), 9–10.

36. The article is reproduced in Annetta G. Dresser, *Philosophy of P. P. Quimby*, 19–20.

37. Cather and Milmine, *Life of Mary Baker Eddy*, 52.

38. See the essay "From Fear to Faith" in Amao, *Beyond Conventional Wisdom*.

39. Regardie, *Romance of Metaphysics*, 131–32.

40. Thomson Jay Hudson, *The Law of Psychic Phenomena* (Chicago: A. C. McClurg, 1893), 157.

41. Quoted in the magazine *Healing Thoughts*, no. 15, Plainfield Christian Science Church (Nov. 1989): 3.

42. See the final chapter in Eddy, *Unity of Good*, entitled "There Is No Matter."

43. Ibid., 31–32.

44. Hudson, *Law of Psychic Phenomena*, 163.

45. Fleta Campbell Springer, *According to the Flesh: A Biography of Mary Baker Eddy* (New York: Coward-McCann, 1930), 299.

46. Ibid., 418.

47. Stephen Barrett, "Some Thoughts about Faith Healing," http://www.quack watch.com/01QuackeryRelatedTopics/faith.html.

48. Hudson, *Law of Psychic Phenomena*, 164.

49. Barrett, "Some Thoughts about Faith Healing."

50. Mary Baker Eddy, *Miscellaneous Writings, 1883–1896*, 249.

Chapter 6. Emma Curtis Hopkins: Teacher of Teachers

1. "Emma Curtis Hopkins," http://desert.xpressdesigns.com/ech.html.

2. "Emma Curtis Hopkins: Teacher of Teachers," http://emmacurtishopkins .wwwhubs.com.

3. "Emma Curtis Hopkins," http://desert.xpressdesigns.com/ech.html.

Chapter 7. Malinda Cramer and the Brooks Sisters: Founders of the Divine Science Church

1. "Malinda Cramer: Founder of Divine Science," http://malindacramer .wwwhubs.com/.

2. Malinda E. Cramer, "Spiritual Experience," *Harmony Magazine* 7:1 (Oct. 1894), http:// divinescience.com/bio_malindaRecord.htm.

3. Divine Science.com, http://divinescience.com/ds_history.htm.

4. Joseph Murphy, *The Power of Your Subconscious Mind* (New York: Penguin, 2008), 82.

5. Divine Science.com, http://divinescience.com/ds_history.htm.

6. Ibid.

7. "Divine Science Founders," http://www.dsschool.org/founders/index.html.

8. Anderson and Whitehouse, *New Thought*, 24–25 (see chap. 4, n. 5).

Chapter 8. Charles and Myrtle Fillmore: Founders of Unity

1. Anderson and Whitehouse, *New Thought*, 1 (see chap. 4, n. 5).

2. Ibid., 25.

3. "Charles Fillmore (1854–1948): A Modern Way-Shower," http://charles fillmore.wwwhubs.com.

Chapter 9. Ernest Holmes: Founder of Religious Science

1. Ernest Holmes, *The Science of Mind: A Philosophy, A Faith, A Way of Life*, rev. ed. (New York: Tarcher/Putnam, 1997 [1938]), 35.

2. Ibid., 168.

3. Donald Curtis, "Who Taught Ernest Holmes?," *Science of Mind* (Jan. 1996), 23.

4. Ibid.

5. Ibid., 24.

6. Ibid., 26.

Chapter 10. Ambroise-Auguste Liébeault and Hippolyte Bernheim: The Nancy School of Hypnosis

1. C. G. Jung, *Psychology and the Occult*, trans. R. F. C. Hull (Princeton: Princeton/Bollingen, 1977), 116.

2. "Ambroise-Auguste Liébeault," obituary, *British Medical Journal*, March 19, 1904, http://www.pubmedcentral.nih.gov/picrender.fcgi?artid=2353478an dblobtype=pdf.

3. Quoted in Hudson, *Law of Psychic Phenomena*, 168–69 (see chap. 5, n. 40).

4. "Sigmund Freud Chronology," http://www.freud-museum.at/freud /chronolg/1889-90e.htm. The letter was dated Dec. 28, 1887.

Chapter 11. William James:
The Father of American Psychology

1. William James, *The Varieties of Religious Experience* (New York: Barnes & Noble, 2004 [1902]), 122.

2. John J. McDermott, *The Writings of William James: A Comprehensive Edition* (Chicago: University of Chicago Press, 1977), 6–7. See also James, *Varieties*, 146–47.

3. John C. Durham, "Understanding the Sacred," http://auss.forumotion.eu /t12-understanding-the-sacred-by-john-c-durham-2001.

4. James, *Varieties*, xxv.

5. "William James," *Stanford Encyclopedia of Philosophy*, http://plato.stanford .edu/entries/james/.

6. Quoted in Claire Dunne, *Carl Jung: Wounded Healer of the Soul* (New York: Parabola, 2000), 3.

7. James, *Varieties*, 39.

8. Quoted in Edward Hoffman, "William James: The Pragmatic Visionary," *Quest: Journal of the Theosophical Society in America*, 98:3 (Summer 2010), 98.

9. James, *Varieties*, 102.

10. McDermott, *Writings of William James*, 7.

Chapter 12. Thomson Jay Hudson:
The Scientific Working Hypothesis

1. Jung, *Psychology and the Occult*, 6 (see chap. 10, n. 1).

2. *The Interpretation of Dreams*, regarded as Freud's masterpiece, first appeared in November 1899, although it is dated 1900. It was followed by *The Psychopathology of Everyday Life* in 1901 and by *Three Essays on the Theory of Sexuality* in 1905.

3. Ervin Seale, "Introduction to the 1968 Edition," Thomas Jay Hudson, *Law of Psychic Phenomena* (see chap. 5, n. 40).

4. Erich Fromm, *Greatness and Limitations of Freud's Thought* (New York: Harper and Row, 1980), 23.

5. Zweig, *Mental Healers*, 291 (see chap. 1, n. 3).

6. See Israel Regardie, *The Golden Dawn* (St. Paul, MN: Llewellyn, 1993).

7. Hudson, *Law of Psychic Phenomena*, 144, 166.

8. Ibid., 323.

9. According to Holmes, "race-suggestion is a very real thing, and each individual carries around with him (and has written into his mentality) many impressions which he never consciously thought of or experienced." He further defines this concept as "the tendency to reproduce what the race has thought and experienced. This race-suggestion is a prolific source of disease" (*Science of Mind*, 348, 624; see chap. 9, n. 1).

10. Quoted in Murphy, *Power of Your Subconscious Mind*, 38 (see chap. 7, n. 4).

11. Hudson, *Law of Psychic Phenomena*, 150.

12. The reader interested in this subject would do well to consult the writings of Allan Kardec (Hippolyte Léon Denizard Rivail, 1804–69) and Léon Denis (1846–1927), promoters of this movement in France.

13. Hudson, *Law of Psychic Phenomena*, 337.

14. Hudson, ibid., 333.

Chapter 13. Thomas Troward: Founder of Mental Science

1. Gaze, *Thomas Troward*, 1–3 (chap. 4, n. 8).

2. Ibid., 3–4.

3. Ibid., viii.

4. Troward uses the word "personality" as equivalent to "image" or "picture."

5. Thomas Troward, *Edinburgh Lectures on Mental Healing* (New York: Dodd, Mead, 1909), thomastroward.wwwhubs.com/elomstitle.htm.

6. Ibid.

7. Ibid.

8. Ibid.

9. *Jesus mihi omnia* was the Rosicrucian motto. According to Paul Foster Case, the name Jesus signifies "Self-existence liberates." Connected with *omnia* ("all things"), this intimates the characteristic Rosicrucian point of view, which is that everything contributes to liberation. See Paul Foster Case, *The True and Invisible Rosicrucian Order* (York Beach, ME: Weiser, 1985), 121.

10. Ibid.

11. Case, *The True and Invisible Rosicrucian Order*, 53.

12. Troward, *Edinburg Lectures*, 122.

13. Those interested in this subject are encouraged to read the article "Jesus the Nazarene: The True Rose and Cross," by V. H. Frater T. S. O., published on the website of the Esoteric Order of the Golden Dawn, http://www.esoteric goldendawn.com/rosicrucian_jesusnazarene.htm.

Chapter 14. Émile Coué: Autosuggestion and the Placebo Effect

Epigraph: Émile Coué, *Self-Mastery through Conscious Autosuggestion* (New York: American Library Services, 1922), 14.

1. Hudson, *Law of Psychic Phenomena*, 148 (see chap. 5, n. 40).

2. Michael McThoerosen, "The Discoveries of Emile Coué," http://www .spiritual-mind-control.com/emilie-coue.html.

3. Émile Coué, *Self Mastery through Conscious Autosuggestion* (New York: American Library Services, 1922), 7. Free copy can be found online at http://api.ning.com/files/GtJDVS4lBqE41PyKuBxNpJt85XqRUH7jkOty WD4SmbW1hqCcoUp8oHLmE2VjVGbUEg8wti4nTX-PDOBpDSIpkw __/selfmasterythrou00coue.pdf

Chapter 15. Sigmund Freud: Father of Psychoanalysis

1. C. L. Rich and F. N. Pitts Jr., "Suicide by Psychiatrists: A Study of Medical Specialists among 18,730 Consecutive Physician Deaths during a Five-Year Period, 1967–72," *Journal of Clinical Psychiatry*, 41:8 (Aug. 1980), 261–63, http://www.ncbi.nlm.nih.gov/pubmed/7400103.

2. René DesGroseillers, "Sigmund Freud: Life and Work," http://www.freudfile .org/charcot.html.

3. Peter Gay, "Sigmund Freud: A Brief Life," in Sigmund Freud, *The Ego and the Id*, trans. James Strachey (New York: W. W. Norton, 1990), xiii–xiv.

4. James Durlacher, *Freedom from Fear Forever* (Tempe, AZ: Van Ness, 1995), 18.

5. Mikkel Borch-Jacobsen and Douglas Brick, "Neurotica: Freud and the Seduction Theory," *October*, vol. 76 (Spring 1996), 15–43, http://www .revalvaatio.org/wp/wp-content/uploads/borch-jacobsen-neurotica.pdf.

6. "Sigmund Freud: Biography," http://www.freud-sigmund.com/file/bio graphy/.

7. "Sigmund Freud (1856–1939)," *Internet Encyclopedia of Philosophy*, http://www.iep.utm.edu/f/freud.htm.

8. See, for example, Lenore Terr, *Unchained Memories: True Stories of Traumatic Memories Lost and Found* (New York: Basic Books, 1995); Elizabeth Loftus and Katherine Ketcham, *The Myth of Repressed Memory: False Memories and Allegations of Sexual Abuse* (New York: St. Martin's, 1996); Mark Pendergrast and Melody Gavigan, *Victims of Memory: Incest Accusations and Shattered Lives*, 2d ed. (Hinesburg, VT: Upper Access, 1996); and Richard Ofshe and Ethan Watters, *Making Monsters: False Memories, Psychotherapy, and Sexual Hysteria* (Berkeley: University of California Press, 1996).

9. Judy Siegel-Itzkovich, "Freud's Theory of Repression Should Be Dropped," *Jerusalem Post*, April 13, 2008, http://www.jpost.com/HealthAndSci-Tech /Health/Article.aspx?id=98064.

10. Zweig, *Mental Healers*, 357–58.

11. "Sigmund Freud (1856–1939)," *Internet Encyclopedia of Philosophy*.

12. See Frederick Crews, *The Memory Wars: Freud's Legacy in Dispute* (New York: New York Review Books, 1990), http:// human-nature.com/articles/crews .html.

13. Jeffrey Moussaieff Masson, ed., *The Complete Letters of Sigmund Freud to Wilhelm Fliess (1887–1904)* (Cambridge: Harvard University Press, 1985), 272.

14. C. G. Jung, *Memories, Dreams, Reflections*, ed. Aniela Jaffé, trans. Richard and Clara Winston (New York: Pantheon, 1973), 150.

15. Robert I. Simon, "Great Paths Cross: Freud and James at Clark University, 1909," http://www.uky.edu/~eushe2/Pajares/JamesSimon1967.pdf.

16. Jeffrey Moussaieff Masson, *The Assault on Truth: Freud's Suppression of the Seduction Theory* (New York: Harper, 1984), 233–50.

17. Sigmund Freud, *The Interpretation of Dreams*, trans. A. A. Brill (New York: Barnes & Noble, 2005), xii.

18. E. M. Thornton, *The Freudian Fallacy* (New York: Dial, 1984); see also Masson, *Assault on Truth*, 7.

19. Jürgen vom Scheidt, "Sigmund Freud and Cocaine," *Psyche* 27, (1973), 385–430, http://www.pep-web.org/document.php?id=paq.043.0693c. See also "Freud and Cocaine—The Deal," http://www.historyhouse.com/in_history/cocaine.

20. Thornton, *Freudian Fallacy*, ix.

21. Thomas Szasz, *The Myth of Psychotherapy* (Syracuse, NY: Syracuse University Press, 1978), xi.

Chapter 16. Carl Gustav Jung: Doctor of the Soul

1. Dunne, *Carl Jung*, 21 (see chap. 11, n. 6).

2. "Carl G. Jung," http://en.wikipedia.org/wiki/Carl_Jung#cite_note-10.

3. "Carl Jung Biography," http://soultherapynow.com/articles/carl-jung.html.

4. Joseph Campbell, ed., *The Portable Jung* (New York: Viking, 1971), xv.

5. Jung, *Memories, Dreams, Reflections*, 149 (see chap. 15, n. 14).

6. Quoted in Dunne, *Carl Jung*, 28.

7. Ibid.

8. Jung, *Memories, Dreams, Reflections*, 155.

9. Sigmund Freud, *Moses and Monotheism*, trans. Katherine Jones (New York: Vintage, 1967), 71.

10. Szasz, *Myth of Psychotherapy*, 173 (see chap. 15, n. 21).

11. C. G. Jung, *The Red Book*, trans. Sonu Shamdasani et al. (New York: W. W. Norton, 2009), back cover.

12. Richard Wilhelm and Cary F. Baynes, trans., *The Secret of the Golden Flower: A Chinese Book of Life* (New York: Causeway Books, 1975).

13. Quoted in Dunne, *Carl Jung*, 3 (see chap. 11, n. 6).

14. David Allen Hulse, *New Dimensions for the Cube of Space* (York Beach, ME: Samuel Weiser, 2000), 126–27.

15. Eva Pierrakos, "The Language of the Unconscious," lecture 124, Pathwork Center, http://pathwork.org/lectures/the-language-of-the-unconscious.

16. There are rich spiritual lessons transcribed from Mrs. Pierrakos's channeling sessions for anyone interested in them. These materials can be found on the Internet for free at the Pathwork Center website, http://pathwork.org

/the-lectures/. The lectures "What Is the Path?" and "The Language of the Unconscious" are particularly recommended.

Chapter 17. New Thought and the Law of Attraction

1. Napoleon Hill, *Think and Grow Rich*, audio book, pt. 1, "Definiteness and Purpose," http://www.youtube.com/watch?v=tq2jIDwleLA&list=PL02D2A EF294A36BBA. When you click on the above link, please wait for Hill to begin speaking; he will state the quoted material more than once. Watch also: http://www.youtube.com/watch?v=UmCtWskzmAQ.

2. "Three Initiates," *The Kybalion: Hermetic Philosophy* (Chicago: Yogi Publication Society, 1940 [1908]), 171. Atkinson has been identified as the author of this pseudonymous work: see the introduction to Philip Deslippe, ed., *The Kybalion: The Definitive Edition* (New York: Tarcher/Penguin, 2011); also Mitch Horowitz, *Occult America: The Secret History of How Mysticism Shaped Our Nation* (New York: Bantam, 2009), 210.

3. "Gary E. Schwartz, PhD," http://authors.simonandschuster.com/Gary-E -Schwartz-Ph-D/16578798/books.

4. See also Wayne W. Dyer, *The Power of Intention: Learning to Co-Create Your World Your Way* (Carlsbad, CA: Hay House, 2004).

5. See the chapter "The Fallacy of Predictions" in Amao, *Beyond Conventional Wisdom*.

6. Richard C. Henry, "The Mental Universe," *Nature* 436:29 (July 7, 2005), http://henry.pha.jhu.edu/The.mental.Universe.pdf.

Chapter 18. The Concept of the Egregore

1. "Egregore," http://en.wikipedia.org/wiki/Egregore.

2. Dion Fortune, *Applied Magic* (York Beach, ME: Samuel Weiser, 2000), 14.

3. Jung, *Memories, Dreams, Reflections*, 183 (see chap. 15, n. 14).

4. Mircea Eliade, *The Myth of the Eternal Return* (Princeton: Princeton University Press, 2005), 3–4.

5. "Inca Mythology," http://en.wikipedia.org/wiki/Apu_Illapu.

6. Jack Ensign Addington, *The Secret of Healing* (Los Angeles: Science of Mind, 1979), 18.

7. "Bernadette Soubirous," http://en.wikipedia.org/wiki/Bernadette_Soubirous.

8. Addington, *Secret of Healing*, ibid.

9. James Randi, *The Faith Healers* (Amherst, New York: Prometheus, 1989), 22–23.

10. According to James Randi, five million people visit the shrine annually, occupying 400 hotels: ibid., 20.

11. Ibid., 21.

Chapter 19. Spontaneous Healing and the Placebo Effect

Epigraph: Quoted in Marilyn Ferguson, *The Aquarian Conspiracy: Personal and Social Transformation in the 1980s* (Los Angeles: Tarcher, 1980), 249.

1. R. Barker Bausell, *Snake Oil Science: The Truth about Complementary and Alternative Medicine* (New York: Oxford University Press, 2007), 275.

2. James Harvey Young, "Why Quackery Persists," http://www.quackwatch.com/01QuackeryRelatedTopics/persistance.html.

3. Bruce H. Lipton, *The Biology of Belief* (New York: Hay House, 2008).

4. Bruce H. Lipton, "Mind over Genes," http://okbodytalk.com/bruce-lipton-mind-over-genes/.

5. Stephen Barrett, "Spontaneous Remission and the Placebo Effect," http://www.quackwatch.org/04ConsumerEducation/placebo.html.

6. Quoted in Jeanne Achterberg, *Imagery in Healing: Shamanism and Modern Medicine* (Boston: New Science Library, 1985), 97.

7. Murphy, *Power of Your Subconscious Mind*, 46 (see chap. 7, n. 4).

8. Young, "Why Quackery Persists." See also Stephen Barrett and William T. Jarvis, *The Health Robbers: A Close Look at Quackery in America* (Amherst, NY: Prometheus, 1993).

9. Young, "Why Quackery Persists."

10. Ibid.

Chapter 20. The Role of Imagery in Healing

1. Quoted in Szasz, *Myth of Psychotherapy*, 62 (see chap. 15, n. 21).

2. Murphy, *Power of Your Subconscious Mind*, 47, 67 (see chap. 7, n. 4).

3. Paul Foster Case, *The Secret Doctrine of the Tarot* (Los Angeles, CA: Builders of the Adytum), 1919. See also Case, *Occult Fundamentals and Spiritual Unfoldment, vol. 1: The Early Years* (Laguna Niguel, CA: Fraternity of the Hidden Light, 2008).

4. "The Academy for Guided Imagery," http://www.academyforguidedimagery. com/about/index.html. The website indicates that "the Academy is a postgraduate training provider for health professionals, and a source of self-care products and programs for those struggling with a chronic, difficult, or painful illness."

5. Simonton Cancer Center, http://www.simontoncenter.com.

6. Achterberg, *Imagery in Healing*, 8 (see chap. 19, n. 6).

7. Ibid., 3.

8. Daniel Reid, *The Complete Book of Chinese Health and Healing* (New York: Barnes & Noble, 1994), 76.

9. Achterberg, *Imagery in Healing*, 12.

10. Ibid., 13.

11. Ibid., 6.

Chapter 21. The Healing Power of the Subconscious Mind

Epigraph: Murphy, *Power of Your Subconscious Mind*, 64 (see chap. 7, n. 4).

1. Zweig, *Mental Healers*, 31 (see chap. 1, n. 3).

2. C. George Boeree, "Carl Jung," http://webspace.ship.edu/cgboer/jung.html.

3. Ralph Waldo Emerson, "Self-Reliance", *Essays: First Series*, http://www .emersoncentral.com/selfreliance.htm.

4. Ibid.

5. Henry, "Mental Universe." See also Lynne McTaggart, *The Field: The Quest for the Secret Force of the Universe*, rev. ed. (New York: Harper, 2008) and

Elisabet Sahtouris, "A Scientist's Thoughts about Redefining Our Concept of God," http://www.ratical.org/LifeWeb/Articles/whatsgod.html.

6. Paul Foster Case, *Wisdom of Tarot: The Golden Dawn Tarot, Series 1* (Laguna Niguel, CA: Rosicrucian Order of the Golden Dawn, 2009), 43; also see his correspondence lessons on Tarot.

7. Paul Foster Case, *The Secret Doctrine of the Tarot* (Laguna Niguel, CA: Rosicrucian Order of the Golden Dawn, 2009). See also his correspondence lessons on Tarot.

Chapter 22. Suggestion and Autosuggestion

1. Holmes, *Science of Mind*, 605 (see chap. 9, n. 1).

2. Murphy, *Power of Your Subconscious Mind*, 66 (see chap. 7, n. 4).

3. Roger and Joanne Callahan, *Thought Field Therapy and Trauma: Treatment and Theory* (Indian Fields, CA: Callahan Techniques, 1996).

4. Troward, *Edinburgh Lectures* (see chap. 13, n. 5).

Chapter 23. Self-Help and Self-Empowerment

1. "Coffee, Tea, or Pee?," http://www.heartlandhealing.com/pages/archive/urine_therapy/index.html.

2. Aubrey de Grey, "Mr. Immortality," *The Week* (Nov. 16, 2007), 52–53.

3. Marianne Williamson, *A Return to Love: Reflections on the Principles of A Course in Miracles* (New York: Harper Collins, 1992), 190–91.

Chapter 24. The Healing Power of Love and Forgiveness

1. "Dr. Harold G. Koenig Establishes Duke Center for the Study of Religion, Spirituality, and Health," http://www.thenewmedicine.org/timeline/spirituality_research; Duke Center for Spirituality, Theology and Health, http://www.spiritualityandhealth.duke.edu/about/hkoenig/.

2. "Endorphins: Natural Pain and Stress Fighters," http://www.medicinenet.com/script/main/art.asp?articlekey=55001.

3. See Larry Dossey's website, http://www.dosseydossey.com/larry/default.html.

4. "Norman Cousins," http://en.wikipedia.org/wiki/Norman_Cousins.

Chapter 25. The Qabalistic Method of Treatment

1. Israel Regardie, "The Art of True Healing," in *Foundations of Practical Magic* (Wellingborough, Northamptonshire, UK: Aquarian Press, 1979), http://www.hermetics.org/pdf/TheArtofTrueHealing.pdf.

2. Ibid., 138.

3. Ibid., 143.

4. Ibid., 150

5. Ibid.

Chapter 26. Rational and Cognitive Behavioral Therapies

1. Reid, *Complete Book of Chinese Health*, 76 (see chap. 20, n. 8).

2. Cognitive Behavior Therapy Self-Help Resources, Epictetus—quotes (55–135 AD), http://www.get.gg/epictetus.htm.

Chapter 27. Energy Psychology and Energy Healing

1. Quoted in Durlacher, *Freedom from Fear*, 2 (see chap. 15, n. 4).

2. Reid, *Complete Book of Chinese Health*, 77 (see chap. 20, n. 8).

3. Quoted in ibid., 78.

4. Durlacher, *Freedom from Fear*, 3.

5. Ibid., 7.

6. Quoted in Zweig, *Mental Healers*, 31 (see chap. 1, n. 3).

7. See Gallo's website, http://energypsych.com.

Chapter 28. Faith Healing and Fake Healers

1. Murphy, *Power of Your Subconscious Mind*, 70 (see chap. 7, n. 4).

2. See the following websites: http://www.randi.org/site, http://www.skepdic
.com/randi.html, http://en.wikipedia.org/wiki/James_Randi.

3. See Randi, *Faith Healers* (see chap. 18, n. 9); also http://www.pointofinquiry
.org/james_randi_the_faith_healers.

4. Tijn Touber, "How I Lost Faith: How the End of Religion Can Be the Beginning
of God," *ODEwire*, http://odewire.com/52717/how-i-lost-faith-how-the
-end-of-religion-can-be-the-beginning-of-god.html.

5. Addington, *Secret of Healing*, 28 (see chap. 18, n. 6).

Chapter 29. The Power of the Mind to Heal

1. Norman Doidge, *The Brain That Changes Itself: Stories of Personal Triumph
from the Brain Sciences* (New York: Penguin, 2007).

2. Daniel G. Amen, *Change Your Brain and Change Your Life* (New York:
Random House, 2010).

3. Henry, "Mental Universe," (see chap. 17, n. 6).

4. See Wayne Dyer, "When you change the way you look at things," http://you
tube.com/watch?v=urQPraeeYOw.

5. Bruce H. Lipton, "Insight Into Cellular Consciousness," http://www
.brucelipton.com.

6. Lipton, "Mind over Genes," http://okbodytalk.com/bruce-lipton-mind-over
-genes/.

7. Lipton, "Embracing the Immaterial Universe," http://www.brucelipton.com
/media/embracing-immaterial-universe

8. Lipton, "Mind over Genes."

Chapter 30. Spiritual Mind Healing

1. Addington, *Secret of* Healing, viii (see chap. 18, n. 6).

2. University of Michigan Health System, http://www.med.umich.edu/1libr /aha/umpsysom.htm.

3. Henry, "Mental Universe," (see chap. 17, n. 6)

4. See *The Kybalion*; also Stanley Sobottka, *A Course on Consciousness*, http://faculty.virginia.edu:80/consciousness/home.html.

5. For example, medical doctors such as James Harvey Young and Stephen Barrett consider this kind of treatment to be a mental narcotic or anesthetic to alleviate the suffering of naive people. See http://www.quackwatch.org /index.html.

6. Lipton, *Biology of Belief*, 17 (see chap. 19, n. 3).

Epilogue

1. See Albert Amao, *The Dawning of the Golden Age of Aquarius: Redefining the Concepts of God, Man, and the Universe* (Bloomington, IN: AuthorHouse, 2012).

2. See Paul Foster Case, *The Name of Names* (Los Angeles: Builders of the Adytum, 1981); David A. Cooper, *God Is a Verb: Kabbalah and the Practice of Mystical Judaism* (New York: Riverhead, 1998); and Arthur Green, *Ehyeh: A Kabbalah for Tomorrow* (Woodstock, VT: Jewish Lights, 2004).

3. Paul Foster Case, *Occult Fundamentals and Spiritual Unfoldment* (Laguna Niguel, CA: Fraternity of the Hidden Light, 2008), 148.

Bibliography

Achterberg, Jeanne. *Imagery in Healing: Shamanism and Modern Medicine*. Boston: New Science Library, 1985.

Addington, Jack Ensign. *The Secret of Healing*. Los Angeles: Science of Mind, 1979.

Allen, James. *As a Man Thinketh*. New York: Barnes & Noble, 1992.

Amao, Albert. *Beyond Conventional Wisdom*. Bloomington, IN: AuthorHouse, 2006.

———. *The Dawning of the Golden Age of Aquarius*. Bloomington, IN: AuthorHouse, 2007.

Amen, Daniel G. *Change Your Brain and Change Your Life*. New York: Random House, 2010.

Anderson, C. Alan, and Deborah Whitehouse. *New Thought: A Practical American Spirituality*. New York: Crossroad, 1995.

Anonymous. "The Academy for Guided Imagery." http://www.academyforguidedimagery.com/about/index.html.

———. "Ambroise-Auguste Liébeault," obituary, *British Medical Journal*, March 19, 1904, 706. http://www.pubmedcentral.nih.gov/picrender.fcgi?artid=2353478&blobtype=pdf.

———. "Andrew Jackson Davis." http://www.fst.org/ajdavis.htm.

———. "Andrew Jackson Davis: The First American Prophet and Clairvoyant." http://www.andrewjacksondavis.com.

———. "Annetta and Julius Dresser: Early Practitioners of the Quimby System of Mental Treatment of Diseases." http://jadresser.wwwhubs.com.

———. "Bernadette Soubirous." http://en.wikipedia.org/wiki/Bernadette
_Soubirous.

———. "Carl G. Jung." http://en.wikipedia.org/wiki/Carl_Jung#cite
_note-10.

———. "Carl Jung Biography." http://soultherapynow.com/articles/carl
-jung.html.

———. "Charles Fillmore (1854–1948): A Modern Way-Shower."
http://charlesfillmore.wwwhubs.com.

———. "Coffee, Tea, or Pee?" http://www.heartlandhealing.com/pages
/archive/urine_therapy/index.html.

———. "Divine Science Founders." http://www.dsschool.org/founders
/index.html.

———. "Dr. Harold G. Koenig Establishes Duke Center for the Study
of Religion, Spirituality, and Health." http://www.thenewmedicine
.org/timeline/spirituality_research.

———. "Egregore." http://en.wikipedia.org/wiki/Egregore.

———. "Emma Curtis Hopkins." http://desert.xpressdesigns.com/ech
.html.

———. "Emma Curtis Hopkins: Teacher of Teachers." http://emma
curtishopkins.wwwhubs.com.

———. "Endorphins: Natural Pain and Stress Fighters." http://medicine
net.com/script/main/art.asp?articlekey=55001.

———. "Franz Anton Mesmer." http://anton-mesmer.com/index.htm.

———. "Franz Anton Mesmer." http://knowledgerush.com/kr/encyclo
pedia/Franz_Anton_Mesmer.

———. "Freud and Cocaine—The Deal." http://historyhouse.com/in
_history/cocaine.

———. "Gary E. Schwartz, PhD." http://authors.simonandschuster.com
/Gary-E-Schwartz-Ph-D/16578798/books.

———. "Great Theosophists: Anton [*sic*] Mesmer." *Theosophy* 26:10
(Aug. 1938), 434–440. http://wisdomworld.org/setting/mesmer
.html.

————. "Heavy Metal Medicine." http://pubs.acs.org/subscribe/journals /tcaw/10/i01/html/01chemch.html.

————. "Inca Mythology." http://en.wikipedia.org/wiki/Apu_Illapu.

————. "Larry Dossey, MD: Biography." http://dosseydossey.com/larry /default.html.

————. "Malinda Cramer: Founder of Divine Science." http://malinda cramer.wwwhubs.com.

————. "Mary Baker Eddy (1821–1910): Founder of Christian Science." http://marybakereddy.wwwhubs.com.

————. "Mercury(I) Chloride." http://en.wikipedia.org/wiki/Mercury %28I%29_chloride.

————. "Norman Cousins." http://en.wikipedia.org/wiki/Norman _Cousins.

————. "People: The Universal Friend." http://www.yatescounty.org /upload/12/historian/friend.html.

————. "Sigmund Freud (1856–1939)." *Internet Encyclopedia of Philosophy*. http://iep.utm.edu/f/freud.htm.

————. "Sigmund Freud: Biography." http://freud-sigmund.com/file /biography.

————. "Sigmund Freud Chronology." http://freud-museum.at/freud /chronolg/1889-90e.htm.

————. "William James." *Stanford Encyclopedia of Philosophy*. http://plato .stanford.edu/entries/james.

Bair, Deirdre. *Jung: A Biography*. Boston: Little, Brown, 2003.

Barrett, Stephen. "Some Thoughts about Faith Healing." http://quack watch.com/01QuackeryRelatedTopics/faith.html.

————. "Spontaneous Remission and the Placebo Effect." http://quack watch.com/04ConsumerEducation/placebo.html.

Barrett, Stephen, and William T. Jarvis. *The Health Robbers: A Close Look at Quackery in America*. Amherst, NY: Prometheus, 1993.

Bausell, R. Barker. *Snake Oil Science: The Truth about Complementary and Alternative Medicine*. New York: Oxford University Press, 2007.

Boeree, C. George. "Carl Jung." http://webspace.ship.edu/cgboer/jung.html.

Borch-Jacobsen, Mikkel, and Douglas Brick. "Neurotica: Freud and the Seduction Theory," *October* 76 (Spring 1996): 15–43. http://revalvaatio.org/wp/wp-content/uploads/borch-jacobsen-neurotica.pdf.

Calgary New Thought Centre. "New Thought: What It Is and How It Can Help YOU!" http://cornerstone.wwwhubs.com/history2.htm.

Callahan, Roger and Joanne. *Thought Field Therapy and Trauma: Treatment and Theory.* Indian Fields, CA: Callahan Techniques, 1996.

Campbell, Joseph, ed. *The Portable Jung.* New York: Penguin, 1971.

Case, Paul Foster. *The Early Writings*, vol. 1: *Occult Fundamentals and Spiritual Unfoldment.* Laguna Niguel, CA: Fraternity of the Hidden Light, 2008.

———. *The Early Writings*, vol. 2: *Esoteric Secrets of Meditation and Magic.* Covina, CA: Fraternity of the Hidden Light, 2008.

———. *The Name of Names.* Los Angeles: Builders of the Adytum, 1981.

———. *The Secret Doctrine of the Tarot.* Los Angeles: Rosicrucian Order of the Golden Dawn, 2009.

———. *The True and Invisible Rosicrucian Order.* York Beach, ME: Samuel Weiser, 1985.

———. *Wisdom of Tarot: The Golden Dawn Tarot, Series 1.* Laguna Niguel, CA: Rosicrucian Order of the Golden Dawn, 2009.

Cather, Willa, and Georgine Milmine. *The Life of Mary Baker G. Eddy and the History of Christian Science.* Lincoln: University of Nebraska Press, 1993 [1909].

Cooper, David A. *God Is a Verb: Kabbalah and the Practice of Mystical Judaism.* New York: Riverhead, 1998.

Coué, Émile. *Self Mastery through Conscious Autosuggestion.* New York: American Library Services, 1922.

Cramer, Malinda E. "Spiritual Experience." *Harmony Magazine* 7, no. 1 (Oct. 1894). http://divinescience.com/bio_malindaRecord.htm.

Crews, Frederick. *The Memory Wars: Freud's Legacy in Dispute*. New York: New York Review Books, 1990.

Curtis, Donald. "Who Taught Ernest Holmes?" *Science of Mind* (Jan. 1996): 22–28.

Della Cava, Marco R. "The Secret History of *The Secret.*" *USA Today*, March 29, 2006. http://usatoday30.usatoday.com/life/books/news /2007-03-28-the-secret-churches_N.htm.

DesGroseillers, René. "Sigmund Freud: Life and Work." http://freudfile .org/charcot.html.

Deslippe, Philip, ed. *The Kybalion: The Definitive Edition*. New York: Tarcher/Penguin, 2011.

Dispenza, Joe. *Evolve Your Brain: The Science of Changing Your Mind*. Deerfield Beach, FL: HCI, 2007.

Doidge, Norman. *The Brain That Changes Itself: Stories of Personal Triumph from the Brain Sciences*. New York: Penguin, 2007.

Dresser, Annetta G. *The Philosophy of P. P. Quimby*. Boston: Builders Press, 1895.

Dresser, Horatio W. *A History of the New Thought Movement*. New York: Thomas Crowell, 1919.

Dresser, Horatio W., ed. *The Quimby Manuscripts, Showing the Discovery of Spiritual Healing and the Origin of Christian Science*. New York: Thomas Crowell, 1921.

Dresser, Julius A. *The True History of Mental Science*. Boston: Alfred Mudge, 1887.

Dunne, Claire. *Carl Jung, Wounded Healer of the Soul*. New York: Parabola, 2000.

Durham, John C. "Understanding the Sacred." auss.forumotion.eu/t12 -understanding-the-sacred-by-john-c-durham-2001.

Durlacher, James V. *Freedom from Fear Forever*. Tempe, AZ: Van Ness, 1995.

Dyer, Wayne W. *The Power of Intention: Learning to Co-Create Your World Your Way*. Carlsbad, CA: Hay House, 2004.

Eddy, Mary Baker. *Miscellaneous Writings, 1883–1896*. Boston: First Church of Christ, Scientist, 1924 [1896].

———. *Retrospection and Introspection*. Boston: Trustees under the Will of Mary Baker Eddy, 1891.

———. [Mary Baker Glover]. *Science and Health*. Boston: Christian Scientist Publishing Company, 1875.

———. *Science and Health with Key to the Scriptures*. Boston: The First Church of Christ, Scientist, 1971.

———. *Unity of Good*. Boston: The Trustees under the Will of Mary Baker Eddy, 1908.

Eliade, Mircea. *The Myth of the Eternal Return*. Princeton: Princeton University Press, 2005.

Emerson, Ralph Waldo. "Self-Reliance." *Essays: First Series*. http://emersoncentral.com/selfreliance.htm.

Ferguson, Marilyn. *The Aquarian Conspiracy: Personal and Social Transformation in the 1980s*. Los Angeles: Tarcher, 1980.

Fortune, Dion. *Applied Magic*. York Beach, ME: Samuel Weiser, 2000.

Frankl, Viktor E. *Man's Search for Ultimate Meaning*. New York: Plenum, 1997.

Freud, Sigmund. *The Ego and the Id*. Translated by James Strachey. New York: W. W. Norton, 1990.

———. *The Interpretation of Dreams*. New York: Barnes & Noble, 2005.

———. *Moses and Monotheism*. Translated by Katherine Jones. New York: Vintage, 1967.

———. *Three Essays of the Theory of Sexuality*. Translated by James Strachey. New York: Basic Books, 1962.

Fromm, Erich. *Greatness and Limitations of Freud's Thought*. New York: Harper and Row, 1980.

Gardner, Martin. *The Healing Revelations of Mary Baker Eddy: The Rise and Fall of Christian Science*. Buffalo, NY: Prometheus Books, 1993.

Gaze, Harry. *Thomas Troward: An Intimate Memoir of the Teacher and the Man*. Los Angeles: DeVorss, 1993.

Green, Arthur. *Ehyeh: A Kabbalah for Tomorrow.* Woodstock, VT: Jewish Lights, 2004.

Hoffman, Edward. "William James: The Pragmatic Visionary." *Quest: Journal of the Theosophical Society in America*, 98, no. 3 (Summer 2010): 96–99.

Henry, Richard C. "The Mental Universe." *Nature* 436, no. 29 (July 7, 2005). http://henry.pha.jhu.edu/The.mental.Universe.pdf.

Holmes, Ernest. *The Science of Mind: A Philosophy, a Faith, a Way of Life.* Rev. ed. New York: Tarcher/Putnam, 1997 (1938).

Horowitz, Mitch. *Occult America: The Secret History of How Mysticism Shaped Our Nation.* New York: Bantam, 2009.

Hudson, Thomson Jay. *The Law of Psychic Phenomena.* Salinas, CA: Hudson-Cohan, 1977 [1893].

Hulse, David Allen. *New Dimensions for the Cube of Space.* York Beach, ME: Samuel Weiser, 2000.

James, William. *The Varieties of Religious Experience.* New York: Barnes & Noble, 2004 [1902].

Jung, C. G. *Memories, Dreams, Reflections.* Edited by Aniela Jaffe. Translated by Richard and Clara Winston. New York: Vintage, 1989.

———. *Psychology and the Occult.* Translated by R. F. C. Hull. Princeton: Princeton/Bollingen, 1977.

———. *The Red Book.* Translated by Sonu Shamdasani, et al. New York: W. W. Norton, 2009.

Lipton, Bruce H. *The Biology of Belief.* New York: Hay House, 2008.

———. "Embracing the Immaterial Universe." http://brucelipton.com.

———. "Insight Into Cellular Consciousness." http://brucelipton.com.

———. "Mind over Genes." http://okbodytalk.com/bruce-lipton-mind-over-genes.

Loftus, Elizabeth, and Katherine Ketcham. *The Myth of Repressed Memory: False Memories and Allegations of Sexual Abuse.* New York: St. Martin's, 1996.

Masson, Jeffrey Moussaieff. *The Assault on Truth: Freud's Suppression of the Seduction Theory.* New York: Harper, 1984.

Masson, Jeffrey Moussaieff, ed. *The Complete Letters of Sigmund Freud to Wilhelm Fliess (1887–1904)*. Cambridge: Harvard University Press, 1985.

McDermott, John, ed. *The Writings of William James: A Comprehensive Edition*. Chicago: University of Chicago Press, 1977.

McGee, Micki. *Self-Help, Inc.: Makeover Culture in American Life*. New York: Oxford University Press, 2005.

McTaggart, Lynne. *The Field: The Quest for the Secret Force of the Universe*, rev. ed. New York: Harper, 2008.

McThoerosen, Michael. "The Discoveries of Emile Coué." http://spiritual-mind-control.com/emilie-coue.html.

Murphy, Joseph. *The Power of Your Subconscious Mind*. New York: Penguin, 2008.

Ofshe, Richard, and Ethan Watters. *Making Monsters: False Memories, Psychotherapy, and Sexual Hysteria*. Berkeley: University of California Press, 1996.

Pendergrast, Mark. *Victims of Memory: Incest Accusations and Shattered Lives*. 2d ed. Hinesburg, VT: Upper Access, 1996.

Peschek-Böhmer, Flora, and Gisela Schreiber. *Urine Therapy: Nature's Elixir for Good Health*. Rochester, VT: Healing Arts, 1999.

Pierrakos, Eva. "The Language of the Subconscious." Lecture 124, Pathwork Center. http://pathwork.org/lectures/the-language-of-the-unconscious.

Randi, James. *The Faith Healers*. Amherst, NY: Prometheus, 1989.

Regardie, Israel. *Foundations of Practical Magic*. Wellingborough, Northamptonshire, UK: Aquarian, 1979. http://hermetics.org/pdf/TheArtofTrueHealing.pdf.

———. *The Golden Dawn*. St. Paul, MN: Llewellyn, 1993.

———. *The Romance of Metaphysics*. Chicago: Aries, 1946.

Reid, Daniel. *The Complete Book of Chinese Health and Healing*. New York: Barnes & Noble, 1994.

Rich, C. L., and F. N. Pitts, Jr. "Suicide by Psychiatrists: A Study of Medical Specialists among 18,730 Consecutive Physician Deaths during a

Five-Year Period, 1967–72." *Journal of Clinical Psychiatry* 41, no. 8 (Aug. 1980): 261–63. http://ncbi.nlm.nih.gov/pubmed/7400103.

Riley, Isaac Woodbridge. "The Faith, the Falsity, and the Failure of Christian Science." *Journal of the American Medical Association*, 1925, 85, no. 12: 924. http://jama.jamanetwork.com/article.aspx?art icleid=237520#qundefined.

Sahtouris, Elisabet. "A Scientist's Thoughts about Redefining Our Concept of God." http://ratical.org/LifeWeb/Articles/whatsgod .html.

Siegel-Itzkovich, Judy. "Freud's Theory of Repression Should Be Dropped." *Jerusalem Post*, April 13, 2008. http://jpost.com/Health AndSci-Tech/Health/Article.aspx?id=98064.

Simon, Robert I. "Great Paths Cross: Freud and James at Clark University, 1909." http://uky.edu/~eushe2/Pajares/JamesSimon1967.pdf.

Simonton Cancer Center. http://www.simontoncenter.com.

Sobottka, Stanley. *A Course on Consciousness.* http://faculty.virginia .edu:80/consciousness/home.html.

Springer, Fleta Cambell. *According to the Flesh: A Biography of Mary Baker Eddy.* New York: Coward-McCann, 1930.

Stone, Robert B. *The Silva Method.* Nightingale Conant, audiocassettes.

Szasz, Thomas. *The Myth of Psychotherapy.* Syracuse, NY: Syracuse University Press, 1978.

Terr, Lenore. *Unchained Memories: True Stories of Traumatic Memories Lost and Found.* New York: Basic, 1995.

Thornton, E. M. *The Freudian Fallacy.* New York: Dial, 1984.

"Three Initiates." [William Walker Atkinson.] *The Kybalion: Hermetic Philosophy.* Chicago: Yogi Publication Society, 1940 [1908].

Touber, Tijn. "How I Lost Faith: How the End of Religion Can Be the Beginning of God." *ODE* (Jan.-Feb. 2005). http://odewire.com /52717/how-i-lost-faith-how-the-end-of-religion-can-be-the -beginning-of-god.html.

Troward, Thomas. *The Edinburgh and Dore Lectures on Mental Science.* New York: Dodd, Mead, 1909. http://thomastroward.wwwhubs.com /elomstitle.htm.

V. H. Frater T. S. O. "Jesus the Nazarene, The True Rose and Cross." http://esotericgoldendawn.com/rosicrucian_jesusnazarene.htm.

vom Scheidt, Jürgen. "Sigmund Freud and Cocaine." *Psyche* 27 (1973): 385–430. http://pep-web.org/document.php?id=paq.043.0693c.

Wilhelm, Richard, and Cary F. Baynes, trans. *The Secret of the Golden Flower: A Chinese Book of Life.* New York: Causeway, 1975.

Williamson, Marianne. *A Return to Love: Reflections on the Principles of a Course in Miracles.* New York: Harper Collins, 1996.

Young, James Harvey. "Why Quackery Persists." http://quackwatch.com /01QuackeryRelatedTopics/persistance.html.

Zweig, Stefan: *Mental Healers.* New York: Frederick Ungar, 1932.

Index